SHORTER
SPANISH GRAMMAR

By RALPH E. HOUSE *and* ERWIN K.
MAPES, *of the State University of Iowa*

With the Assistance of RUTH HOUSE, *of*
Albion College

GINN AND COMPANY

BOSTON · NEW YORK · CHICAGO · LONDON · ATLANTA · DALLAS
COLUMBUS · SAN FRANCISCO

PREFACE

THE PRESENT TEXT is to a considerable extent a revision of Part I
of *The Essentials of Spanish Grammar*, by R. E. House and E. K.
Mapes, which was published in 1932. For some years the authors,
who had continued as colleagues in the department of Spanish
at the University of Iowa, had discussed the desirability of revising the *Essentials*, particularly Part I. During the university
year of 1939–1940 work was begun on the project: some general
plans were made, and some tentative exercises prepared and tried
out in university classes.

In April, 1940, the work was halted by the sudden death of
Dr. House. Nothing more was done on the project during the
remainder of that year. Early in the academic year of 1940–1941
work was resumed, with Miss Ruth House, daughter of Dr.
House and instructor in Spanish in Albion College, taking her
father's place in the work of revision.

With regard to scope, the present text adheres to the same
principle of language teaching as the *Essentials*: the concentra-
tion of attention upon words and constructions of high frequency,
at the expense of the unusual. As in the earlier book, the authors
have been guided, with respect to relative frequency of words
and constructions, by such studies as Buchanan's *A Graded
Spanish Word Book* and Keniston's *Spanish Idiom List*.

The differences between the two texts, however, are numerous
and fundamental. In recognition of the fact that many teachers
prefer the reading method, the lesson pattern has been changed
so as to permit this type of approach. The section in Spanish
has been considerably lengthened, particularly in the earlier lessons; vocabulary has been introduced somewhat more rapidly;
and, as a completely new feature, a varied and relatively long
recognition-type exercise has been introduced in each lesson.
The paragraph of questions in Spanish and the two reproduction-
type exercises now designated as Exercises D and E, a type of
exercise which was highly effective in the older text, have been

retained, though the latter have been somewhat reduced in length.

Another completely new feature is the introduction of six review lessons at suitable intervals in the text. The use of these lessons is optional with the teacher. They are numbered independently of the regular lessons and contain no new grammar or vocabulary. They consist of new and searching exercises covering every essential detail of grammar taken up in the lessons reviewed. As in the regular lessons, there are in each review lesson a long and varied recognition-type exercise and two relatively short reproduction-type exercises, one for drill on specific points of grammar and the other containing sentences for translation into Spanish.

It is not intended that any teacher shall use all the exercises which have been provided. The lesson pattern has been so planned as to make the text suitable for two different types of approach : that of the reading method and that of the grammar-composition method. When the reading method is used, Exercise A (the section in Spanish), Exercise B (questions in Spanish), and Exercise C (recognition-type drill) are recommended. When the grammar-composition method is used, Exercises A, D, and E are recommended, either with or without Exercise B. A similar choice may be made in the review lessons, the reading-method students using Exercise A, corresponding to Exercise C in the regular lessons, and the grammar-composition students using Exercises B and C, corresponding to Exercises D and E. A deviation from this pattern is recommended in Review Lessons I and II, in which both types of students should use the parts of Exercise A dealing with pronunciation.

It is evident that the book can be readily adapted to an eclectic method, by using material from the two types of exercises in whatever proportion is desired.

An important change not connected with the lesson pattern is to be found in the Introduction. In the *Essentials* the consonants were taken up in alphabetical order; but in the present text they are classified according to the nature of the difficulties that they present to the learner. This arrangement, it is believed, will prove much more satisfactory than the earlier one.

Extensive changes have also been made in the order of presentation of grammatical material (particularly in Lessons VI to X) and in the wording of the grammar statements in several lessons.

A number of persons have rendered invaluable aid in the preparation of the text. Recognition is due first of all to Miss Ruth House, who, since her father's death, has shared with the surviving author the labor of revising the text and seeing it through the press. Dr. Juan López-Morillas, of the department of Spanish at the University of Iowa, has read the entire manuscript, much of it more than once, with special attention to the idiomatic correctness of the Spanish exercises. Dr. Ruth Davis and Dr. Ilse Probst Laas, also of the department of Spanish at the University of Iowa, have read and reread the material at various stages in its elaboration and have made many extremely valuable suggestions. Their help has been particularly important because of their several years' experience in teaching the *Essentials*.

E. K. MAPES

CONTENTS

vii

CONTENTS

SHORTER
SPANISH GRAMMAR

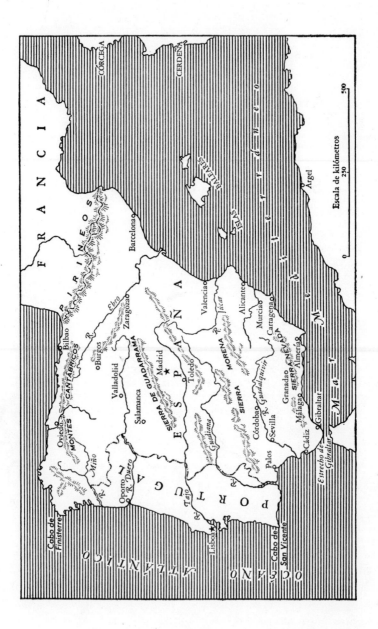

INTRODUCTION

1. *Standard of Pronunciation.* The pronunciation here discussed is that of Castilian Spanish, and the authority followed is Tomás Navarro Tomás's *Manual de Pronunciación Española.* It is not feasible to attempt in this book an extended discussion of Spanish-American pronunciation, because there is no generally accepted standard. However, those differences from Castilian pronunciation which are most common in Spanish America as a whole will be mentioned in connection with the individual letters concerned.

2. *General Comparison of English and Spanish Sounds* In the discussion of pronunciation which follows, Spanish sounds are explained as far as possible by comparing them with English sounds. Certain differences are discussed under individual sounds. In addition, the following fundamental differences between the two languages should be kept in mind:

1

Though Spanish, like English, has syllable stress, unaccented vowels are pronounced almost as clearly and carefully as those which are accented. Slurring of unaccented vowels, as in the English words *letter, nasal, method,* never occurs in the Spanish language.

2

Spanish vowels are brief (about half the length of the English ones) and absolutely uniform in quality. There is never the off-glide noticeable in English long vowels, as in *mate* (ā + ē) or *lone* (ō + ōō).

3

In English the consonants are pronounced with greater vigor than in Spanish, so much so that certain consonants — for example, **p, t, k** — seem to a Spaniard to be followed by a puff of air (*pʰarking, tʰable, cʰamel*). In pronouncing Spanish the consonants must be kept relatively light.

3. *The Alphabet.* The Spanish alphabet consists of thirty different characters, as follows:

CHARACTER	SPANISH NAME	CHARACTER	SPANISH NAME
a	a	n	ene
b	be *or* be alta	ñ	eñe
c	ce	o	o
ch	che	p	pe
d	de	q	cu
e	e	r	ere
f	efe	rr	erre
g	ge	s	ese
h	hache	t	te
i	i	u	u
j	jota	v	ve *or* u-ve
k	ka	w	doble u *or* doble v
l	ele	x	equis
ll	elle	y	ye *or* i griega
m	eme	z	zeda *or* zeta

Note that **ch, ll,** and **rr** are regarded as single characters, and that they and **ñ** occur in addition to the letters of the English alphabet. In dictionaries *ch, ll,* and *ñ* follow **c, l,** and **n** respectively.

4. *Vowels.* Spanish vowels have approximately the following sounds:

a

a is pronounced like English *a* in *father*:

casa   cama

e

e has two sounds: (1) When it ends its syllable it is a little more open than English *a* in *take*, that is, it is between that sound and the sound of *e* in *met*:

queso   compré   mesa

(2) In all other cases the sound is that of English *e* in *met*:

papel   perder   hacer

If the weak vowel has the accent mark → 2 separate syllables
If the first of weak vowels has accent mark → 2 sep. syll.

i

i is like English *i* in *machine*:

silla   vida

o

o has two sounds: (1) When it ends its syllable it is a little more open than English *o* in *note*, that is, it is between that sound and the sound of *o* in *for*:

coche   moda   nota

(2) In all other cases it has the sound of English *o* in *for*:

amor   sol   contar

u

u is pronounced like English *oo* in *moon*:

cura   agudo

y

y as a vowel has the sound of Spanish **i**. The only common example is the conjunction **y**.

5. *Diphthongs*. A diphthong is a combination of two vowel sounds in the same syllable. It must be made up of a strong vowel (**a**, **e**, or **o**) and a weak one (**i**, **y**, or **u**) or of two weak ones. In accented syllables the vocal stress is on the strong vowel or on the second of two weak ones, but in all cases both are clearly heard. When a weak vowel stands first, **i** has the sound of **y** in the English word *yes*, and **u** that of English **w**. The diphthongal combinations are:

ai, ay: aire, hay	**ia:** diablo, Asia
au: causa, gaucho	**ua:** guardar, suave
oi, oy: oigo, soy	**io:** comió, serio
ou: bou	**uo:** antiguo, cuota
ei, ey: seis, ley	**ie:** piedra, bien
eu: deuda, feudal	**ue:** bueno, fuego
iu: viuda, ciudad	
ui, uy: cuidado, muy	

Observe that two strong vowels, a strong-weak combination with accent on the weak vowel, or two weak vowels with accent on the first, do not constitute diphthongs:

Ja-én   te-ní-a   flú-i-do

6. *Triphthongs.* These are combinations of three vowel sounds in a single syllable, and occur only when a strong vowel stands between two weak ones. The existing combinations are:

> **iai:** estudiáis   **uai, uay:** acentuáis, Paraguay
>
> **iei:** estudiéis   **uei, uey:** acentuéis, buey

7. *Consonants.* In the following presentation the consonants are divided into four groups:

1. Those pronounced very nearly like the corresponding English letters.

2. Those similar to English, but requiring some modification.

3. Those which represent sounds occurring in English, but with different spelling.

4. Those which represent sounds unknown in English.

NOTE. The letter **h** is always silent: **hablar, heno**. The letters **k** and **w** occur only in foreign words, and are usually pronounced as in English:

kantismo   **kilo**   **watt**   **Wáshington**

1

Consonants Pronounced as in English

a. Of these, the following have only one sound, which occurs in all positions:

> *ch* as in *church*: **escuchar, muchacho.**
> *f* as in *find*: **fácil, familia.**
> *l* as in *long*: **libro, lápiz.**
> *m* as in *man*: **maestro, mesa.**
> *n* as in *not*: **nada, noche.**
> *p* as in *pen*: **para, papel.**
> *y* as in *yes*: **desayuno, ayer.**

But no diphthong
a strong vowel + a strong vowel →
2 separate syll.

b. Those discussed below have two or more different sounds, only one of which is represented in English by the same letter:

b, v

The sound represented by English *v* does not exist in Spanish, **b** and **v** being pronounced in all combinations exactly alike.

When **b** or **v** is initial or follows **m** or **n**, the sound of either is that of English *b*[1]:

baño	costumbre	vino	invierno

c

Before a consonant or the vowels **a**, **o**, or **u**, Spanish **c** is pronounced like English *c* in *can*:

clase	campo	color	cultivar

g, gu

The Spanish sound corresponding to English *g* in *go* occurs only initially and following **n**. It is spelled **g** before **a**, **o**, **u**, or a consonant, and **gu** before **e** or **i**:

gana	grande	guerra	guisar	tengo	renguera

NOTE: **gu** before **a** or **o** is like English *gw*: **lengua, averiguó.** Before **e** or **i** the same sound is represented by **gü**: **averigüé, pingüino.**

2

Consonants Differing Somewhat in Pronunciation from Their English Equivalents

b, v

When not initial and not following **m** or **n**, Spanish **b** (or **v**) differs from English *b* in that it is fricative. That is, air passes through a small aperture between the lips during articulation:

saber	tabla	cubre	uva	óvalo

---

[1] The combination **nv** is pronounced **mb**: **invierno** sounds like **imbierno.**

d, t

Spanish **t** in all positions, and **d** initial or following **l** or **n**, differ from the corresponding English sounds in that the tip of the tongue is pushed farther forward, against the upper teeth:

tiza   cuatro   contar   doble   falda   conde

g

When not initial, when not following **n**, and when not followed immediately by **e** or **i**, Spanish **g** becomes slightly fricative. That is, some air passes between the organs involved during articulation (compare fricative **b**, above):

pagar   preguntar   siglo   negro

s

Spanish **s** is similar to its English equivalent, except that the frication occurs between the tip of the tongue and the palate, just above the upper teeth, instead of between the front of the palate and the arched upper surface of the tongue, as in English. In most positions (*a*) the sound is hissed (unvoiced), corresponding to English *s* in *this*:

saber   casa   sastre   esperar

(*b*) Before the voiced consonants (**b, d, g, l, ll, m, n, ñ, v, y**) the sound is voiced, corresponding to English *s* in *is*:

esbelto   desde   esgrima   isla   mismo   asno

x

Between vowels, Spanish **x** has approximately the sound of English *gs*, not that of English *x* in either *examination* (*gz*) or *execute* (*ks*):

examen   éxito   exacto   exótico

Note. Before consonants, Spanish **x** has the same sound as unvoiced Spanish **s**:

sexto   mixto   explicar   exclamar

3

*Letters Representing Sounds Which Occur in English, but
Usually with a Different Spelling*

c

Before **e** or **i**, Spanish **c** is pronounced like English *th* in *think* :

docena   cerrar   decir   preciso

In most parts of Spanish America the sound is that of a hissed
Spanish **s** (see page 8).

d

When not initial and not following **n** or **l**, Spanish **d** has the
sound of English *th* in *this*, pronounced lightly :

modo   estado   madre   ciudad

q

Spanish **q** occurs only in the combination **qu**, before the vowels
e and **i**. The sound is that of English *k* :

queso   bosque   pequeño   mosquito   quinina   Iquique

z

Spanish **z** has two sounds : (*a*) In most positions the sound is
that of Spanish **c** before **e** and **i**, or English *th* in *think* :

zapato   pez   capaz   lozano   mozo

In most parts of Spanish America **z** in these positions is pronounced like a hissed Spanish **s**.

(*b*) Before the voiced consonants (**b, d, g, l, ll, m, n, ñ, v, y**)
the sound is voiced, corresponding to English *th* in *then* or a
vigorously articulated Spanish intervocalic **d** :

juzgar   hallazgo   gozne   Luzbel

4

Consonants Which Represent Sounds Unknown in English

g, j

Spanish **g** before **e** and **i**, and Spanish **j** under all circumstances, are pronounced by placing the speech organs in about the position for English *k*, but leaving a small opening through which the air passes with audible friction :

diligente   ligero   dirigir   girar   paisaje   pájaro   joven   lejos

ll

ll is produced by placing the tip of the tongue behind the lower teeth and arching its upper surface against the palate. It thus differs very considerably from English *lli* in *million*, which consists of two distinct articulations, *l* and *y*.

[handwritten margin note: In Spanish it is a single sound]

> **gallina   caballo   llamar   billete**

In most of Spanish America the sound is that of *y* in the English word *yes*. In Argentina and Uruguay both **ll** and **y** are pronounced like *s* in the English word *pleasure*.

ñ *[handwritten: tilde]*

ñ is a palatilized **n**, like French *gn* in *digne*. To form it, the speech organs are in position for **ll**, but approximate an **n** instead of an **l**. A comparison with English *ny* in *canyon* is unsatisfactory, since the latter consists of two distinct articulations, **n** and **y**.

[handwritten margin note: It closely resembles ny onion but in Sp. it is a single sound]

mañana   año   español   acompañar

r, rr

r, rr consists of a vibration of the tip of the tongue against the palate just above the upper teeth. It has two degrees of intensity : (*a*) Single **r** initial or following **n**, **l**, and **s**, and **rr** in all positions, are strongly rolled (three or four vibrations) :

rato   honra   alrededor   los ratones   arreglo

[handwritten note at bottom: long trill - rr — single r in certain cases]

(*b*) Single **r**, except as above, consists of a single tap of the tongue:

para **escribir** **padre**

8. *Differences in Spelling of Certain Consonantal Sounds.* It has been noted that certain consonantal sounds require a different spelling before **e** and **i** than before the other vowels. The sounds concerned are tabulated below. The drill syllables given should be read and repeated in every possible order until the sound involved is recognized instantly wherever found.

SOUND	SPELLING VARIATIONS					EXAMPLES
k as in *make*	ca	que	qui	co	cu	café, querer, aquí, color, cumbre
th as in *thin*	za	ce	ci	zo	zu	zapato, cerca, cinco, zona, zurdo
g as in *go*	ga	gue	gui	go	gu	gana, guerra, guía, gota, gusto
gu as in *language*	gua	güe	güi	guo		agua, averigüé, güiro, antiguo
ch as in German *nach*	ja	ge	gi	jo	ju	coger, giro, hija, rojo, julio
		je	ji			dije, jirón,

9. *Syllabication.* 1. In syllable division, single consonants (including the symbols **ch**, **rr**, and **ll**) and the so-called inseparable combinations (consonant + **r** and consonant + **l**) are placed with the following vowel:

mo-no-sí-la-bo pe-rro pa-dre
mu-cha-cho si-lla ta-bla

2. When two or more consonants occur together, the last consonant or inseparable combination (see 1, above) goes with the following vowel:

ac-to trans-pi-rar ins-truir
tin-ta an-cho an-clar
con-lle-var

Begin a syllable with a consonant or consonant group if possible. In Spanish a syllable must not begin with s + a consonant ∴ always separate s + a consonant.

10. *Accentuation.* 1. Words ending in a vowel or in **n** or **s** are accented on the next to the last syllable:

co-no-cí-do   a-ma-ban   man-za-nas

2. Those ending in a consonant other than **n** or **s** are accented on the last syllable:

can-tar   mi-tad   mi-ne-ral

3. Exceptions to the above rules are indicated by a written accent:

co-mún   des-pués   mé-di-co

4. Written accents are frequently used to distinguish certain parts of speech from others which have the same spelling:

el the, **él** he   **mas** but, **más** more   **si** if, **sí** yes

11. *Punctuation.* In general, the marks of punctuation and their uses are the same as in English. Notable differences are:

1. The use of an inverted interrogation or exclamation point at the beginning of the interrogative or exclamatory word, phrase, or sentence, in addition to the usual one at the end:

¿Qué ha dicho Vd.? What did you say?

¡Qué tiempo tan caluroso! What warm weather!

Si lo prohibe ¿qué haremos? If he forbids it, what shall we do?

En este caso ¡cuántas dificultades encontraremos! In this case how many difficulties we shall encounter!

2. In dialogue, the use of a dash (—) to indicate a change of speaker.

12. *Capitalization.* Capitals are less used than in English, small letters being employed for: 1. Adjectives of nationality, used either as adjectives or nouns:

pan francés French bread   **los mejicanos** the Mexicans

2. Names of languages:

Habla italiano. He speaks Italian.

3. The names of the months and days of the week:

Hoy es lunes, 21 de octubre. Today is Monday, October 21.

4. The pronoun **yo** (I).

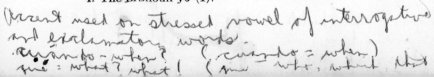

LESSON I

13. *Gender.* In Spanish all nouns are of either masculine or feminine gender. Nouns denoting male beings are masculine; those denoting female beings are feminine. The gender of nouns that denote things must be committed to memory, but generally nouns ending in -o are masculine, and those ending in -a are feminine. Two very common exceptions are **la mano** (the hand), and **el día** (the day).

14. *The Singular of the Definite Article.* **El** is the masculine form :

> **el maestro** the schoolmaster
> **el papel** the paper

La is feminine :

> **la maestra** the schoolmistress
> **la mesa** the table

15. *The Indefinite Article.* **Un** is masculine :

> **un libro** a book

Una is feminine :

> **una pluma** a pen

16. *Interrogation.* In questions a noun subject regularly follows the verb. It usually follows also noun objects and words in the predicate, particularly when they are shorter than the subject.

¿Tiene papel el maestro? Has the schoolmaster paper?
¿Tiene una mesa el alumno? Has the pupil a table?

VOCABULARY

el **alumno** the pupil, student
el **libro** the book
el **maestro** the teacher, schoolmaster
la **mesa** the table
el **papel** the paper
la **pluma** the pen
la **sala de clase** the classroom
el **señor** sir, Mr., gentleman
qué (*interrog. pron. and adj.*)
what

entonces then
sí yes
también also
con with
en in, on
y and
escribe (he) writes
hay there is, there are
lee (he) reads
tiene (he) has
toma (he) takes

EXERCISES

A

En la sala de clase hay un alumno y un maestro. El maestro tiene una mesa. En la mesa hay papel, una pluma y un libro. El maestro toma la pluma y escribe en el papel. Entonces toma el libro y lee. El alumno tiene un libro y una pluma. Lee en el libro. Entonces toma papel. Escribe en el papel con la pluma. — ¿Qué tiene el alumno? — El alumno tiene un libro. — ¿Qué hay en la mesa? — Hay papel en la mesa. Hay también en la mesa una pluma y un libro. — ¿Qué toma el maestro? — El maestro toma una pluma. — ¿En qué escribe el maestro? — El maestro escribe en papel. — ¿Qué lee el maestro? — El maestro lee en el libro. — ¿Toma papel el alumno? — Sí, señor, el alumno toma papel. — ¿Escribe el alumno con una pluma? — Sí, señor, el alumno escribe con una pluma.

B

1. Which of the nouns in the vocabulary can be identified as masculine or feminine by actual gender (sex)? 2. Can they also be identified by their endings? 3. Which of them cannot be identified by sex? 4. Can all of these be identified by endings? 5. Of

which of these eight nouns must you memorize the gender?
6. What person of the verb is **tiene**? **lee**? **escribe**? **toma**?
7. What person is used when the subject is a noun? 8. What is
the position in the sentence of an interrogative word like **qué**?

C

Put the correct form of the indefinite article before each of
the following words:

__?__ mesa   __?__ papel   __?__ maestro   __?__ señor
__?__ día   __?__ pluma   __?__ alumno   __?__ mano

D

1. Is there a table in the classroom? 2. Yes, sir, there is a
table in the classroom. 3. What is there on the table? 4. There
are a pen and paper on the table. 5. Is there also a book on the
table? 6. Yes, sir, there is also a book on the table. 7. The
teacher reads the book. 8. The teacher takes the pen and writes
on the paper. 9. The pupil also has a pen. 10. The pupil writes
on the paper with the pen.

NOTE: In connected speech in any language one unconsciously
separates sentences into small, closely connected groups of words,
pronouncing each group practically as a single word. These groups are
called "stress" or "breath" groups. Such groups may consist, for
instance, of a noun and its modifiers, a preposition and its object, or
a verb and its object. The faster one reads or speaks, the longer the
breath groups tend to be. The first sentence of Exercise A, if pro-
nounced slowly, would normally be read "En la sala de clase | hay
un alumno | y un maestro."

This grouping of words often affects the sounds of letters. For
example, the **d** of **Le doy un libro** and the **b** of **la buena muchacha** are
considered intervocalic and therefore fricative, though in isolated
words they would be explosive. Similarly, the **n** and **v** of **un vaso** are
pronounced **mb**, like the **nv** of **invierno** (see footnote, p. 7).

Another phenomenon is the linking of vowels in contiguous words.
Because of this, **y** followed by a vowel becomes a consonant (**y una**
becomes **yu-na**), and the contiguous **a** and **i** in **habla inglés** are like
the diphthong **ai** in **aire**. Two like vowels in contact become practically a single vowel (**escribe en** is pronounced **escriben**). The
teacher will call attention to other combinations as they occur.

LESSON II

17. *Plural of Nouns.* 1. Nouns ending in a vowel add -s to form the plural; those ending in a consonant add -es:

> **alumno, alumnos**
> **mesa, mesas**
> **papel, papeles**

2. Nouns ending in -z in the singular change z to c when -es is added:

> **lápiz, lápices**

3. The masculine plural may refer to both sexes:

> **los alumnos** the pupils

18. *Plural of the Definite Article.* The plural of **el** is **los**; that of **la** is **las**.

el libro the book	**los libros** the books
la mesa the table	**las mesas** the tables
el papel the paper	**los papeles** the papers

19. *Omission of the Indefinite Article.* The indefinite article is generally omitted before an unmodified predicate noun denoting occupation or nationality.

> **María es alumna.** Mary is a pupil.
> **Juan López es maestro.** John López is a teacher.
> **El señor es francés.** The gentleman is a Frenchman.

20. *Negation.* In a negative sentence **no** is placed before the verb:

> **Juan no tiene papel.** John has no paper.
> **No hay sillas.** There are no chairs.

16

VOCABULARY

la **alumna** the girl student
el **cuaderno** the notebook
el **lápiz** the pencil
la **maestra** the schoolmistress
la **silla** the chair
la **tinta** the ink
Juan John
María Mary
no not, no

a to, at, on
para for
pero but
es (he) is
escriben (they) write
leen (they) read
son (they) are
tienen (they) have

EXERCISES

A

Hay alumnos en la sala de clase. En la sala de clase hay también una mesa y sillas. Hay una silla y una mesa para el maestro. Hay sillas para los alumnos. No hay mesas para los alumnos. Juan es alumno, María es alumna. Juan y María son alumnos. No son maestros. El maestro tiene un libro, un lápiz y papel. El maestro lee en el libro a los alumnos. Entonces escribe con el lápiz en papel. Los alumnos tienen libros y lápices, pero no tienen papel. Tienen cuadernos, y escriben en los cuadernos. Entonces los alumnos leen en los libros. Juan tiene un lápiz, pero no escribe con el lápiz en el cuaderno. María no tiene papel, pero tiene una pluma y tinta. María escribe en el cuaderno. No hay libros en la mesa, pero hay papel y tinta.

B

Answer in Spanish : 1. ¿Qué hay en la sala de clase? 2. ¿Qué hay para el maestro? 3. ¿Qué es María? 4. ¿Qué son Juan y María? 5. ¿Qué tiene el maestro? 6. ¿Tienen libros los alumnos? 7. ¿Qué hay para los alumnos? 8. ¿En qué escribe María? 9. ¿Tienen mesas los alumnos? 10. ¿Qué tiene Juan? 11. ¿Con qué escribe el maestro? 12. ¿En qué escriben los alumnos? 13. ¿Hay libros en la mesa?

C

1. What do you think should be the plural of the following nouns? Give reasons for your answer:

la cruz	el joven	el árbol
la sala de clase	el cañón	la nariz
el balcón	el baúl	el país

2. If **los alumnos** may mean **el alumno y la alumna**, what may **los maestros** mean? **los señores**?

3. Indicate, using (*sing.*) and (*pl.*), whether singular or plural nouns should be used as subjects of

tienen _ _ ? _ _	son _ _ ? _ _	toma _ _ ? _ _
es _ _ ? _ _	escriben _ _ ? _ _	leen _ _ ? _ _
tiene _ _ ? _ _	lee _ _ ? _ _	escribe _ _ ? _ _

D

1. Place the proper form of the indefinite article before the following nouns:

_ _ ? _ _ cuaderno

_ _ ? _ _ silla

_ _ ? _ _ lápiz

_ _ ? _ _ alumna

_ _ ? _ _ sala de clase

2. Form the plural of each of the following nouns, and place before each one the proper form of the definite article:

_ _ ? _ _ alumna _ _	_ _ ? _ _ maestro _ _
_ _ ? _ _ alumno _ _	_ _ ? _ _ mesa _ _
_ _ ? _ _ cuaderno _ _	_ _ ? _ _ papel _ _
_ _ ? _ _ lápiz _ _	_ _ ? _ _ pluma _ _
_ _ ? _ _ libro _ _	_ _ ? _ _ señor _ _
_ _ ? _ _ maestra _ _	_ _ ? _ _ silla _ _

E

Translate into Spanish: 1. The schoolmaster has a chair and a table. 2. There is a book on the table. 3. The chair and the pencil are for Mary. 4. The schoolmaster has a table, but he does not have paper. 5. The pupils have books and pencils. 6. Are John and Mary students? 7. Yes, sir; John is a boy student and Mary is a girl student. 8. Are there students in the classroom? 9. Yes, sir; there are a boy student and a girl student in the classroom. 10. The students write in the notebooks.

LESSON III

21. *First Conjugation. Infinitive and Present Indicative.* The infinitive ends in **-ar**:

hablar to speak	
PRESENT INDICATIVE	
Singular	Plural
(yo) hablo I speak I am speaking I do speak **(tú) hablas** thou speakest thou art speaking, *etc.* **(él, ella, usted) habla** he speaks she speaks you speak, *etc.*	**(nosotros, nosotras) hablamos** we speak, *etc.* **(vosotros, vosotras) habláis** ye speak, *etc.* **(ellos, ellas, ustedes) hablan** they speak you speak, *etc.*

22. *Comparison with English Verb Forms.* It should be kept in mind that English verbs have three forms: simple (I speak), progressive (I am speaking), and emphatic (I do speak), the last-named being used chiefly in negative and interrogative sentences (I do not speak; Do you speak?). In Spanish the progressive form is less used than in English (Article **54**, 4), and the emphatic form does not exist at all. The beginning student of Spanish should use only the simple form (**hablo** etc.).

23. *Use and Omission of Subject Personal Pronouns.* Subject personal pronouns, except **usted** and **ustedes**, are usually omitted, but are expressed when emphatic. This most frequently occurs when it is desired to call attention to a change of subject, as in the second example on page 21.

20

Hablo inglés, pero no hablo español. I speak English, but I do not speak Spanish.

El maestro habla español, pero yo hablo inglés. The teacher speaks Spanish, but I speak English.

24. Usted, ustedes, commonly abbreviated to **Vd.** and **Vds.**, are used for *you* in formal speech. They are pronouns of the third person (in origin like the English titles Your Grace, Your Excellency). They are now used, with the verb in the third person, as the current form of polite address. **Tú** (thou) and **vosotros** (ye) are familiar forms, not archaic as the translation given might imply, but used between members of the same family and intimate friends. Familiar forms will be met frequently in reading, but students should not use them in composition or conversation.

25. *Definite Article with Names of Languages.* With names of languages the definite article is used regularly, except immediately after forms of the verb **hablar** and following the prepositions **de** and **en**.

Estudiamos el español. We are studying Spanish.

Los norteamericanos hablan inglés. The North Americans speak English.

Un maestro de español. A teacher of Spanish.

Un libro en español. A book in Spanish.

VOCABULARY

la lengua the language

el norteamericano the North American, particularly of the United States

el sudamericano the South American

los Estados Unidos the United States

estudiar to study

hablar to speak

necesitar to need

tratar (de) to try (to)

español Spanish; **el español** the Spaniard, Spanish language

inglés English; **el inglés** the Englishman, English language

mejicano Mexican; **el mejicano** the Mexican

de of, from

o ·or

EXERCISES

A

Los ingleses hablan inglés. En los Estados Unidos hablamos inglés también. Nosotros los norteamericanos no hablamos español, pero estudiamos el español. Los mejicanos son norteamericanos, pero hablan español. Juan y María son norteamericanos. Hablan inglés, pero estudian el español. El maestro habla inglés, pero habla español también. Es norteamericano, pero es maestro de español. Un maestro de español en los Estados Unidos necesita hablar inglés y español. Los maestros de inglés en España también necesitan hablar inglés y español. Los mejicanos y los españoles en los Estados Unidos leen libros en inglés. Tratan también de hablar inglés. Nosotros tratamos de hablar español en la sala de clase.

B

Answer in Spanish: 1. ¿Qué lengua hablan los españoles? 2. ¿Habla Vd. español? 3. ¿Hablan Vds. inglés? 4. ¿Hablo (yo) inglés? 5. ¿Hablan español los mejicanos? 6. ¿Estudia Vd. el español? 7. ¿Estudian Vds. libros en español? 8. ¿Qué lengua estudian Vds.? 9. ¿Hablan Vds. la lengua también? 10. ¿Qué lengua hablamos en los Estados Unidos? 11. ¿Qué lengua necesitan hablar los españoles en los Estados Unidos? 12. ¿Qué lenguas necesita hablar el maestro de español? 13. ¿Qué lengua tratamos de hablar en la sala de clase? 14. ¿Necesita Vd. hablar inglés o español?

C

I. Translate into English:

estudiamos	hablan	son	tiene
hay	estudio	estudia	estudian
tienen	habla	hablo	es

Old Moorish Castle, Cádiz, Spain. Cádiz (Founded by the Phoeni-
cians about 1100 B. C.) Is Believed to Be the Oldest City in Europe

James Sawders

The Cathedral of Seville, Spain, Showing the Famous
Tower, la Giralda

II. In the following sentences indicate whether each of the italicized personal pronouns or articles should be used or omitted :

1. (*Vds.*) hablan (*el*) español, pero (*nosotros*) hablamos (*el*) inglés.

2. (*Nosotros*) estudiamos (*el*) español, y (*el*) inglés también.

3. Juan estudia (*un*) libro en (*el*) inglés.

4. Juan y (*yo*) hablamos (*el*) inglés, y (*él*) **habla también** (*el*) español.

5. Hay en la sala de clase (*un*) maestro de (*el*) español.

6. María tiene (*los*) libros en (*el*) español y en (*el*) inglés.

7. (*El*) inglés es la lengua de los norteamericanos; (*el*) español es la lengua de los mejicanos.

8. María y (*yo*) estudiamos; (*ella*) estudia (*el*) español, pero (*yo*) estudio (*el*) inglés.

9. Un alumno tiene (*un*) lápiz, pero no tiene (*el*) papel.

D

I. In the following sentences put all words (that admit of a plural) in the plural: 1. Hablo inglés. 2. El maestro habla español. 3. El alumno es español. 4. El español estudia el inglés. 5. Tiene una mesa. 6. Vd. es norteamericano. 7. Estudio el español.

II. Translate into Spanish the English words in parentheses, and supply the definite article where necessary :

1. Yo (*speak*) inglés.

2. Nosotros (*study*) español.

3. Juan y María (*are*) españoles.

4. Los alumnos (*have*) papel.

5. Vds. (*speak*) inglés.

6. Vd. (*study*) inglés.

7. Juan (*has*) un libro.

8. El maestro (*is*) mejicano.

9. El maestro (*reads*) un libro en español.

E

Translate into Spanish: 1. John speaks English. 2. We are studying an English book (a book in English).[1] 3. The teacher has a pencil for Mary. 4. I speak English, but I am studying Spanish. 5. The pupil is a Spaniard. 6. The English study Spanish also. 7. We speak Spanish in the classroom. 8. The language of the United States is English. 9. John, you are a Mexican, but you are studying English. 10. John and Mary, you study books in Spanish and English.

---

[1] In the translation exercises, words or letters enclosed in square brackets are to be omitted; those in parentheses are to be added or are explanatory.

LESSON IV

26. *Infinitive and Present Indicative of Regular Verbs.* Verbs are classified by the infinitive ending: the first-conjugation infinitive ends in **-ar**, the second in **-er**, the third in **-ir**.

INFINITIVE	PRESENT INDICATIVE					
	Singular			Plural		
	First Person	Second Person	Third Person	First Person	Second Person	Third Person
First Conj. **-ar**	-o	-as	-a	-amos	-áis	-an
Second Conj. **-er**	-o	-es	-e	-emos	-éis	-en
Third Conj. **-ir**	-o	-es	-e	-imos	-ís	-en

aprender to learn	**escribir** to write
aprendo I learn	escribo I write
aprendes thou learnest	escribes thou writest
aprende he learns; you (**Vd.**) learn	escribe he writes; you (**Vd.**) write
aprendemos we learn	escribimos we write
aprendéis ye learn	escribís ye write
aprenden they learn; you (**Vds.**) learn	escriben they write; you (**Vds.**) write

VOCABULARY

la **casa** the house; en **casa** at home
la **clase** the class, kind
el **ejercicio** the exercise
la **falta** the mistake
la **lección** the lesson
la **palabra** the word
la **pizarra** the blackboard
la **tiza** the chalk
España Spain

aprender to learn
escribir to write
escuchar to listen
leer to read
notar to note, remark
tomar to take, get
vivir to live
dónde (*interrog.*) where
si if

25

EXERCISES

A

Vivimos en los Estados Unidos. Hablamos inglés, pero aprendemos el español. Estudiamos las lecciones en casa. Aprendemos las palabras y estudiamos los ejercicios. Escribimos los ejercicios en los cuadernos o en papel. En la clase el maestro lee los ejercicios en español. Los alumnos escuchan. Entonces un alumno lee. El maestro escucha y nota las faltas. Los alumnos escriben el ejercicio en la pizarra con tiza. Entonces el maestro nota las faltas de los alumnos. Si tratamos de escribir en español, hay faltas. Escribimos en papel con lápiz o con pluma, pero necesitamos tiza si escribimos en la pizarra. En casa el maestro lee los ejercicios de los alumnos. Lee también libros en español. En casa yo leo libros en inglés, pero no leo libros en español.

B

Answer in Spanish: 1. ¿Vivimos en España? 2. ¿Viven los españoles en los Estados Unidos? 3. ¿Qué estudiamos en casa? 4. ¿En qué escribimos los ejercicios? 5. ¿Qué lee el maestro? 6. ¿Qué lengua aprenden Vds.? 7. ¿Qué lengua hablan Vds.? 8. ¿Con qué escribo en la pizarra? 9. ¿Con qué escribimos en papel? 10. ¿Escribe Vd. en papel con tiza? 11. ¿Qué nota el maestro? 12. ¿Hay faltas? 13. ¿Qué lee el maestro en casa? 14. ¿Lee Vd. libros en español en casa?

C

I. 1. Why is it usually unnecessary to express the pronoun subjects of Spanish verbs? 2. Why is it almost always necessary in English? Give examples. 3. The infinitive of most verbs minus the infinitive ending is called the *present stem*. What is the present stem of (1) **estudiar**, (2) **leer**, (3) **deletrear**, (4) **creer**, (5) **pronunciar**, (6) **descubrir**, (7) **anunciar**, (8) **partir**, (9) **prometer**, (10) **subir**? 4. Give orally the present tense of each of the above verbs. 5. What differences are there between the present-tense endings of the second and third conjugations?

II. Translate into English and give the infinitive in each case:

escriben	lee	vivimos	aprendemos
aprenden	escuchamos	aprendo	Vds. viven
leo	hablo	escribimos	estudia
Vd. vive	leemos	escuchan	escribo

D

I. Translate into Spanish: 1. He lives, learns, reads, listens, writes. 2. We live, learn, etc. 3. I live, learn, etc. 4. They live, learn, etc. 5. You (*sing.*) live, learn, etc. 6. You (*pl.*) live, learn, etc.

II. Translate into Spanish the English words in parentheses:

1. Nosotros (*live*) en los Estados Unidos.
2. Juan y María (*listen*).
3. Vds. (*are learning*) el español.
4. Yo (*read*) la lección.
5. El maestro (*writes*) en la pizarra.
6. Vd. (*read*) la palabra.
7. Nosotros (*write*) el ejercicio.
8. Yo (*study*) en casa.

E

Translate into Spanish: 1. John and I live in the United States. 2. The Mexicans speak Spanish, but we speak English. 3. The teacher writes an exercise on the blackboard. 4. Then he reads the words in Spanish. 5. The pupils study the lesson, and then they learn the exercise. 6. John and Mary, where do you study Spanish? 7. We study at home, but we read the exercises in the classroom. 8. I write on the blackboard with chalk. 9. John, you are talking; you are not listening. 10. Is there a table in the classroom? 11. Yes, sir, there is a table for the teacher. 12. There are books on the table, and paper also.

LESSON V

27. *Position of the Adjective.* 1. Articles, numerals, pronominal adjectives, and, in general, limiting words that point out rather than describe, usually precede the noun.

> **dos palabras** two words
> **la primera lección** the first lesson
> **muchos ejercicios** many exercises

2. The position of the descriptive adjective must be learned largely by observation. Such descriptive adjectives as the beginning student is likely to use generally follow the noun.

> **un libro interesante** an interesting book
> **una lección fácil** an easy lesson

3. Two descriptive adjectives following the noun are joined by a conjunction, usually **y.**

> **cuentos cortos y fáciles** short, easy stories
> **cuadernos rojos y blancos** red and white notebooks

28. *Forms and Agreement of the Adjective.* 1. The adjective agrees in gender and number with the noun it qualifies.

2. Adjectives ending in **-o** in the masculine singular change **-o** to **-a** to form the feminine:

> **papel blanco** white paper   **tiza blanca** white chalk

3. Other adjectives usually have the same form for both genders:

> **un libro interesante** an interesting book
> **una lección interesante** an interesting lesson

4. Adjectives of nationality ending in a consonant in the masculine singular add **-a** to form the feminine.

> **un alumno español** a Spanish student
> **la lengua española** the Spanish language
> **un maestro inglés** an English schoolmaster
> **una casa inglesa** an English house

28

29. *Plural of Adjectives.* The rule for the plural of nouns (Article **17**) applies also to adjectives.

blanco, blancos ⎫
blanca, blancas ⎭ white

español, españoles ⎫
española, españolas ⎭ Spanish

fácil, fáciles (*m.* and *f.*) easy

feliz, felices (*m.* and *f.*) happy

30. *Apocopation of Adjectives.* By apocopation is meant the dropping of the final letter or syllable of a word.

1. **Bueno** (good), **malo** (bad), **uno** (one), and **primero** (first), drop the final **-o** of the masculine singular when placed before the noun they modify, as is usually the case :

[handwritten: tercero) - Third
algún(o) - some]

un **buen** alumno a good pupil

el **primer** libro the first book

In any other form or position these adjectives are written in full :

la **primera** lección the first lesson

los **buenos** libros the good books

El libro es **malo.** The book is bad.

2. **Grande** usually becomes **gran** before a singular noun of either gender. In this position it means *great*; following the noun it means *large* :

un **gran** maestro a great teacher *[handwritten: figurative*

una casa **grande** a large house *[handwritten: literal - concrete]*

31

tener to have	
tengo I have	**tenemos** we have
tienes thou hast	**tenéis** ye have
tiene he has, you (**Vd.**) have	**tienen** they have, you (**Vds.**) have

VOCABULARY

el cuento the story	**grande** large, great
la gramática the grammar	**interesante** interesting
la lectura the reading	**malo** bad, poor
el libro de ejercicios exercise book, workbook	**mucho** (*adj.* and *adv.*) much, a great deal; **muchos** many
el libro de lectura the reader	**negro** black
Méjico Mexico	**nuevo** new
tener to have, possess	**otro** other, another
blanco white	**primero** (*adj.*) first
bueno good	**rojo** red
corto short	**uno** one
difícil difficult	**dos** two
fácil easy	**tres** three

EXERCISES

A

Necesitamos tres libros en la clase de español. Uno es la gramática de la lengua española. El libro de gramática no es difícil. Las lecciones son interesantes y cortas. Pero la lengua española no es fácil; es difícil. Tenemos también un libro de ejercicios. Estudiamos mucho en casa. Estudiamos la lección de gramática. Escribimos los ejercicios en los cuadernos con pluma y tinta. Escribimos con tinta negra en papel blanco. En la sala de clase escribimos con tiza blanca en la pizarra negra. Leemos los ejercicios en español, y notamos las faltas. Los dos primeros libros son rojos. La gramática es roja y grande. El libro de ejercicios es también rojo, pero no es grande. El otro libro es el libro de lectura. Hay en el libro de lectura muchos cuentos fáciles mejicanos. Leemos los cuentos, y aprendemos muchas palabras nuevas. En la clase el maestro habla mucho de Méjico.

B

Answer in Spanish: 1. ¿Con qué escribimos en el papel?
2. ¿Con qué escribimos en la pizarra? 3. ¿Es blanca la pizarra?
4. ¿Es negra la tiza? 5. ¿Es rojo el papel? 6. ¿Qué libros
necesitamos? 7. ¿Es difícil la gramática? 8. ¿Dónde estudiamos
la lección? 9. ¿Qué escribimos en los cuadernos? 10. ¿Es grande
el libro de ejercicios? 11. ¿Qué aprendemos en el libro de lectura? 12. ¿De qué habla el maestro? 13. ¿Es fácil la lengua
española?

C

I. Choose the proper form of each of the adjectives in parentheses and place it in correct position, either before or after the
noun. (Do not write in this book.)

1. Un __?__ alumno __?__ (*buen, bueno, buena, buenos,
buenas*).

2. Los __?__ libros __?__ (*primer, primero, primera, primeros, primeras*).

3. Las __?__ casas __?__ (*negro, negra, negros, negras*).

4. La __?__ lectura __?__ (*interesante, interesantes*).

5. __?__ papel __?__ (*mucho, mucha, muchos, muchas*).

6. Las __?__ lecciones __?__ (*fácil, fáciles*).

7. La __?__ tiza __?__ (*blanco, blanca, blancos, blancas*).

8. __?__ lápices __?__ (*corto, corta, cortos, cortas*).

9. __?__ cuadernos __?__ (*dos*).

10. La __?__ casa __?__ (*gran, grande, grandes*).

II. In each of the following groups of words, put the noun and
adjectives in the proper relative positions, using **y** if necessary.
Select proper form of **un** (-o), etc.

1. libros, nuevos, muchos
2. casas, primeras, las
3. maestro, español, buen(-o), un(-o)
4. lápiz, nuevo, un(-o)
5. maestro, buen(-o), español, un(-o)
6. cuento, fácil, un(-o), corto

7. ejercicio, difícil, primer(-o), el
8. roja, silla, negra, una
9. españolas, alumnas, inglesas
10. maestro, norteamericano, un(-o), mal(-o)

D

I. Supply the proper form of **tener** in the following sentences:

1. ¿Qué (*have*) Vds.?
2. (*We have*) muchos libros
3. (*I have*) un lápiz rojo, pero Juan (*has*) un lápiz negro.
4. Los alumnos (*have*) un buen maestro.
5. ¿(*Have*) Vds. libros de lectura?
6. Sí; (*we have*) gramáticas también.

II. Supply the proper endings for the adjectives in the following sentences: 1. Gramáticas español__. 2. La gramática nuev__ es difícil__. 3. Lápices blanc__ y roj__. 4. Palabras fácil__ y difícil__. 5. Alumnos ingles__. 6. La casa es gran__.

III. Translate into Spanish: 1. Two easy words. 2. A good Spanish schoolmaster. 3. The English language is difficult. 4. The first lessons. 5. A great teacher. 6. A large table.

E

Translate into Spanish: 1. John has a red pen. 2. He also has a black notebook. 3. He writes with the pen in the black notebook. 4. I have a new pen, but it is not red. 5. We have a new grammar. 6. We are studying Spanish in the new book. 7. There are many difficult words in the Spanish grammar. 8. There are interesting stories in the reader. 9. We read the lesson in Spanish. 10. Then we write the new words on the blackboard. 11. I learn the new words, and write the exercises on paper. 12. The first two lessons are easy, but in the others there are many new words.

REVIEW LESSON I

[Introduction (except paragraph 4, Article 7, and Article 8) and Lessons I–V]

A

I. Indicate in the following words the letters pronounced like (a) English o in *for*, (b) o in *mode*, (c) e in *met*, (d) a in *take*, (e) b in *but*, (f) c in *can*, (g) g in *go* :

gana	víbora	otorgo	dolor	capa
enviar	regla	tercero	lector	general
cocer	alforjas	gitano	lácteo	guitarra
docto	beber	vivo	sol	pera
papel	cinco	bóveda	acecha	invierno

II. In the following words identify the diphthongs and the triphthongs. Tell where each word should be accented.

naipe	continúa	comía	hacéis	cambiéis
poeta	leía	averiguáis	león	fuera
puede	Paraguay	bueno	Callao	Uruguay
Bilbao	baúl	aureola	Europa	taconeo
apreciáis	hacia	hacía	envío	deudo

III. Point out in the following words (a) the consonants pronounced as in English, (b) those which differ slightly from English, and (c) those represented in English by a different spelling. Give the correct pronunciation of each word.

fatal	título	queso	leche	celda
cheque	zeta	zampa	nata	quinto
guisa	maceta	cepa	tácito	cinco
cesta	góndola	gafa	chancla	ciencia
dado	cayó	empaque	moza	duda

IV. Divide the following words into syllables, and indicate the position of the accent :

hombre	alforjas	tablón	taconeo	cecear
carrera	caballo	bacalao	ataúd	ancla
reportar	perro	destrucción	héroe	cicatriz
heroico	doble	subterráneo	heroína	peligro
acecha	patria	leer	feudal	bello
Pedro	construir	calle	temblar	gorra

V. Determine the gender of the following nouns, giving in each case the reason for your decision :

libro	alumna	ejercicio	pizarra	cuaderno
mesa	tinta	clase	inglés	alumno
señor	maestro	falta	español	casa
lápiz	lección	cuento	lengua	papel

VI. Select the correct ending (if any is needed) of the adjective in each of the following word groups:

> papeles blanc(-o, -a, -os, -as)
> pluma negr(-o, -a, -os, -as)
> maestro ingles(-o, -a, -os, -as)
> alumnos español(-s, -es, -os, -as)
> alumnas ingles(-s, -es, -os, -as)
> un(-e, -o, -a) gran(-de, -des) maestro
> casas gran(-de, -des)
> primer(-o, -a, -os, -as) libro
> lecciones fácil(-s, -es, -os, -as)
> un(-e, -o, -a) buen(-e, -o, -a) gramática
> cuentos cort(-s, -es, -os, -as) y fácil(-s, -es, -os, -as)
> lecturas interesant(-s, -es, -os, -as)
> un(-e, -o, -a) alumna ingles(-e, -o, -a)
> El libro es buen(-e, -o, -a)
> un(-e, -o, -a) maestro mal(-e, -o, -a)
> un mal(-e, -o, -a) libro

B

Translate into Spanish: 1. Red books. 2. A good Spanish student. 3. Easy lessons. 4. Many Englishmen. 5. We have. 6. Difficult reading. 7. An easy story. 8. Many short, interesting stories. 9. They read. 10. I have. 11. A good black pencil. 12. John is good. 13. A good student. 14. We study. 15. I live. 16. You (*sing.*) are speaking. 17. Do you (*pl.*) read Spanish? 18. We do not listen. 19. Are the pupils reading? 20. The house is large.

C

Translate into Spanish: 1. We have a large house. 2. I am studying a good Spanish grammar. 3. The first reader is not difficult. 4. Mary is writing with a short red pencil. 5. The pencil is good, but the paper is bad. 6. We have a good reader; they have a bad reader. 7. Are you an Englishman or a Spaniard? 8. Have you easy lessons in the Spanish grammar? 9. An English student is studying the Spanish language. 10. You are studying English, but we are studying Spanish.

32. *Ser and estar.* In Spanish there are two verbs, **ser** and **estar**, translated into English by *to be*. They are not interchangeable. To use them correctly is for the foreigner one of the serious difficulties of Spanish.

ser to be	**estar** to be
soy I am	**estoy** I am
eres thou art	**estás** thou art
es he is; you (**Vd.**) are	**está** he is; you (**Vd.**) are
somos we are	**estamos** we are
sois ye are	**estáis** ye are
son they are; you (**Vds.**) are	**están** they are; you (**Vds.**) are

33. 1. **Ser** is used (*a*) whenever a predicate noun follows:

> **Es maestro.** He is a teacher.
> **Es una casa grande.** It is a large house.

(*b*) with a predicate adjective which denotes an essential or permanent quality:

> **La nieve es fría.** The snow is cold (has to be).
> **La casa es grande.** The house is large.

(*c*) to express origin, ownership, or material:

> **Es de España.** He is from Spain.
> **La pluma es de María.** The pen is Mary's.
> **Los libros son de papel.** The books are of paper.

2. **Estar** is used (*a*) to denote place:

> **Está aquí.** He is here.
> **Madrid está en España.** Madrid is in Spain.

36

Es bueno – He is good (in character)
Está bueno – He is well (in health)

(*b*) with a predicate adjective which denotes a temporary or accidental condition :

> **El agua está fría.** The water is cold (happens to be).
> **Juan está enfermo.** John is sick.

VOCABULARY

el amigo the friend
la biblioteca the library
la cocina the kitchen
el comedor the dining room
la comida the dinner, meal
la criada the servant (girl)
el cuarto the room
la madre the mother
los negocios (*pl.*) business
el padre the father
los padres the fathers *or* the parents
el país the country
el periódico the newspaper
la sala the living room, parlor

la visita the visit ; **tener visita** to have a visitor *or* visitors
Cuba Cuba
Josefa Josephine
comer to eat
estar to be
preparar to prepare
ser to be
cansado tired
diligente diligent
enfermo sick
limpio clean
mi, mis my
donde where
hoy today
mañana tomorrow

EXERCISES

A

No hay clases hoy. Estamos en casa. María está en la biblioteca. La biblioteca es un cuarto donde hay muchos libros, una mesa y sillas. Los libros en la biblioteca son de muchos países : de España, de Cuba y de Méjico. María estudia las lecciones para mañana. Yo estoy también en la biblioteca. Juan no está en la biblioteca ; está enfermo. Yo no estudio hoy ; estoy cansado. Leo el periódico. Tengo también un libro interesante. Mi padre tiene visita. Está en la sala con un amigo. El amigo es de España. Hablan de negocios. Mi padre tiene también negocios con señores de Méjico y de Cuba. Mi madre habla con la criada

Josefa. Están en la cocina. Hablan de la casa y de la comida. Josefa prepara la comida. Josefa _es_ diligente, y la casa _está_ limpia. Comemos en el comedor.

B

Answer in Spanish : 1. ¿Dónde estamos hoy? 2. ¿Qué hay en la biblioteca? 3. ¿De dónde son los libros? 4. ¿Lee Vd. periódicos? 5. ¿Son interesantes los periódicos? 6. ¿Está Vd. enfermo? 7. ¿Dónde está Josefa? 8. ¿Es diligente Josefa? 9. ¿Está limpia la casa? 10. ¿Hay libros y periódicos en la cocina? 11. ¿Dónde tiene visita mi padre? 12. ¿De dónde es el amigo? 13. ¿Qué hay en el comedor? 14. ¿De qué habla mi padre? 15. ¿Dónde están mi madre y Josefa? 16. ¿De qué hablan?

C

Choose the verb form which correctly completes each sentence :

1. Juan (_soy, es, estoy, está_) un buen alumno; (_estudio, estudia_) mucho.

2. Hoy dos alumnos (_es, son, está, están_) enfermos.

3. Los libros (_soy, son, estoy, están_) rojos, pero no (_soy, son, estoy, están_) limpios.

4. Los alumnos (_es, son, está, están_) en la sala de clase. (_Prepara, preparan_) las lecciones.

5. Josefa (_soy, es, estoy, está_) diligente; (_soy, es, estoy, está_) una buena criada.

6. El libro de lectura (_es, son, está, están_) interesante, pero no (_es, son, está, están_) fácil.

7. Yo (_soy, es, estoy, está_) en la biblioteca; no (_soy, es, estoy, está_) en el comedor.

8. Mi madre y yo (_tengo, tenemos, tienen_) visita; (_somos, son, estamos, están_) en la sala.

9. Mi padre (_soy, es, estoy, está_) maestro. No (_son, están, hay_) clases hoy, y él (_es, son, está, están_) en casa.

10. La gramática (_es, somos, está, estamos_) roja.

11. El maestro (_es, está, son, están_) de España.

12. Los cuadernos (_soy, son, estoy, están_) de papel.

The Old and the New in Transportation. Andean Plateau

Summit of a Pass across the Andes, Bolivia

2

Largest Tin Mine in the World, Llallagua, Bolivia

Prehistoric Indian Terraces, Urubamba Valley, Peru

D

Fill in the blanks with the correct forms of **ser** or **estar**. (Do not write in this book.)

1. (Nosotros) __?__ en casa.
2. Juan __?__ enfermo.
3. Las casas __?__ grandes.
4. Yo no __?__ diligente: no __?__ buen alumno.
5. La sala no __?__ limpia hoy; la nueva criada no __?__ diligente.
6. Yo __?__ en la sala, pero mis padres __?__ en la biblioteca.
7. Juan y yo __?__ alumnos.
8. ¿__?__ grande la sala de clase?
9. ¿Dónde __?__ Vds.?
10. __?__ en mi cuarto.
11. ¿__?__ Vd. enfermo, Juan?
12. Sí, señor; __?__ en mi cuarto; __?__ enfermo.
13. María, Vd. __?__ una alumna diligente.
14. Las alumnas __?__ diligentes y buenas.

E

Translate into Spanish: 1. The chairs and the table are in the dining room. 2. The kitchen is not large, but it is clean. 3. The table is in the library, where we study the lessons. 4. Many books in the library are from Cuba. 5. I am in my room, but I am not sick. 6. John and Mary are diligent. 7. Today we do not have classes. 8. The pupils are not in the classroom. 9. They are at home. 10. I have visitors today. 11. I am talking with my friends in the living room, but my parents are in the library. 12. My friends are from Spain.

LESSON VII

34. *Cases.* 1. Spanish nouns and pronouns, with the exception of personal pronouns (Lesson IX), have no distinguishing case forms. Although Spanish word order is freer than English, the subject usually precedes the verb, and noun objects usually follow it.

2. The possessive case is represented by **de** followed by the name of the possessor:

> **el lápiz de Juan** John's pencil
> **los libros de los alumnos** the pupils' books

3. With the exception of some personal-pronoun forms, the indirect object is preceded by the preposition **a**:

> **Hablo a la criada.** I speak to the servant.
> **Doy el libro a Juan.** I give John the book.

4. If the direct object of the verb is an inanimate thing, usually nothing other than the meaning or its position in the sentence is necessary to show its grammatical construction:

> **El muchacho come pan.** The boy is eating bread.
> **María escribe una carta.** Mary is writing a letter.

5. If the direct object refers to a definite person or is the name of a person or place, it is regularly preceded by the preposition **a**:

> **El maestro enseña a los alumnos.** The teacher instructs the pupils.
> **María ve a Juan.** Mary sees John.
> **Visito a Madrid.** I visit Madrid.

35. The preposition **a** followed by the article **el** is always contracted to **al**, and **de** plus the article **el** is always written **del**:

> **Voy a la casa del maestro.** I am going to the teacher's house.
> **Hablo al maestro.** I am speaking to the teacher.

40

All other forms are written in full:

> **El maestro habla a las muchachas.** The teacher is speaking to the girls.
> **Tengo los libros de los alumnos.** I have the pupils' books.

36. *Forms of the Personal Pronouns Used with Prepositions.* The forms of the personal pronouns used with prepositions are the same as those used as subjects, with the exception of **yo**, which becomes **mí**, and **tú**, which becomes **ti**:

> **El libro es para mí.** The book is for me.
> **Van con nosotros.** They are going with us.
> **Hablamos de él.** We are speaking of him.

When used with the preposition **con**, the pronoun forms **mí** and **ti** are combined with it and followed by the syllable **-go**:

> **Va conmigo.** He is going with me.
> **¿Quién está contigo?** Who is with thee?

consigo — with himself, herself, oneself, themselves

37.

ir to go	**dar** to give
voy I go	**doy** I give
vas thou goest	**das** thou givest
va he goes; you (**Vd.**) go	**da** he gives; you (**Vd.**) give
vamos we go	**damos** we give
vais ye go	**dais** ye give
van they go; you (**Vds.**) go	**dan** they give; you (**Vds.**) give

VOCABULARY

la **carne** the meat
la **carnicería** the butcher shop
el **carnicero** the butcher
la **cosa** the thing; **otra cosa** anything else
el **día** the day; **buenos días** good day
la **docena** the dozen
las **gracias** the thanks
el **kilogramo** or el **kilo** the kilogram (about two pounds)
el **pan** the bread
la **panadería** the bakery
el **panadero** the baker
el **panecillo** the roll

la **peseta** Spanish coin, par value about twenty cents
comprar to buy
contestar to answer
dar to give
desear to wish
entrar to enter; **entrar en la casa** to enter the house
ir to go; **ir a** to be going to
preguntar to ask
unos, unas some
quién (*interrog.*) who, whom
cuando when
cuánto (*interrog.*) how much
primero (*adv.*) first
dice (he) says

EXERCISES

A

La criada, Josefa, va a comprar unas cosas para la comida. Yo voy con ella. Primero va a comprar pan. Entramos en una panadería. El panadero dice a la criada: — Buenos días, Josefa. — Ella contesta: — Buenos días, señor. — Él pregunta: — ¿Qué desea Vd.? — Josefa contesta: — Deseamos pan y una docena de panecillos. — El panadero da el pan y los panecillos a la criada. — ¿Cuánto es? — pregunta Josefa. — Dos pesetas — contesta él. Ella da las dos pesetas al panadero y toma el pan. Necesitamos también carne para la comida, y la criada va conmigo a la carnicería. Cuando entramos, el carnicero dice: — Buenos días. ¿Qué desean Vds.? — La criada contesta: — Deseamos un kilo de carne. — El carnicero da la carne a Josefa. Josefa da tres pesetas al carnicero y toma la carne. — ¿Necesita Vd. otra cosa? — pregunta él. — No, señor, gracias — contesta la criada. Entonces va conmigo a la casa de mis padres, donde va a preparar la comida.

B

Answer in Spanish : 1. ¿Quién es Josefa? 2. ¿Qué va a comprar? 3. ¿Quién va con ella? 4. ¿Qué dice el panadero? 5. ¿Qué pregunta entonces? 6. ¿Qué desea la criada? 7. ¿Qué da el panadero a la criada? 8. ¿Qué da la criada al panadero? 9. ¿Dónde compramos carne? 10. ¿Quién da la carne a la criada? 11. ¿Cuánto es la carne? 12. ¿Qué pregunta entonces el carnicero? 13. ¿Necesita la criada otra cosa? 14. ¿Para qué deseamos el pan y la carne? 15. ¿Quién va a preparar la comida?

C

I. Translate into English and give the infinitive of each :

estoy	es	estamos	son	tienen
dan	tiene	tengo	va	da
somos	damos	están	soy	Vd. está
vamos	tenemos	voy	van	doy

II. Translate into English : 1. La criada del carnicero. 2. Los lápices de las alumnas. 3. La lengua de los mejicanos. 4. La peseta de la criada. 5. La mesa del maestro. 6. El cuarto de María. 7. La biblioteca del inglés. 8. El libro de lectura de Juan. 9. El periódico de mi padre. 10. La casa de mis padres. 11. La lección de los alumnos.

III. Choose the correct form from each parenthesis :

1. Voy (*a los, a las, al, a la*) biblioteca.
2. El maestro habla (*a la, el, al*) alumno.
3. Estamos (*en, en el, en las*) casa hoy.
4. Entran (*en la, la*) sala de clase.
5. María da la gramática (*a, al*) Juan.
6. El panecillo es para (*yo, mí*).
7. La criada habla (*a, al, a la*) panadero.
8. El carnicero contesta (*la, a la*) criada.
9. Los alumnos van (*con yo, con mí, conmigo*).
10. Josefa toma (*el, la, al*) pan

D

I. Translate, and explain the use or omission of **a**: 1. He gives Mary the bread. 2. John talks to Josephine. 3. The pupils write the exercise. 4. They give the teacher the pencil. 5. The servant takes the meat. 6. We give the books to the pupils.

II. Translate: 1. Mary's teacher. 2. The baker's house. 3. The servant girl's friends. 4. The pupils' books. 5. The teachers' readers. 6. The mother's table.

III. Translate into Spanish the English words in parentheses:

1. Van con (*us*).
2. Los libros son para (*you*).
3. María va con (*me*).
4. Juan estudia con (*her*).
5. Hablan de (*you*).
6. Entran con (*me*).
7. El pan es para (*them*).
8. Vamos con (*him*).

E

Translate: 1. The baker has good bread and rolls in the bakery. 2. When we want things for (the) dinner, we go to the bakery and the butcher shop. 3. Josephine goes with me to buy bread. 4. The baker says: " Good day," and asks: " What do you want? " 5. The servant answers: " I want a dozen rolls." 6. We take the rolls, and give the baker two pesetas. 7. John's father has a butcher shop. 8. The butcher shop is clean, but the meat is not good. 9. Many servants buy meat in [an]other butcher shop. 10. Mary, I am going with you to buy a newspaper. 11. In the newspaper there are many interesting things. 12. The servant [girl] does not read difficult books; she reads easy stories.

Otro, otra = another
el otro, la otra = the other

38. *The Possessive Adjective.* When it precedes the noun it modifies, as is usually the case, the possessive adjective has the forms given below. In the first column is the personal pronoun to which each corresponds.

SUBJECT PRONOUN	Singular		Plural		
	Masculine	Feminine	Masculine	Feminine	
yo I	mi	mi	mis	mis	my
tú thou	tu	tu	tus	tus	thy
él he, it					his, its
ella she, it	su	su	sus	sus	her, its
usted you					your
nosotros *m.* we nosotras *f.*	nuestro	nuestra	nuestros	nuestras	our
vosotros *m.* ye vosotras *f.*	vuestro	vuestra	vuestros	vuestras	your
ellos *m.* they					their
ellas *f.* they	su	su	sus	sus	their
ustedes you					your

39. 1. Like all Spanish adjectives, the possessive adjective agrees in gender and number with the noun it modifies. In contrast with the English possessive adjective in such expressions as *his book* and *her book*, the Spanish possessive adjective never indicates by its form the gender of the possessor. It is repeated before each noun to which it refers:

> **nuestro libro** our book
> **nuestra casa** our house
> **mis hermanos** my brothers
> **su libro y su papel** his book and paper
> **¿Tiene usted su pluma y sus cuadernos?** Have you your pen and notebooks?

2. As the forms **su** and **sus** have many possible meanings (his, her, its, their, your), a phrase such as **de él, de ellos, de Vd.**, etc. is often used in addition to the possessive adjective to make the meaning clear. More frequently the definite article is substituted for **su** or **sus** in the construction just described :

> **su libro de él** or **el libro de él** his book
> **sus hermanos de Vd.** or **los hermanos de Vd.** your brothers

40. *Change of Stem Vowel.* Many Spanish verbs change **e** of the stem to **ie** and **o** to **ue** when the accent falls on the last syllable of the stem. This change occurs in the present tense only, throughout the singular and in the third person plural. The first person singular of such verbs will be written out in the lesson vocabularies.

pensar to think, intend	**volver** to turn, return
pienso I think	vuelvo I turn
piensas	vuelves
piensa	vuelve
pensamos	volvemos
pensáis	volvéis
piensan	vuelven

VOCABULARY

el **árbol** the tree
la **calle** the street
la **escuela** the school, schoolhouse
la **familia** the family
la **hermana** the sister
el **hermano** the brother
los **hermanos** brothers and sisters
el **jardín** garden, yard

la **muchacha** the girl
el **muchacho** the boy
el **tiempo** time
contar to count, relate ; **cuento**, etc.
pensar to think, intend ; **pienso**, etc.
perder to lose, waste ; **pierdo**, etc.
volver to turn, return ; **vuelvo**, etc.

inteligente intelligent
todo all
que (*rel. pron.*) who, whom,
  which, that
más more
más que more than
menos que less than

muy very
siempre always
cerca de near (to)
para in order to
porque because
que (*conj.*) that, than

EXERCISES

A

Vivimos en una casa grande cerca de la escuela. La casa está
en un jardín donde hay muchos árboles. Cerca de la casa está
la calle. Nuestros padres necesitan una casa grande, porque su
familia es grande. Tengo tres hermanos, y nuestra criada tiene
también su cuarto. Mi hermano Juan y mi hermana María
estudian el español. María es una muchacha muy inteligente.
Aprende más que Juan porque estudia más. No pierde el tiempo.
Cuando vuelve de la escuela, cuenta muchas cosas interesantes
que dice el maestro. Piensa ir a España o a Méjico para aprender
el español. Estudia siempre todas sus lecciones y escribe todos
sus ejercicios. Juan es un buen muchacho, pero estudia menos
que María. En la escuela pierde el tiempo. Cuando vuelve, no
cuenta a la familia las cosas que aprende. Piensa ir a Méjico
porque es interesante, no para aprender la lengua.

B

Answer in Spanish : 1. ¿Dónde viven nuestros padres? 2. ¿Es
grande su familia? 3. ¿Dónde está la casa? 4. ¿Qué hay en el
jardín? 5. ¿Tengo yo hermanos? 6. ¿Qué estudian Juan y
María? 7. ¿Aprende Juan más que María? 8. ¿Estudia mucho
María? 9. ¿Pierde el tiempo? 10. ¿Qué cuenta en casa? 11. ¿Es
malo Juan? 12. ¿Estudia María menos que Juan? 13. ¿Dónde
piensa María aprender el español? 14. ¿Qué estudia y qué
escribe María? 15. ¿Piensa Juan estudiar en Méjico?

C

I. Choose the correct form of the possessive adjective in each case, and translate:

1. (*Mi, -s*) padres compran (*su, -s*) pan en otra panadería.
2. (*Nuestro, -a, -os, -as*) escuela está cerca de (*nuestro, -a, -os, -as*) casas.
3. (*Mi, -s*) gramática es fácil, pero Juan necesita estudiar mucho (*su, -s*) libro de lectura.
4. ¿Es interesante (*su, -s*) libro de Vd.?
5. (*Mi, -s*) hermano estudia en (*su, -s*) cuarto.
6. (*Su, -s*) criadas de ellos no son muy diligentes.
7. (*Nuestro, -a, -as, -os*) maestro es muy inteligente, pero (*su, -s*) clases no son siempre interesantes.
8. Vd. aprende más que (*su, -s*) hermana porque estudia (*su, -s*) lecciones.

II. Translate into English: 1. Juan y María vuelven a la escuela con la hermana de él y el hermano de ella. 2. Juan pierde el libro de él y el cuaderno de Vd. 3. Mi amigo y yo volvemos a la casa de él. 4. Pienso leer el libro de Vd. 5. La casa de ellos está cerca de la escuela. 6. Piensan volver a la casa de Vds. 7. ¿Piensa aprender el español el amigo de Vd.? 8. El hermano de él es más grande que el padre de ella. 9. ¿Desean libros los hermanos de Vd.? 10. ¿Piensan Juan y María estudiar la gramática de ella o el libro de lectura de él?

D

I. Continue throughout the six forms of the present tense: 1. Yo tengo mi pluma y mis libros, tú tienes tu pluma y tus libros, etc. 2. Yo pienso estudiar mis libros en mi cuarto, etc. 3. Yo pierdo mi cuaderno y mis libros, etc. 4. Yo vuelvo a mi casa con mis hermanos, etc.

II. Translate into Spanish the English words in parentheses:

1. (*My*) libro es nuevo, pero (*their*) libro es más interesante.

2. María y (*her*) hermano viven con (*their*) padres.

3. (*Their*) casa es grande, pero (*their*) familia es grande también.

4. Juan, ¿tiene Vd. (*your*) cuadernos y (*your*) gramática?

5. Sí, señor, tengo todos (*my*) libros y (*my*) papeles.

6. (*Our*) escuela es nueva.

7. (*Our*) libros de lectura son más interesantes que (*their*) gramáticas.

8. ¿Tienen Vds. (*your*) plumas y (*your*) lápices?

9. No, señor, no tenemos más que (*our*) cuadernos y (*our*) gramáticas.

10. Juan y (*his*) padres viven en (*their*) casa nueva.

E

1. John and Mary have three brothers. 2. Their parents live near the schoolhouse. 3. Our schoolhouse is very large. 4. Mary studies more than John. 5. She intends to study Spanish in Mexico. 6. She relates to her family the things that she learns in (the) school. 7. My brother is not very intelligent. 8. He has more books than I, but he loses his books and papers. 9. He does not read stories in Spanish. 10. John and Mary, when do you return from (the) school? 11. John, do you intend to study your reading lesson (lesson of reading) at home? 12. No, sir, but I intend to write my exercises.

41. *The Personal Pronoun.* In addition to the subject and prepositional forms already given, the personal pronoun has distinctive forms for the indirect object and for the direct object of a verb.

SUBJECT	AFTER PREPOSITIONS	INDIRECT OBJECT	DIRECT OBJECT
yo	mí	me to me	me me
tú	ti	te to thee	te thee
él	él {	{ to him	le him
		{ to it	lo it
ella	ella	le { to her, to it	la her, it
usted	usted	{ to you	{ le you *m.*
			{ la you *f.*
nosotros *m.*	nosotros }		
nosotras *f.*	nosotras }	nos to us	nos us
vosotros *m.*	vosotros }		
vosotras *f.*	vosotras }	os to you	os you
ellos *m.*	ellos		los them *m.*
ellas *f.*	ellas	les { to them *m.*	las them *f.*
		{ to them *f.*	
ustedes	ustedes	{ to you	{ los you *m.*
			{ las you *f.*

42. *Position of Object Pronouns.* 1. The personal-pronoun direct and indirect objects are placed immediately before the verb:

El muchacho toma el pan y lo come. The boy takes the bread and eats it.

2. Contrary to the above rule, personal-pronoun objects follow the infinitive and are joined to it:

Voy a verle. I am going to see him.

3. When a direct and an indirect object personal pronoun are used together, the indirect object precedes the direct object:

Me lo da. He gives it to me.

Desean dárnoslo. They wish to give it to us.

4. **Se** *for* **le** *or* **les.** When both pronouns are in the third person, **se** is substituted for the indirect object **le** or **les**:

Se lo da. He gives it to him (to her, to them, to you).

Tengo unos libros para los alumnos, y voy a dárselos. I have some books for the pupils, and I am going to give them to them.[1]

5. When the meaning of an object pronoun is not clear from the context, it is made so by adding the prepositional form:

Se lo doy. I give it to him (to her, to them, to you).

Se lo doy a él. I give it to him.

VOCABULARY

el **carro** the cart, wagon
la **fruta** the fruit
el **hombre** the man
la **legumbre** the vegetable
la **mujer** the woman
la **naranja** the orange
la **patata** the potato
la **pera** the pear
la **tienda** the shop
el **tomate** the tomato
el **vendedor, la vendedora** the vender

pasar to pass, spend (time); go; happen
vender to sell
lleno full
cerca near, near by
todos los días every day
por through
vale it is worth
valen they are worth
ve (he) sees

---

[1] The following suggestions may help the student to remember the positions of double object pronouns:

1. The relative position of two object pronouns in Spanish is the reverse of the usual English order:

Nos lo dan. They give it to us.

2. Since the student should not use the informal **te** and **os**, and since **se** has many meanings, it is necessary to learn only three combinations:

me lo (la, los, las), it (or them) to me
nos lo (la, los, las), it (or them) to us
se lo (la, los, las), it (or them) to him, her, it, them, you (*sing.* and *pl.*)

EXERCISES

A

Todos los días pasan por nuestra calle carros de vendedores. Un día pasa una mujer con un carro lleno de legumbres. Josefa y yo estamos en la calle. Josefa ve a la mujer y le pregunta: — ¿Tiene Vd. patatas? — La vendedora de legumbres contesta: — Sí, las tengo. — ¿Cuánto valen? — le pregunta nuestra criada. — Tres kilogramos valen una peseta — dice la vendedora. — ¿Tiene Vd. tomates también? — pregunta Josefa. — Sí, los tengo, y muy buenos. Valen una peseta el kilo. — Josefa compra dos kilos de tomates y tres de patatas. La vendedora nos da las legumbres. Josefa le da tres pesetas, y la mujer le da las gracias. Cerca hay una tienda donde venden frutas. Josefa entra conmigo en la tienda. Un vendedor nos pregunta: — ¿Qué desean Vds.? — ¿Cuánto valen las peras y las naranjas? — dice la criada. El hombre le contesta: — Las naranjas valen dos pesetas la docena, pero no tengo peras. — Josefa compra una docena de naranjas. El vendedor las cuenta, y nosotros las contamos también. Entonces Josefa me las da, y volvemos a nuestra casa.

B

Answer in Spanish: 1. ¿Dónde está la mujer? 2. ¿Qué tiene en el carro? 3. ¿Qué desea Josefa? 4. ¿Las tiene la vendedora? 5. ¿Cuánto valen? 6 ¿Qué otra clase de legumbres desea Josefa? 7. ¿Las tiene también la vendedora? 8. ¿Cuánto valen las patatas y los tomates? 9. ¿Dónde está la tienda de frutas? 10. ¿Quién nos vende frutas, un hombre o una mujer? 11. ¿Tienen peras en la tienda? 12. ¿Qué otra clase de frutas deseamos? 13. ¿Cuánto valen? 14. ¿Quién cuenta las naranjas? 15. ¿A quién las da Josefa?

C

I. Translate into English: 1. La mujer cuenta las peras y nos las da. 2. Josefa ve a la mujer y le habla. 3. El hombre vende los tomates a la criada y se los da. 4. La mujer tiene frutas;

desea vendérmelas. 5. Voy con ellos. 6. Él lo compra para mí.
7. Hablan de nosotros. 8. María tiene en su libro un cuento interesante; desea leérmelo. 9. Nos hablan de ella. 10. Tengo el
libro de Vd. y deseo dárselo. 11. Deseo dárselo a él, no a ella.
12. ¿Desea Vd. ir conmigo?

II. Place the pronoun objects in parentheses in their correct
position in the sentence:

1. El carnicero da la carne (me).
2. El pan es para (nosotros).
3. El vendedor va a vender unas frutas (les).
4. Nuestros padres escriben (nos).
5. María, ¿qué da el maestro (le)?
6. Él da un libro (me).
7. La muchacha escribe todos los días (les).
8. El libro es de (ellos).

III. Choose the correct pronominal form:

1. La criada ve la fruta y (lo, la, le) compra.
2. El maestro (nos, nosotros, nosotras) lee la lección.
3. Tengo muchos libros y deseo vender (los, las, les).
4. — ¿Desea Vd. las naranjas? — No; no (los, las, les) deseo.
5. ¿Quién (los, las, les) vende a Vds. las legumbres?
6. El alumno ve el libro y desea leer (lo, la, le).
7. El muchacho tiene una gramática nueva y va a dar (me la,
me lo, la me, lo me).
8. La criada compra los tomates, (los, las, les) cuenta, y (le
los, se los, se las, las se) da a Vd.

D

I. Translate into Spanish: 1. I give it to him. 2. He reads it
to us. 3. He is going to read it to us. 4. They go with me.
5. They are going to give it to me. 6. He speaks of us. 7. They
speak of me. 8. They want to give it to us. 9. He gives them to
me. 10. He wants to give them to me. 11. We sell it to you.
12. You are going to sell it to him.

II. In the following sentences, substitute pronouns for all the noun objects, place them correctly, and translate: 1. El vendedor da los tomates a María. 2. Las mujeres compran el pan. 3. Juan da dos pesetas a la criada. 4. Los alumnos leen las lecciones. 5. Mi madre da un libro al maestro. 6. Compro la carne. 7. Dan una naranja a Juan. 8. Doy frutas a María. 9. Leo el cuento a mis hermanas.

E

Translate into Spanish: 1. (To) Where are you going, Josephine? 2. I am going to buy vegetables for (the) dinner. 3. Who is going with you? 4. John is going with me. 5. Are you going with us? 6. Yes, I am going with you. 7. I am going to buy fruit. 8. What does the vender have in her cart? 9. Does she have potatoes? 10. Yes, she has (them). 11. She sells them to us every day. 12. Does she sell you tomatoes also? 13. Yes, she has very good ones (has them very good). 14. Do you want some (them)? 15. No, I do not want them. 16. I want fruit. 17. Does she have any (it)? 18. No, she does not have any.

LESSON X

43. *Reflexive Verbs.* 1. Reflexive verbs differ from other verbs only in the fact that each form is accompanied by a reflexive pronoun. This must always be of the same person and number as the verb.

2. In the first and second persons singular and plural the reflexive pronouns have the same forms as other object pronouns (Lesson IX) :

Me lavo. I wash myself.
Nos lavamos. We wash ourselves.

3. In the third person, both singular and plural, the reflexive form is always **se** :

Se lava. He washes himself *or* You (**Vd.**) wash yourself.
Se lavan. They wash themselves *or* You (**Vds.**) wash yourselves.

(Do not confuse this **se** with that discussed in Article **42**, 4.)

4. Reflexive pronouns have the same position as other object pronouns (Article **42**).

5. After prepositions **se** becomes **sí**; **con** combined with **sí** becomes **consigo** :

Habla mucho de sí. He talks a great deal about himself.
Me llevan consigo. They are taking me with them.

44. *Use of the Reflexive.* The reflexive construction is much more frequent in Spanish than in English. Its principal uses are :

1. The usual reflexive use of transitive verbs as in English, with literal meaning :

Se odia. He hates himself.
Me divierto. I amuse myself.

55

2. In certain constructions the English equivalents of which are intransitive:

Me levanto. I get up (raise myself up).
Nos acostamos. We go to bed (put ourselves to bed).

3. As a substitute for the passive voice when the agent is not expressed:

Se venden aquí frutas y legumbres. Fruits and vegetables are sold here.
Se bebe mucho café en España. Much coffee is drunk in Spain.

levantarse to get up	**sentarse** to sit down
me levanto	me siento
te levantas	te sientas
se levanta	se sienta
nos levantamos	nos sentamos
os levantáis	os sentáis
se levantan	se sientan

45. Many stem-changing verbs (Article **40**) are also reflexive:

Se sientan. They sit down (seat themselves).
Me despierto. I wake up (awaken myself).

46.

querer to wish, be fond of	
quiero I wish	queremos
quieres	queréis
quiere	quieren

Note. Hereafter, in giving verb forms, the polite forms with **Vd.**, **Vds.**, will be omitted. Although the second-person forms are given for the sake of completeness, the beginning student should always translate *you* by **usted(es)** with the verb in the third person.

VOCABULARY

la alcoba the bedroom
el baño the bath
el café the coffee
el cuarto de baño the bathroom
el desayuno the breakfast
la escalera the stairway
la oficina the office
bajar to go down; **bajar de (un tren)** to get off (a train)
bañarse to take a bath; **me baño,** etc.
beber to drink
desayunarse to breakfast; **me desayuno,** etc.
despertar to awaken (another); **despertarse** to wake up; **me despierto,** etc.
dormir to sleep; **duermo,** etc.

encontrar to meet, find; **encuentro,** etc.
hacer to do, make
lavar to wash; **lavarse** to wash oneself; **me lavo,** etc.
levantarse to get up; **me levanto,** etc.
querer to wish; be fond of
sentarse to sit down; **me siento,** etc.
listo ready
mismo same
allí there
como like, as
poco (*adv.*) little
después afterwards; **después de** after
antes de before
durante during

EXERCISES

A

Mi hermano y yo dormimos en el mismo cuarto. Yo duermo poco, él duerme mucho. Cuando me despierto, me levanto. Primero voy al cuarto de baño y me baño. Entonces despierto a mi hermano. Es siempre muy difícil despertarle. No quiere levantarse, pero lo hace. Él se baña también. No nos desayunamos en la alcoba como muchos españoles. Cuando mi hermano está listo, bajamos la escalera, y entramos en el comedor. Encontramos allí a nuestros padres y a nuestra hermana. Siempre está lista primero. Mi madre se sienta a la mesa. Entonces mi hermana y yo nos sentamos, y mi padre y mi hermano se sientan. Para el desayuno no se come mucho en España. Se bebe café y se come un panecillo. Durante el desayuno mi padre lee siempre el periódico. Después va a su oficina. Mis hermanos y yo vamos a la escuela. Mi madre va a la cocina para hablar con nuestra criada. Quieren hablar de la comida que la criada va a preparar.

B

1. ¿En qué cuarto duerme mi hermano? 2. ¿Dónde duermo yo? 3. ¿Duerme Vd. en una silla? 4. ¿Duermo más que mi hermano? 5. ¿Me despierto después de mi hermano? 6. ¿Dónde me baño? 7. ¿Se baña también mi hermano? 8. ¿Se desayunan muchos españoles en la alcoba? 9. ¿Dónde nos desayunamos los norteamericanos? 10. ¿Qué hacemos para ir al comedor? 11. ¿Quién se sienta primero a la mesa? 12. ¿Quién se sienta después? 13. ¿Tomamos carne para el desayuno? 14. ¿Va nuestro padre con nosotros a la escuela? 15. ¿Va nuestra madre a la oficina?

C

I. Give all six forms of the following verbs and translate: 1. Me baño, etc. 2. Me lavo, etc. 3. Me desayuno, etc. 4. Encuentro, etc. 5. Me despierto, etc. 6. Me siento, etc. 7. Me levanto, etc.

II. Fill the blanks in the following sentences with the appropriate reflexive pronouns. (Do not write in this book.)

1. __?__ bañamos.
2. Vd. __?__ levanta.
3. Lo toma para __?__.
4. __?__ desayunamos.
5. Voy a bañar__?__.
6. Queremos levantar__?__.
7. Vds. __?__ sientan.
8. __?__ siento.
9. Van a sentar__?__.
10. Hablan de __?__.
11. __?__ desayunan.
12. Juan y yo __?__ sentamos.

13. _ _ ? _ _ despierto.
14. Vd. va a lavar _ _ ? _ _.
15. Vamos a levantar _ _ ? _ _.

D

I. Translate into Spanish the English words in parentheses:

1. Mi padre me (*awakens*).
2. Mi hermano no quiere (*wake up*).
3. Siempre (*I eat breakfast*) en el comedor.
4. No queremos (*sit down*).
5. Mi hermano y yo (*get up*).
6. (*We bathe*) en el cuarto de baño.
7. Mis padres (*wake up*) primero.
8. No quiero (*sit down*).
9. Mi hermana nos (*meets*) en el comedor.
10. Siempre quiero (*bathe*) antes del desayuno.

II. Translate: 1. He meets us. 2. You (*sing.*) sit down. 3. We sleep. 4. I wake up. 5. They get up. 6. You (*pl.*) are breakfasting. 7. We meet him. 8. You (*sing.*) wake up. 9. They bathe. 10. He sleeps.

E

1. John and his brother sleep a great deal. 2. They sleep in the same room. 3. When their parents wake up, their father awakens the boys. 4. John gets up first; then his brother gets up. 5. They go downstairs to the dining room. 6. Many Spaniards breakfast in their bedrooms (the bedroom). 7. We breakfast in the dining room with our parents. 8. We sit down at the table. 9. The Spaniards eat very little for breakfast. 10. They take coffee and rolls. 11. The English and the North Americans eat much more. 12. They eat meat, bread, fruit, coffee, and other things.

REVIEW LESSON II

[Introduction, Articles 7–10, particularly Article 7, 4; Lessons VI–X]

A

I. Every **b**, **v**, and **g** in the following exercise is of the fricative type, described in Article **7**, 2. Read and reread the words slowly, following directions carefully:

haba	cabo	amago	plaga	Pablo
uva	Habana	lugar	paga	tuve
habla	lobo	maga	abogado	mago
habrá	tuvo	lagar	tubo	pagaba
Cuba	lago	haga	siglo	lavabo
lava	amigo	hagamos	pagano	hago

II. Explain how you know that the **g** and **j** sounds in the following exercise are identical. Pronounce each word carefully:

paja	hija	magín	oveja	junto
lujo	coger	magia	conejo	laja
gema	cojo	junto	página	Jorge
jamás	bajo	tejo	justo	gesto
lejos	baja	gemelo	Josefa	giro
gira	Gijón	gemir	gente	lejano

III. Put the speech organs in the correct position for **ll**, as described in Article **7**, 4, and read and reread carefully the following syllables and words:

lla, lle, lli, llo, llu	llave	lleva	callo	bollo
llana	llaga	llora	calla	agalla
llano	llamo	lloro	malla	pillo
llena	lluvia	llovía	mella	cabello
lleno	llega	bello	palla	muralla
llama	llegada	caballo	bellaco	pollo

IV. Apply to **ñ** the directions given in III above for **ll**:

ña, ñe, ñi, ño, ñu	ñanga	ñoque	baña	año
ñame	ñango	ñuto	caña	moño
ñaco	ñaque	ñopo	niño	moña
ñachi	ñatas	ñorba	estaño	hogaño
ñandú	ñato	paño	pequeño	antaño
ñandutí	ñoca	baño	castaño	cabaña

V. 1. Every **rr** and **r** in the following list is multiple (three or four vibrations). In each case be sure you produce a definite lingual vibration.

barra	porra	burra	barro	honra
parra	corro	horrible	ropa	enredo
borra	garra	carro	Roma	el ratón
narra	burro	ahorra	rapa	el robo

2. Every **r** in the first ten examples below is simple (one tap of the tongue). In the remaining examples the **r** is sometimes simple and sometimes multiple. Distinguish carefully.

para	contra	rueda	Paraná	tarro
pero	duro	barrera	el roto	rabo
Pedro	enero	torre	rocío	sombrero
cara	Perú	torero	coro	María
toro	caro	carrera	tira	raro
moro	carro	honrado	ahora	guerrero

VI. Practice until you can read correctly and rapidly the following series of syllables and words:

ca, que, qui, co, cu
za, ce, ci, zo, zu
ga, gue, gui, go, gu
gua, güe, güi, guo
ja, ge, gi, jo, ju
ca, za, ga, gua, ja
ca, ce, gui, guo, ju, gue, gi, güe, gui, zo, cu, ju, gu, zu, jo,
    cocuyo, jícara, guardia, guedeja, zapato, zumo, coge, jota,
    agua, gemir, queso, cuatro, gana, gema, lengua, baja, gimo,
    gigante, zurrón, jipijapa, guerra, contigo, cojo, cesta, cinco.

VII. Read the following words slowly, pausing between syllables and indicating the position of the accent by stress of voice:

bacalao	pingüe	argüir	porque	reyes
ancho	entonces	país	leo	centro
interés	cerquita	paisano	ley	tabla
monosílabo	vengo	baúl	leyendo	escocés
construcción	fuerza	causa	reina	copla
libre	caída	alguno	rey	silvestre

VIII. In each of the following sentences decide whether **ser** or **estar** is required:

1. Madrid (*es, está*) en España.
2. Juan (*es, está*) alumno.
3. (*Soy, estoy*) enfermo.
4. La casa (*es, está*) grande.
5. (*Somos, estamos*) en Méjico.
6. (*Somos, estamos*) de Méjico.
7. El lápiz (*es, está*) rojo.
8. (*Soy, estoy*) en casa.
9. La gramática (*es, está*) interesante.
10. María (*es, está*) cansada.

IX. Translate into English: 1. Juan estudia en su libro. 2. Vivo en mi casa. 3. Doy al maestro la gramática de Juan. 4. Tengo la pluma de él, no el lápiz de ella. 5. Juan escribe con su pluma en el cuaderno de María. 6. María da a Juan mi gramática y mi libro de lectura. 7. El muchacho va al jardín con su hermano. 8. Juan está en su casa; no está en la casa del maestro. 9. Damos una peseta a nuestro panadero. 10. Los amigos de Vd. van con el padre de Juan a su oficina.

X. Select from within each set of parentheses what is needed to make a correct reading, and translate the sentence:

1. Tengo mi libro, y qu(-e-, -ie-, -o-, -ue-)ro estudiar(-le, -la, -lo).

2. Los alumnos c(-o-, -ie-, -ue-)ntan a sus padres las cosas que (*los, las, les*) dice el maestro.

3. Mi padre toma una silla y *(lo, le, la, se)* s(-*e*-, -*ie*-, -*o*-, -*ue*-)nta en *(él, ella, lo, la)*.

4. Juan v(-*e*-, -*ie*-, -*o*-, -*ue*-)lve a casa porque p(-*e*-, -*ie*-, -*o*-, -*ue*-)nsa estudiar.

5. María tiene todos sus libros; no *(los, las, les)* p(-*e*-, -*ie*-, -*o*-, -*ue*-)rde.

6. Mi padre *(lo, le, la, se)* levanta y *(lo, le, la, se)* desayuna.

7. Mi madre va con *(mi, me, -migo, -sigo)* a desp(-*e*-, -*ie*-, -*o*-, -*ue*-)rtar a mi hermano.

8. Enc(-*e*-, -*ie*-, -*o*-, -*ue*-)ntro a mi amigo y *(lo, le, la, se)* doy su pluma.

9. *(Me, nos, los, se)* sentamos a la mesa y *(me, nos, los, se)* desayunamos.

10. Juan enc(-*e*-, -*ie*-, -*o*-, -*ue*-)ntra la pluma de María y *(le lo, se lo, le la, se la)* da.

B

I. Translate correctly into Spanish the English words in parentheses:

1. *(I am)* en la escuela, pero *(I am going)* a casa.
2. Juan *(gives)* el libro *(to the)* maestro; no quiere dar *(it to me)*.
3. Josefa *(wants)* ir *(with me)*.
4. María *(is)* cansada; *(she is not)* enferma.
5. *(His sister)* y *(her brother)* van *(with me)* mañana.
6. Juan encuentra *(the teacher)* en la calle.
7. Mi hermano va con *(us)*.
8. Mucha carne *(is sold)* en *(our)* carnicería.

II. Translate into Spanish: 1. We are from Mexico. 2. I meet John's father. 3. They intend to go. 4. I return with him. 5. They get up. 6. He sits down. 7. They want to go with us. 8. You *(sing.)* see the teacher. 9. I want to give it to you *(pl.)*. 10. She is a student. 11. She is sick. 12. His house. 13. Her father. 14. The teacher's pencil. 15. I go with your *(sing.)* friend.

C

Translate into Spanish: 1. He is going with us to the dining room. 2. My book and my father's newspaper are on the table. 3. I want her pen, not your pencil. 4. They are returning from the schoolhouse with the teacher's brother. 5. They sit down at the table and eat breakfast. 6. He gives it to John; he does not give it to you. 7. Many things are bought and sold in my father's store. 8. We are going with his father, not with their brothers. 9. They intend to go with us. 10. The vender's cart is in our street.

LESSON XI

47. *First Conjugation, Imperfect and Preterit Indicative*

hablar to speak	
IMPERFECT INDICATIVE	PRETERIT INDICATIVE
hablaba I was speaking, used to speak	hablé I spoke
hablabas	hablaste
hablaba	habló
hablábamos	hablamos
hablabais	hablasteis
hablaban	hablaron

48. *Uses of the Imperfect and Preterit.* 1. The imperfect has two principal uses : (*a*) It denotes an action repeated an *indefinite* number of times in the past. If a definite number of repetitions is indicated or implied, the preterit is used.

> **Le encontraba todos los días.** I used to meet him every day.
> **Siempre tomaba un billete de primera clase.** He always got a first-class ticket.

But :

> **Le hablé tres veces, pero no contestó.** I spoke to him three times, but he did not reply.

(*b*) It indicates that an action or state was *in progress* at a specified time in the past. The action or state is always represented as *incomplete,* no indication being given as to when it began or when it ended. The imperfect is employed in past descriptions and in indicating past mental states. Accompanying narration is usually in the preterit.

> **Cuando me levanté, llovía** (*imperf.*). When I got up, it was raining.

65

But :

Llovió (*pret.*) **todo el día.** It rained all day.

Nos visitó cuando vivíamos (*imperf.*) **en Madrid.** He visited us when we were living in Madrid.

But :

Vivimos (*pret.*) **dos años en Madrid.** We lived in Madrid two years.

Tenía (*imperf.*) **unos ojos grandes y negros.** She had large, black eyes.

Pensaba estudiar en España. He was intending to study in Spain.

2. The preterit indicates that an act was completed at a definite time in the past. It is the tense used to denote single past happenings, whether the time occupied was short or long.

El tren se paró en la estación. The train stopped at the station.

Viajó conmigo todo el verano. He traveled with me all summer.

Pasó tres años en Méjico. He spent three years in Mexico.

VOCABULARY

el **asiento** the seat
el **billete** the ticket
el **campo** the country, field
la **estación** the station
la **hora** the hour
la **llegada** the arrival
el **primo** the cousin
la **semana** the week
la **tía** the aunt
el **tío** the uncle
los **tíos** the uncle and aunt
el **tren** the train
la **ventanilla** the (car) window
la **vez** the time ; **a veces** at times : **muchas veces** often ;

de **vez en cuando** sometimes, from time to time
el **viaje** the journey, voyage, trip
el **viajero** the traveler
Dorotea Dorothy
José Joseph
acompañar to accompany
esperar to await, wait for, expect, hope
llevar to carry, take with one
mirar to look, look at, watch
pararse to stop
tomar to get, buy (a ticket) ; eat *or* drink

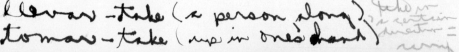

viajar to travel
visitar to visit
pasado past
ayer yesterday

cuándo (*interrog.*) when
ya already
vivía (*imperf.*) he lived, was
living

EXERCISES

A

La semana pasada visité a mis tíos que viven en el campo. Mi padre me acompañó a la estación. Tomé un billete de primera clase, y nos sentamos en la estación para esperar la llegada del tren. Esperamos una hora. Cuando el tren entró en la estación y se paró, encontré un buen asiento. Miré por la ventanilla y noté que mi padre y muchos viajeros entraban ya en la estación. En un asiento cerca de mí dos hombres hablaban. Me miraron dos o tres veces. Entonces uno de ellos me preguntó a dónde pensaba ir. Contesté que pensaba visitar a mi tío, que vivía en el campo. Le pregunté dónde vivía él, y contestó que vivía también en el campo, muy cerca de mi tío. Su hermano, que viajaba con él, también vivía cerca de allí. A veces durante el viaje miraba el campo. De vez en cuando el tren se paraba en una estación. Después de dos horas de viaje el tren se paró en la estación cerca de donde viven mis tíos. Cuando bajé del tren, allí estaba mi tío que me esperaba. Me llevó consigo a su casa, donde encontré a mi tía y a mis primos, José y Dorotea.

B

1. ¿Qué es un tío? 2. ¿Qué es una tía? 3. ¿Un primo? 4. ¿Dónde viven los tíos que visité? 5. ¿Cuándo los visité? 6. ¿Me acompañaron mis hermanos a la estación? 7. ¿Tomó mi padre un billete? 8. ¿Dónde se paró el tren? 9. Cuando viajamos, ¿encontramos siempre un buen asiento? 10. ¿Estaba mi padre en el tren? 11. ¿Hablé yo con él durante el viaje? 12. ¿Dónde estaban los dos hombres? 13. ¿Qué me preguntaron? 14. ¿Dónde bajé del tren? 15. ¿Quién estaba allí? 16. ¿Dónde encontré a mi tía y a mis primos?

C

I. Translate and give the tense and infinitive of each of the following verb forms:

estudiábamos	bajé	Vd. visitaba	nos levantamos
deseó	Vds. se sentaron	pensaban	visité
escucho	cuentan	tomó	viajaron
compra	pensamos	me paraba	mirábamos
entraba	esperó	se bañó	prepara

II. Decide whether the imperfect or preterit should be used in each of the following sentences:

1. Mi amigo me (*visitaba, visitó*) todos los días.

2. (*Pensábamos, Pensamos*) estudiar nuestras lecciones.

3. (*Encontraba, Encontré*) a mi hermano en la calle.

4. Cuando nos (*visitaban, visitaron*) mis primos, (*tomábamos, tomamos*) café todos los días.

5. Me (*levantaba, levanté*) primero ayer.

6. (*Esperaban, Esperaron*) a sus tíos cuando (*bajaban, bajaron*) del tren.

7. Josefa (*pensaba, pensó*) acompañarme a la panadería.

8. Mi padre (*hablaba, habló*) con un amigo cuando yo (*entraba, entré*).

9. María no nos (*hablaba, habló*) porque (*estudiaba, estudió*).

10. Siempre le (*hablábamos, hablamos*) cuando le (*encontrábamos, encontramos*).

D

Translate the English words in parentheses by the Spanish imperfect or preterit, giving reasons for your decision:

1. Cuando mi tío nos (*used to visit*), (*he took*) café todos los días.

2. Un día (*I spoke*) con mi primo.

3. (*We met*) a sus amigos la semana pasada, y nos (*spoke*) de Vd.

4. María (*was preparing*) su lección de gramática cuando (*we entered*).

5. Ayer (*I bought*) un libro y una pluma.

6. ¿Quién (*was talking*) con Vd. cuando yo (*entered*)?

7. El muchacho siempre nos (*used to look at*) cuando nos (*met*).

8. Cuando (*we were*) en la escuela, (*we did not study*) mucho.

9. Mi hermano (*got off*) del tren cuando (*it stopped*).

10. Cuando (*we were traveling*) en España, (*we ate breakfast*) en la alcoba.

E

1. Joseph's parents live in the country. 2. One day he took me with him to (*a*) visit them. 3. My parents accompanied us to the station. 4. Many travelers were getting their tickets when we entered. 5. We got our tickets and sat down in the station. 6. We were talking when the train stopped. 7. We found good seats in the train. 8. Near us two men were talking. 9. We asked them where they lived. 10. When we got off (from) the train, my friend's parents were waiting for us. 11. They took us with them to their house. 12. There I found Joseph's brother and sister.

LESSON XII

49. *Second and Third Conjugations, Imperfect and Preterit Indicative.* The endings of the second and third conjugations are identical throughout the imperfect and preterit indicative.

aprender to learn	
IMPERFECT INDICATIVE	PRETERIT INDICATIVE
aprendía I was learning, used to learn	aprendí I learned
aprendías	aprendiste
aprendía	aprendió
aprendíamos	aprendimos
aprendíais	aprendisteis
aprendían	aprendieron
escribir to write	
escribía I was writing, used to write	escribí I wrote
escribías	escribiste
escribía	escribió
escribíamos	escribimos
escribíais	escribisteis
escribían	escribieron

50. *The Prepositions* **para** *and* **por.** 1. **Para** denotes use, purpose, or destination, and may be translated by *for, to, in order to* :

un vaso para vino a wineglass
dos pesetas al día para carne two pesetas a day for meat
Tomamos café para el desayuno. We take coffee for breakfast.
Estudio para aprender. I study in order to learn.
Tomó el tren para Madrid. He took the train for Madrid.
El libro es para Vd. The book is for you.

James Sawders

The Famous " Silver Mountain," Potosí, Bolivia, Is One of the
Richest Silver Deposits Ever Discovered

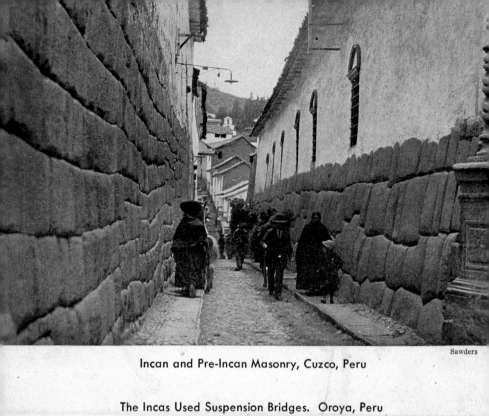

Incan and Pre-Incan Masonry, Cuzco, Peru

The Incas Used Suspension Bridges. Oroya, Peru

2. **Por** denotes reason or cause, exchange, manner or means, duration of time, place through which, and may be translated by *for, in behalf of, by, during, through,* etc. :

Lo hace por Vd. He does it for you (in your behalf).

Compró la fruta por dos pesetas. He bought the fruit for two pesetas.

Viaja por tren. He travels by train.

por la mañana during the morning

Corría por las calles. He used to run through the streets.

VOCABULARY

la aldea the village
el caballo the horse
la casa: a casa (toward) home
el cielo the sky
la ciudad the city
la finca the farm
la flor the flower
la gallina the hen
el huevo the egg
la leche the milk
la mañana the morning, forenoon
el pájaro the bird
la parte the part; **por todas partes** everywhere

la vaca the cow
buscar to look for
correr to run
cultivar to cultivate, till
montar to mount; **montar a caballo** to ride on horseback
parecer to appear, seem
azul blue
hermoso handsome, beautiful
pequeño little
mientras while
temprano early
por for, by, during, through
hasta (*conj.*) even
había there was, there were

EXERCISES

A

Cuando visité a mis tíos, vivían en una finca pequeña cerca de una aldea. Tenían en la finca dos o tres caballos, unas vacas y muchas gallinas. Mi primo y yo nos levantábamos muy temprano todas las mañanas y corríamos por todas partes. En los árboles cerca de la casa había muchos pájaros, y buscábamos sus huevos. Hasta en los campos encontrábamos de vez en cuando huevos de pájaros. Todas las cosas parecían muy hermosas. Hasta el cielo parecía más azul que en la ciudad. Mi tío cultivaba los campos con sus caballos. Mi tía cultivaba sus flores en el jardín. Durante mi visita aprendí a montar a caballo. Las vacas daban leche, y mi tío la vendía en la aldea. Las gallinas también la bebían. Había muchos huevos, y yo los buscaba para mi tía. Tomaba leche y huevos todos los días para el desayuno. Un día mi tía y dos amigas que vivían cerca me llevaron consigo a la aldea. Todas tenían huevos y otras cosas que deseaban vender. Mi tía vendió unas docenas de huevos y compró cosas para mi tío y para la comida. Entonces volvimos a casa.

B

1. ¿Dónde vivían mis tíos? 2. ¿Qué tenían en la finca? 3. ¿Nos levantábamos temprano mi primo y yo? 4. ¿Por dónde corríamos? 5. ¿Qué buscábamos? 6. ¿Qué aprendí a hacer? 7. ¿Qué daban las vacas? 8. ¿Quién cultivaba los campos? 9. ¿Con qué los cultivaba? 10. ¿Qué cultivaba mi tía? 11. ¿A dónde me llevaron mi tía y sus amigas? 12. ¿Qué tenían? 13. ¿Qué deseaban hacer? 14. ¿Qué vendió mi tía? 15. ¿Qué compró? 16. ¿A dónde volvimos?

C

I. Translate the following verb forms and give the infinitive of each:

Vd. bebió	leí	comieron
vivieron	escribimos	bebía
aprendemos	dormimos	come
volvía	vuelvo	duermen
perdían	vendía	Vds. escribían
comíamos	perdió	corrimos

II. Translate the following sentences, accounting for the use of each imperfect and preterit:

1. Yo *estaba* en la sala de clase cuando *entró* mi amigo.
2. *Visitaban* a sus tíos todas las semanas.
3. Mientras *dormíamos* mi hermano *estudiaba* sus lecciones.

4. *Tomaron* huevos para el desayuno.

5. Cuando *estuve* en los Estados Unidos, *aprendí* a hablar inglés.

6. Los *buscó* por todas partes.

7. *Bebimos* café para el desayuno.

8. Siempre se *levantaban* temprano.

III. Supply either **para** or **por**. (Do not write in this book.)

1. Bebe leche _ _ ? _ _ el desayuno.

2. Muchas veces duermo _ _ ? _ _ la mañana.

3. Vamos a Madrid _ _ ? _ _ Irún.

4. Entramos _ _ ? _ _ la cocina.

5. Deseo acompañarle _ _ ? _ _ buscar a su hermano.

6. Va a darle tres pesetas _ _ ? _ _ el libro.

7. La criada preparó la comida _ _ ? _ _ Vd.

8. El vendedor tiene un carro _ _ ? _ _ frutas.

9. Los buscó _ _ ? _ _ todas partes.

10. Los muchachos corrían _ _ ? _ _ los campos.

11. Voy a tomar el tren _ _ ? _ _ Sevilla.

12. Se sienta a la mesa _ _ ? _ _ comer.

D

Translate the English words in parentheses by the Spanish imperfect or preterit, giving reasons for your decision:

1. Mi hermano y yo (*used to live*) en la ciudad.

2. (*We slept*) en el mismo cuarto.

3. Yo (*used to get up*) primero, porque él (*slept*) mucho.

4. Un día él (*got up*) primero, y cuando yo (*woke up*) él (*was writing*) en un cuaderno.

5. Cuando (*we went down*) la escalera nuestros padres (*were eating breakfast*).

6. (*We sat down*) a la mesa.

7. Yo (*ate*) un huevo y (*drank*) leche.

8. Mi hermano (*ate*) pan y carne y (*drank*) café.

9. Mientras (*we were eating*) mi padre (*was reading*) el periódico.

10. Después del desayuno yo (*wrote*) mis ejercicios.

E

1. My uncle and aunt used to live in the country. 2. We lived in the city, but I visited them from time to time. 3. Once when (*Una vez que*) I visited them I took a friend with me. 4. He wanted to ride horseback, and so did I (and I also). 5. One day I rode horseback with one of my cousins. 6. My uncle used to cultivate the fields. 7. Sometimes we accompanied him. 8. One day I found two eggs in the fields and carried them to the house. 9. When I entered the house my aunt was preparing (the) dinner. 10. Sometimes my aunt sold eggs in the village. 11. One day she and I took my friend with us. 12. We sold all our eggs and bought some things for (the) dinner.

LESSON XIII

51. *Some Irregular Verbs*

ser to be	estar to be	tener to have	ir to go	dar to give	querer to wish
		IMPERFECT INDICATIVE			
era eras era éramos erais eran	estaba (regular)	tenía (regular)	iba ibas iba íbamos ibais iban	daba (regular)	quería (regular)
		PRETERIT INDICATIVE			
fuí fuiste fué fuimos fuisteis fueron	estuve estuviste estuvo estuvimos estuvisteis estuvieron	tuve tuviste tuvo tuvimos tuvisteis tuvieron	fuí (same as **ser**)	di diste dió dimos disteis dieron	quise quisiste quiso quisimos quisisteis quisieron

52. *Definite Article with Abstract and General Nouns.* The definite article must be employed before abstract nouns and nouns used in a general sense, that is, to represent an entire class of persons or objects:

> **La vida es interesante.** Life is interesting.
> **Las flores son hermosas.** Flowers are beautiful.

75

VOCABULARY

el **animal** animal
la **avena** oats
el **campesino** countryman, farmer
el **color** color
la **cosecha** harvest, harvesting
el **heno** hay
la **hierba** grass
el **invierno** winter
el **maíz** corn
el **sol** sun; **al sol** in the sun
el **trigo** wheat
el **verano** summer
la **vida** life
ayudar to aid, help

comer: **dar de comer a** to feed (animals), *children*
cortar to cut
dejar to leave, let
gustar to be pleasing; **Me gusta el libro** I like the book
hacerse to be made
recoger to gather, harvest
trabajar to work
alto tall, high
maduro ripe
ocupado busy
seco dry
útil useful
cómo (*interrog.*) how

EXERCISES

A

Durante mi visita con mis tíos encontré muy interesante la vida del campo. Me gustó mucho. Era verano, y los campesinos estaban muy ocupados. La primera semana de mi visita cultivaban el maíz, que estaba ya muy alto. Después trabajaron en otras cosas. Mi tío tenía muchos campos, y yo iba con él muchas veces a mirarle y a ayudarle. Un día fuí a un campo donde él cortaba hierba para hacer heno. Después de cortarla, la dejó unas horas al sol. Cuando estuvo seca ya era heno, y lo llevó a casa. Pensaba darlo de comer a los animales durante el invierno. Otro día notamos por el color de la avena y el trigo que estaban maduros, y que necesitábamos recogerlos. La cosecha me gustó, pero necesitamos trabajar mucho. El trigo es muy útil, porque del trigo se hace el pan. Muchas veces yo daba maíz a las gallinas. Comían también cosas que encontraban en los campos. Los caballos comían maíz, avena y heno cuando trabajaban. Cuando no trabajaban comían hierba en los campos. En el verano las vacas comen hierba, pero en el invierno comen heno y maíz como los caballos.

B

1. ¿Es Vd. campesino? 2. ¿Dónde vive Vd.? 3. ¿Le gusta a Vd. la vida del campo? 4. ¿Están muy ocupados los campesinos en el invierno? 5. ¿Dónde trabajaba mi tío? 6. ¿Iba con él mi tía? 7. ¿Qué cortó un día mi tío? 8. ¿Cómo se hace el heno? 9. ¿A dónde lo llevó mi tío? 10. ¿Qué se hace del trigo? 11. ¿Son útiles la avena y el maíz? 12. ¿Qué comen las gallinas? 13. ¿Comen trigo los caballos? 14. ¿Cuándo está maduro el trigo? 15. ¿Qué comen las vacas en el verano?

C

I. Translate the following verb forms and give the infinitive of each:

dió	estuve	quiso	quise	fué
querían	tuvo	iban	di	quisimos
éramos	tenían	fuimos	somos	tuvimos
fuí	tiene	estuvieron	estoy	Vd. era

II. Choose the correct verb form:

1. Yo (*estaba, estuve, era, fuí*) en casa cuando Vd. me (*visitaba, visité, visitó*).

2. Los alumnos (*dábamos, daban, dimos, dieron*) los libros al maestro ayer.

3. Mi tío (*tenía, tenían, tuvo, tuvieron*) caballos y vacas.

4. Las vacas (*daba, daban, dió, dieron*) mucha leche todos los días.

5. El maíz (*estaba, estuvo, era, fué*) maduro.

6. Un día nosotros (*íbamos, iban, fuimos, fueron*) a mirar los campos.

7. El vendedor (*iba, iban, fuí, fué*) a nuestra calle todos los días.

8. Mi hermano y yo (*fué, fuimos, iba, íbamos*) al campo todos los veranos.

III. Indicate whether or not the articles in the following sentences are correctly used, and translate:

1. Me gustan (*las*) flores.
2. (*Los*) campesinos trabajan mucho.
3. Es (*un*) maestro.
4. Es (*un*) maestro muy inteligente.
5. (*El*) maíz es muy útil.
6. (*El*) café es negro.
7. Es (*un*) inglés.
8. Comemos (*la*) fruta y (*las*) legumbres todos los días.
9. (*La*) vida de (*la*) ciudad me gusta más que (*la*) vida (*del*) campo.
10. (*Los*) muchachos son siempre malos.

D

I. In the following sentences, change the verbs to the tense indicated and translate:

1. Va a casa (*pret.*).
2. Me da lecciones de español (*imp.*).
3. Está en casa (*imp.*).
4. Doy maíz a las gallinas (*pret.*).
5. Tienen caballos (*imp.*).
6. Vamos con mi tía (*pret.*).
7. La casa es grande (*imp.*).
8. Tengo un cuaderno (*imp.*).
9. Le damos el libro (*pret.*).
10. Somos alumnos (*imp.*).

II. Translate: 1. Cows are useful. 2. Milk is white. 3. We ate bread. 4. My aunt gave me coffee. 5. Horses are intelligent. 6. He bought meat. 7. Meat is red. 8. We write with chalk.

III. Translate: 1. I like bread. 2. We like eggs. 3. He likes the book. 4. They do not like flowers. 5. Do you (*pl.*) like the city? 6. We don't like our seat. 7. Do you (*sing.*) like oranges?

E

1. We liked country life (The life of the country was pleasing to us). 2. We were busy every day. 3. One day we went to the fields to look at the wheat. 4. The wheat and oats were ripe, but the corn was not ripe. 5. The farmers were cultivating the corn. 6. Corn is very useful, because horses and cows eat it. 7. We buy white bread, which is made of wheat. 8. My uncle's horses ate corn every day. 9. One day I gave them wheat, but they did not eat it. 10. They do not like wheat. 11. The cows used to eat grass during the day. 12. One day my cousin and I went for (looked for) them and took them home. 13. They gave good milk, which we liked [very] much. 14. For breakfast we used to drink milk and eat bread, potatoes, and eggs.

LESSON XIV

53.   *Forms of the Participles*

INFINITIVE	PRESENT PARTICIPLE	PAST PARTICIPLE
-ar	-ando	-ado
-er ⎱ -ir ⎰	-iendo	-ido
hablar to speak comer vivir ir	hablando speaking comiendo viviendo yendo (irregular)	hablado spoken comido vivido ido

The participles of **ser, estar, tener, dar,** and **querer** are regular. Give them.

54. *The Present Participle.* 1. The present participle always ends in **-ndo,** as indicated in the diagram above.

2. It is usually translated by the English present participle:

Encontré a mi hermano escribiendo en su cuaderno. I found my brother writing in his notebook.

It is almost never used, however,. as the object of a preposition. For this and certain other constructions the infinitive is employed (see Article **58**).

3. As in the case of the infinitive (Article **42**, 2), a personal-pronoun object follows the present participle and is joined to it. A written accent is necessary, for the participle has the same stress as if it stood alone:

hablándome speaking to me   **comiéndolo** eating it

4. The present participle is used with **estar** to form the progressive tenses, which are similar in form and use to the English progressive. They are more emphatically progressive, and less frequently used, than the Spanish simple tenses. (Compare Article **22**.)

Estoy comiendo or Como. I am eating.

Estaba escuchando or Escuchaba. He was listening.

55. *The Past Participle.* 1. The past participle is used with the auxiliary verb **haber** to form the perfect tenses. When so used it always ends in **-o**.

2. Used as an adjective it agrees in gender and number with the noun or pronoun it modifies:

> **la semana pasada** last week
> **campos cultivados** cultivated fields

3. The past participle is used with **ser** to form the passive voice, similar to the English passive but less common. When so used it agrees in gender and number with the subject. In Spanish the passive is usually employed only when the agent is expressed, other English passive constructions being translated by the reflexive (Article **44**, 3):

La carta fué recibida por el maestro. The letter was received by the teacher.

Fuimos acompañados por tres muchachos. We were accompanied by three boys.

56. *Uses of* **tener** *and* **haber.** 1. There are two verbs in Spanish which mean *to have.* The one so far used in this text is **tener**, usually meaning *to possess*:

Mi tío tiene vacas y caballos. My uncle has cows and horses.

2. *a.* **Haber** is used principally as an auxiliary verb to form the perfect tenses (Articles **55**, 1, and **57**).

b. The third person singular of **haber** may be used impersonally in every tense. It means, according to the tense, *there is, there are; there was, there were; there will be;* etc. In this impersonal use, **hay**, which has been used from the beginning of the book, takes the place of **ha** in the present indicative.

Hay dos libros en la mesa. There are two books on the table.

Había muchos alumnos en la sala de clase. There were many students in the classroom.

Ha habido siempre guerras. There have always been wars.

haber to have (auxiliary)		
PRESENT INDICATIVE	IMPERFECT INDICATIVE	PRETERIT
he hemos	había (regular)	hube hubimos
has habéis		hubiste hubisteis
ha han		hubo hubieron

57. *Perfect Tenses*

THE PERFECT INDICATIVE	
he hablado I have spoken	hemos hablado
has hablado	habéis hablado
ha hablado	han hablado
THE PLUPERFECT INDICATIVE	
había hablado I had spoken	habíamos hablado
habías hablado	habíais hablado
había hablado	habían hablado

VOCABULARY

el automóvil automobile
la carta letter
la invitación invitation
el plan plan
la puerta door
la tarde afternoon
Carlos Charles
Enrique Henry
aceptar to accept
formar to form
invitar to invite
llegar to arrive
mostrar to show; muestro, etc.

recibir to receive
subir to go up; subir a un tren, un automóvil to get into a train, an automobile
ver to see
próximo next, near by
ahora now
cordialmente cordially
pronto soon
rápidamente rapidly
sin embargo nevertheless
diciendo saying

EXERCISES

A

Carlos había pasado unas semanas en el campo cuando recibió una carta de su amigo Enrique invitándole a pasar unos días con él en la ciudad. No le gustaba dejar el campo, porque veía allí todos los días cosas muy interesantes. Sin embargo, quería ver la ciudad donde vivía Enrique, porque sus padres le habían hablado mucho de ella. Contestó a la carta de Enrique diciéndole que aceptaba su invitación. Hoy tomó el tren y ahora ha llegado a la ciudad donde vive su amigo. Cuando bajó del tren, vió a Enrique esperándole. Subió con él a un automóvil. Pasaron rápidamente por las calles, y llegaron pronto a la casa de Enrique. Sus padres estaban a la puerta. Recibieron cordialmente a Carlos, diciéndole que Enrique había hablado mucho de él. Le invitaron a entrar. Ahora le han llevado a la sala, todos se han sentado, y han hablado mucho de la visita de Carlos en el campo, de sus padres y sus hermanos, y de su viaje en el tren. Han hablado Enrique y sus padres de muchas cosas que piensan mostrar a Carlos en la ciudad, y han formado muchos planes para el próximo día.

B

1. ¿Qué recibió Carlos? 2. ¿De quién la recibió? 3. ¿Dónde había estado Carlos? 4. ¿Le había gustado el campo? 5. ¿Dónde vivía Enrique? 6. ¿Cómo fué Carlos a la ciudad? 7. ¿Dónde se paran los trenes? 8. ¿Quién le esperaba? 9. ¿En qué fueron a la casa de Enrique? 10. ¿Van rápidamente los automóviles? 11. ¿Estaban en casa los padres de Enrique? 12. ¿Dónde recibieron a Carlos? 13. ¿Se sentaron en la biblioteca? 14. ¿De qué hablaron? 15. ¿Qué han formado?

C

I. Give the tense of each of the following verb forms and translate each form. What is the infinitive?

dando	han sido	ha perdido
habían tomado	cultivándolo	vendiéndoselo
queriendo	he estado	Vd. había dormido
hemos ido	nos habíamos parado	teniéndolos

II. Choose correct verb forms and translate:

1. (*Hubimos, Tuvimos*) visita ayer.
2. (*Había, Tenía*) tres cartas en la mesa cuando entró.
3. La criada (*ha, tiene*) preparado una buena comida para nosotros.
4. Ahora (*he, tengo*) un automóvil.
5. (*Había, Tenía*) pasado una semana en la ciudad.
6. (*Estoy, Soy*) comiendo la fruta.
7. El maestro (*estuvo, fué*) recibido por los alumnos.
8. ¿Qué planes (*estuvieron, fueron*) formados por los muchachos?
9. (*Estamos, Somos*) estudiando nuestras lecciones.
10. El campo (*está, es*) cultivado por el campesino.

D

Translate: 1. Having them (*masc.*). 2. We had wished. 3. Giving it to me. 4. He had received. 5. It (*fem.*) was received by him. 6. We have given. 7. They had had. 8. There were books on the table. 9. Wishing it. 10. Writing it (*fem.*). 11. He has arrived. 12. Saying it to me. 13. You (*sing.*) had read. 14. They were showing (*progressive*). 15. You (*pl.*) have had. 16. Taking us to the house. 17. She was saying (*prog.*). 18. She was invited by Henry. 19. Looking for them (*fem.*). 20. We were writing (*prog.*).

E

1. John and I had visited his parents in the country. 2. We had received a letter from friends in the city, inviting us to spend a week with them. 3. John's parents had accompanied us to the station. 4. We had spent two or three hours on the train. 5. When we arrived our friends were at the station waiting for us. 6. They had arrived at the station in an automobile. 7. They received us cordially. 8. We got into the automobile, and they took us to their house. 9. Their mother was expecting us. 10. She and the servant had prepared a good dinner. 11. When we had eaten we sat down in the living room. 12. We spent the afternoon talking with our friends. 13. Now we have talked of many interesting things in the city. 14. We have formed many plans for our visit.

LESSON XV

58. *The Infinitive as Verbal Noun.* Both Spanish and English have verb forms which are used as nouns, that is, as subjects or objects of verbs or as objects of prepositions. In English the form so used is the gerund (ending in *-ing*):

Stealing is a crime.   We heard the ringing of a bell.

Spanish employs for this purpose the infinitive (compare Article **54**, 2). When not governed by a preposition it generally takes the definite article.

Al followed by the infinitive is translated into English by *on* and the gerund.

El escribir es más difícil que el leer. Writing is more difficult than reading.
Mi madre odia el fumar. My mother detests smoking.
el arte de escribir the art of writing
Al llegar entró en la casa. On arriving he entered the house.

59. *The Future Indicative Tense.* 1. The endings for the future tense for all verbs, regular and irregular, are **-é, -ás, -á, -emos, -éis, -án.**

2. In all regular verbs, and in many irregular ones, these endings are added to the infinitive. In some irregular verbs they are added to a shortened or modified form of the infinitive, called an irregular future stem.

FUTURE		
hablaré I shall speak	**aprenderé** I shall learn	**escribiré** I shall write
hablarás thou wilt speak	**aprenderás**	**escribirás**
hablará he will speak	**aprenderá**	**escribirá**
hablaremos we shall speak	**aprenderemos**	**escribiremos**
hablaréis ye will speak	**aprenderéis**	**escribiréis**
hablarán they will speak	**aprenderán**	**escribirán**

86

3. The future indicative of ser, estar, dar, ir is regular:

| seré | estaré | daré | iré |

The future stems of tener, haber, and querer are irregular:

tendré, tendrás, etc.
habré, habrás, etc.
querré, querrás, etc.

4. *a.* The future indicative expresses simple future time:

Iré mañana. I shall go tomorrow.

b. It may also express present conjecture or probability:

Será la una. It must be about one o'clock.

is probably

60. *The Future Perfect Indicative.* This tense is formed by adding the past participle to the future of haber:

habré hablado I shall have spoken, etc.

It is used practically as in English. It may, however, like the simple future, indicate probability:

Habrán llegado ayer. They probably arrived yesterday.

must have completed action or state

VOCABULARY

el **centro** center; ir al centro de la ciudad to go downtown
la **compra** purchase
la **corbata** necktie
la **hora**: a qué hora at what time
la **librería** bookstore
la **medida** measure
el **par** pair
el **sastre** tailor
la **sastrería** tailor's shop
el **sombrero** hat

el **traje** suit of clothes
el **tranvía** streetcar
la **zapatería** shoe store
el **zapatero** shoemaker *or* shoe dealer
el **zapato** shoe
acostarse to go to bed; me acuesto, etc.
encontrarse to be found; me encuentro, etc.
llamarse to be called, named
bien well

EXERCISES

A

Carlos y Enrique se han acostado, después de hablar mucho tiempo con la familia. Dormirán bien, y mañana se levantarán temprano, porque Carlos quiere hacer muchas compras antes de volver a casa. Se desayunarán con los padres de Enrique. Después de desayunarse irán en el tranvía al centro de la ciudad. Allí visitarán muchas tiendas, porque el encontrar las cosas que se desean es siempre más difícil que el comprarlas. Carlos comprará corbatas y un sombrero. Necesita también un par de zapatos. El hombre que hace o vende zapatos se llama zapatero, y su tienda es una zapatería. Carlos irá a una zapatería a comprar zapatos. Una tienda donde se venden libros es una librería. Carlos y Enrique no irán allí, porque el leer necesita mucho tiempo, y estarán muy ocupados en hacer sus compras. Si hay tiempo, los muchachos irán también a una sastrería. El sastre tomará la medida a Carlos para un traje. El hacer un traje es muy difícil, pero Carlos lo recibirá muy pronto. Después de hacer sus compras, los dos amigos volverán a casa. Hablarán con la familia de todas las cosas interesantes que hay en las tiendas.

B

1. ¿A qué hora se levantarán Carlos y Enrique? 2. ¿Qué quieren hacer? 3. ¿A dónde irán? 4. ¿En qué irán? 5. ¿Dónde se encuentran las tiendas? 6. ¿Qué comprará Carlos? 7. ¿Qué es un zapatero? 8. ¿Qué es una zapatería? 9. ¿Comprará Carlos zapatos? 10. ¿Dónde los comprará? 11. ¿Se compran libros en una zapatería? 12. ¿Dónde se compran? 13. ¿Qué es un sastre? 14. ¿Qué es una sastrería? 15. ¿Qué hace un sastre antes de hacer un traje?

C

I. Translate the following verb forms:

me encontraré	habremos dejado	entramos
me encontré	iré	Vds. comprarán
querremos	correrá	querrá
habrá tenido	se habrán levantado	tendremos
tendrán	entrará	habré dado

II. Form the proper person and number of the future tense:

1. Él (*ir*) mañana a la ciudad.
2. Nosotros lo (*tener*) mañana.
3. Vds. (*haber*) visitado a sus amigos en el campo.
4. Yo (*viajar*) por tren.
5. El tren se (*haber*) parado en la estación.
6. Mis padres (*llegar*) mañana.
7. Nosotros (*volver*) temprano.
8. Yo no (*tener*) tiempo para ir.
9. Nosotros no lo (*querer*) hacer.
10. Mañana nosotros (*haber*) recibido la carta.

III. Translate the following sentences:

1. Al entrar en la casa le vi.
2. Es más facil el recibir que el dar.
3. Antes de volver, compró una corbata.
4. Me gusta mucho vivir en la ciudad.
5. El viajar es muy interesante.
6. Al llegar a Madrid, fuimos a visitarles.

D

I. Continue the following verbs through all six forms and translate: 1. Estaré ocupado mañana. 2. Los querré visitar. 3. Tendré un sombrero nuevo. 4. Me despertaré temprano. 5. Iré con Enrique. 6. Habré recibido la carta. 7. Lo habré comprado.

II. Change all verbs to the future and translate: 1. Tengo zapatos. 2. Vuelven a casa. 3. Necesita un sombrero. 4. Nos bañamos. 5. Va a la tienda. 6. Le doy un billete. 7. Les damos la carta. 8. Nos paramos.

III. Translate: 1. We shall give. 2. I shall get up. 3. He will go. 4. We shall have. 5. You (*sing.*) will have bought. 6. I shall return. 7. He will have arrived. 8. They will run. 9. You (*pl.*) will stop. 10. They will have gone.

E

1. Charles and I are now at Henry's house. 2. The house is not in the center of the city. 3. It is not near the large stores. 4. We shall get up very early tomorrow. 5. Henry will have awakened us. 6. We shall eat breakfast with Henry's parents. 7. After (the) breakfast Henry's father will go to his office. 8. Charles, Henry, and I shall visit some stores. 9. I shall visit first a shop where they sell ties and hats. 10. Charles and Henry will go to a shoe store. 11. Charles will buy himself a pair of shoes. 12. Then they will go to a tailor's shop. 13. We shall return home on the streetcar. 14. The servant will have prepared (the) dinner.

LESSON XVI

61. *The Conditional Tense.* 1. The endings of the conditional for all verbs are **-ía, -ías, -ía, -íamos, -íais, -ían.**

2. As in the future tense, the endings are normally added to the infinitive.

3. When the stem of the future indicative is irregular (Article **59**, 2), the same irregularity is always found in the conditional.

CONDITIONAL	
hablaría I should speak [1]	**hablaríamos** we should speak
hablarías thou wouldst speak	**hablaríais** ye would speak
hablaría he would speak	**hablarían** they would speak

Similarly, **aprendería** (I should learn) and **escribiría** (I should write).

The conditional of **ser, estar, dar,** and **ir** is regular:

sería	estaría	daría	iría

Since **tener, haber,** and **querer** have irregular future stems, the conditional has the same irregularity:

tendría	habría	querría

4. The conditional expresses time future to a point in the past. For this reason it is sometimes called the past future tense.

> **Dice que irá.** He says that he will go.
> **Dijo que iría.** He said that he would go.

5. It may also express conjecture or probability in past time (compare Article **59**, 4):

Sería la una cuando llegaron. It was perhaps one o'clock when they arrived.

---

[1] Do not confuse this English wording with *should* in the sense of *ought.*

91

62. *The Conditional Perfect.* This tense is formed by adding the past participle to the conditional of **haber**:

> **habría hablado** I should have spoken, etc.

63. *The True or Informal Imperative.* The imperative mood in Spanish has only two forms: a singular and a plural. These are in the second person, the subjects (generally not expressed) being **tú** and **vosotros**. The use of the informal imperative is restricted to familiar speech, as are second-person forms in general (Article **24**). It is further restricted to affirmative commands, the negative being expressed by the subjunctive (Article **69**, 2). Beginners should learn to recognize the informal imperative, but should not attempt to use it in composition or conversation.

64. *Forms of the True Imperative.* In regular verbs and some irregular ones the singular of the informal imperative has the same form as the third person singular of the present indicative. This is not true of most irregular verbs, whose singular imperatives, therefore, should be committed to memory. The plural in all verbs is formed by changing the final **-r** of the infinitive to **-d**.

REGULAR VERBS		
	Singular	Plural
hablar	habla	hablad
aprender	aprende	aprended
escribir	escribe	escribid
SOME IRREGULAR VERBS		
ser	sé	sed
estar	está	estad
ir	ve	id
tener	ten	tened

65. *Peculiarities of the Imperative.*[1] 1. The personal-pronoun objects follow the affirmative imperative and are joined to it:

Véndemelo. Sell it to me.   **Habladle.** Speak to him.

Observe again that if there are two personal-pronoun objects the indirect precedes the direct, also that a verb form followed by an object pronoun or pronouns has the same stress as if it stood alone (Articles **42**, 3, and **54**, 3).

2. In reflexive verbs (Article **43**) the final **-d** of the plural is dropped when **-os** is added:

Sentaos. Sit down.   **Levantaos.** Get up.

VOCABULARY

la **camisa** shirt
la **causa** cause; **a causa de** on account of
la **lluvia** rain
el **mercado** market place
el **restaurante** restaurant
la **ventana** window
almorzar to lunch; **almuerzo,** etc.
creer to believe

llover to be raining; **llueve,** etc.
salir to go out; **salir de la casa** to leave the house
bonito pretty
tarde late
dijo (he) said
dijeron (they) said
hecho (from **hacer**) made

EXERCISES

A

Una de las cosas que Carlos pensaba hacer durante su visita era visitar el mercado. Enrique y su familia le dijeron ayer que encontraría muy interesante el mercado, porque los campesinos estarían allí con sus huevos, su leche, sus legumbres, sus frutas

---

[1] No exercises on the informal imperative have been provided, lest the student confuse it with the much more frequent formal imperative (Lesson XVII). If drill is desired, the teacher can adapt to that purpose the exercises of Lesson XVII.

y muchas otras cosas. Carlos dijo que iría primero al mercado, porque le dijeron que los campesinos llegarían muy temprano. No creían entonces que llovería. Pero cuando se levantó hoy, llovía. Le dijeron que los campesinos no estarían en el mercado a causa de la lluvia. Después de desayunarse Carlos y Enrique fueron a una tienda grande. Carlos dijo que compraría unas corbatas, pero las corbatas no le gustaban. Compró unas camisas muy bonitas y un sombrero. Dijeron que volverían a almorzar en casa con la familia, pero era muy tarde cuando salieron de la tienda. Fueron a almorzar en un restaurante. Ya no llovía, y vieron muchas cosas interesantes mientras pasaban por las calles. Sin embargo, no entraron en más tiendas. Ahora han almorzado bien, y toman el café sentados a una mesa cerca de una ventana.

B

1. ¿A dónde quería ir Carlos? 2. ¿Por qué? 3. ¿Fué allí? 4. ¿Por qué no estarían los campesinos en el mercado? 5. ¿Dónde se desayunaron Carlos y Enrique? 6. ¿Era grande o pequeña la tienda que visitaron? 7. ¿Qué dijo Carlos que compraría? 8. ¿Las compró? 9. ¿Por qué no? 10. ¿Eran bonitas las camisas que compró? 11. ¿Dónde dijeron que almorzarían? 12. ¿Por qué no fueron allí? 13. ¿Dónde almorzaron? 14. ¿Dónde están ahora? 15. ¿Qué hacen?

C

I. Translate the following verb forms and give the tense of each:

lloverá	perdían	Vds. tendrían
almorzaríamos	Vd. vería	bebía
habría vendido	subiré	bebería
habían aprendido	iremos	pensaré
me llamaría	nos habríamos levantado	creíamos

II. Choose the proper tense of the verb in each case:

1. Creo que ellos (*llegan, llegarán, llegarían*) muy pronto.
2. Contestó que nos (*visita, visitará, visitaría*) pronto.

depart - leave on a long journey - partir
depart from - partir de

3. Dijeron que (*tenemos, tendremos, tendríamos*) una buena comida.

4. Escribe que (*quiere, querrá, querría*) vivir siempre en el campo.

5. Creía que Vds. (*vuelven, volverán, volverían*) antes de la hora de comer.

6. Dice que yo (*encuentro, encontraré, encontraría*) a mis amigos.

III. Translate into idiomatic English the following sentences expressing present or past probability : 1. Habrá llegado ayer. 2. Serían las dos (*two o'clock*) cuando llegó. 3. Serán ahora las dos. 4. Habrán vendido su casa. 5. Vivirán cerca de aquí. 6. Juan estaría entonces en el jardín. 7. Lo habremos perdido. 8. Estaría allí, pero no le vi.

D

I. In the following sentences replace the infinitives in parentheses with the future or conditional, as the sense requires, and translate :

1. Creo que él (*estar*) en casa mañana.
2. Dijo que él (*tener*) pronto el libro.
3. Creían que nosotros (*llegar*) más pronto.
4. Yo creía que Vd. me (*encontrar*).
5. Cree que yo (*comprar*) el automóvil.
6. Creíamos que Vds. nos (*acompañar*) a casa.
7. Creen que (*llover*) mañana.
8. Dice que el tren (*pararse*) en la estación.

II. Translate : 1. We believed that they would return. 2. He said that he would be at home. 3. I believed that it would rain. 4. He says that they will go. 5. They said that they would be busy. 6. We believe that the train will stop. 7. You (*sing.*) said that you would visit me. 8. You (*pl.*) said that you would wait for him.

E

1. When we woke up yesterday Charles said that it would rain. 2. He had wanted to go to the market, because it was very interesting. 3. The farmers used to sell vegetables there every morning. 4. We did not want to go to the market while it was raining. 5. We believed that many farmers would not be there. 6. He said that he would go to a store to buy some shirts. 7. We did not like the shirts, and Charles said that he would not buy them. 8. Then we looked for ties. 9. Charles told (said to) me that they had good ties there. 10. We found three ties that we liked. 11. We had believed that we should lunch at home. 12. Henry's mother said that she would prepare a good meal. 13. But when we left the store it was raining hard (much). 14. We lunched in a restaurant and then talked with some friends who had entered.

REVIEW LESSON III

[Lessons XI–XVI]

A

I. Give the tense, person, and number of each of the following verb forms, and translate:

hablé	era	está comiendo
quería	estaban aprendiendo	fué ayudado
hemos hablado	recibía	tendríamos
estoy escribiendo	darán	habrán tenido
fuimos invitados	escribirían	tuve
habían llegado	habremos tomado	querrán
quisieron	comíamos	habremos querido
han aprendido	íbamos	dió
di	fuí	está dando
tuvimos	habrían dado	quiso

II. In each of the following sentences indicate which verb form is correct:

1. Cuando yo entré, Juan (*escribió, escribía*) una carta.
2. Le (*di, daba*) el libro ayer.
3. Mi padre (*fué, iba*) a su oficina todos los días.
4. Cuando los visité, (*vivieron, vivían*) en el campo.
5. El hombre me preguntó dónde (*viví, vivía*).
6. (*Ayudé, ayudaba*) a mi tío todo el verano.
7. Siempre me (*habló, hablaba*) cuando me (*encontró, encontraba*).
8. Le (*encontré, encontraba*) tres veces, pero no me (*habló, hablaba*).
9. Durante el verano que (*pasé, pasaba*) con mis tíos, (*fuí, iba*) muchas veces con mi tío a los campos.
10. La casa (*fué, era*) muy grande.
11. Cuando me (*levanté, levantaba*) ayer (*llovió, llovía*), y (*llovió, llovía*) todo el día.
12. Mi padre dijo que no (*pensó, pensaba*) almorzar en casa.

97

III. Fill each of the following blanks with **para** or **por**, and translate the sentence. (Do not write in this book.)

1. El libro es _ _ ? _ _ mí.
2. Le di tres pesetas _ _ ? _ _ las naranjas.
3. Está tomando el tren _ _ ? _ _ Méjico.
4. Necesitamos comer _ _ ? _ _ vivir.
5. La comida fué preparada _ _ ? _ _ nuestra criada.
6. Pasamos _ _ ? _ _ las calles de la ciudad.
7. Compramos panecillos _ _ ? _ _ el desayuno.
8. Me levanté temprano _ _ ? _ _ ir al mercado.
9. Siempre estudio _ _ ? _ _ la tarde.
10. Un pájaro entró en el cuarto _ _ ? _ _ la ventana.

IV. In the following sentences point out (*a*) abstract or general nouns, (*b*) infinitives as nouns, and (*c*) informal imperatives, and translate: 1. Dámelo. 2. El hablar una lengua es más difícil que el leerla. 3. Levantaos de la mesa. 4. El trigo es más útil que la avena. 5. Pensad mucho, pero hablad poco. 6. Las vacas y los caballos comen heno. 7. La vida del campo me gusta mucho. 8. Al entrar en el cuarto, me dió una carta. 9. Después de levantarse, se bañó. 10. Los carniceros venden carne. 11. Ve a la panadería y compra un kilo de pan. 12. Sé bueno, y aprende tu lección.

B

I. Translate into Spanish the English words in parentheses:
1. Me dió dos pesetas (*for*) la carne.
2. Dijo que (*he would buy*) el pan.
3. Me gusta mucho (*reading*).
4. Estudiamos (*in order to*) aprender.
5. (*On seeing me*) me dió una carta.
6. Habla de (*selling*) su casa.
7. Carlos (*had gone*) al campo.
8. (*Birds*) viven en (*trees*).
9. El maíz (*was*) alto, pero (*it was not*) maduro.
10. (*There will be*) muchos campesinos en el mercado.

II. Translate into Spanish: 1. There was wheat in the field.
2. Has the letter arrived? 3. Horses and cows eat hay. 4. Give
(*sing.*) me the pencil. 5. He was reading when I entered. 6. He
gave me fruit and vegetables. 7. The letter is for you. 8. My
uncle's house was small. 9. I used to go with him to the village.
10. He said that he would go with me.

C

Translate into Spanish: 1. When I was a boy, I used to go
often to the country. 2. I went in order to help my uncle. 3. Working in the country was interesting, but it was not easy. 4. Boys
who live in the city often work in the country in the summer.
5. Animals and birds are more interesting than streets and houses.
6. My uncle liked living in the country. 7. The house had been
bought by his father, and he had lived there all his (the) life. *N. B*
8. He always had good wheat and corn, and sold them in the
village. 9. In the morning my cousin and I used to wake up very
early. 10. He used to say (*Decía*): "Get up, Charles, and wash
yourself. 11. My parents have already got up and are working.
12. We shall eat breakfast, and then we shall help my father."

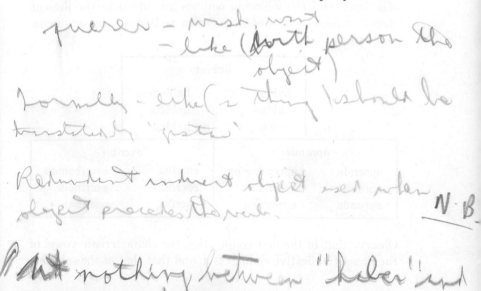

LESSON XVII

66. *General Characteristics of the Subjunctive.* All the verb forms studied up to this point (except the informal imperative) have been in the indicative mood. The indicative is used in dealing with actual facts: what is known or believed to be true. The subjunctive, on the other hand, expresses what is unreal, untrue, doubtful, indefinite, subject to some condition, or affected by will, emotion, etc. It nearly always stands in a subordinate clause.

I know that he is in the city. (*Known fact*)
He insists that it be done immediately. (*Will*)
I do not know anyone who can speak Spanish. (*Unidentified person*)
I will pay you well, provided you work faithfully. (*Proviso*)

67. *Forms of the Present Subjunctive.* To form the present subjunctive of regular verbs the following endings are added to the present stem of first-conjugation verbs: **-e, -es, -e, -emos, -éis, -en**; and the following endings are added to the present stem of second- and third-conjugation verbs: **-a, -as, -a, -amos, -áis, -an**.

hablar	
hable	hablemos
hables	habléis
hable	hablen

aprender		escribir	
aprenda	aprendamos	escriba	escribamos
aprendas	aprendáis	escribas	escribáis
aprenda	aprendan	escriba	escriban

Observe that in the first conjugation the characteristic vowel of the present indicative endings is **a**, and that that of the subjunctive is **e**. In the second and third conjugations the reverse is true, **e** occurring in the indicative and **a** in the subjunctive.

For convenience in verb drills, the present subjunctive may be translated *may*.

hable I may speak etc.

Its translation in any given sentence depends on the construction.

68. *The Formal Imperative.* The formal imperative, in both positive and negative commands, is formed by using the third person singular and plural of the present subjunctive with **Vd.** and **Vds.** **Vd.** and **Vds.** regularly follow the verb. The formal imperative is by far the most common form of command.

Vuelva Vd. temprano. Come back early.
No escriba Vd. en su libro. Do not write in your book.
Aprendan Vds. bien la lección. Learn the lesson well.
No abran Vds. las ventanas. Do not open the windows.

69. *Other Subjunctive Forms Used in Commands.* In addition to those just mentioned, the following subjunctive forms are used imperatively: 1. The first person plural (the hortatory subjunctive):

Hablemos un rato. Let us talk awhile.
Escribamos los ejercicios en la pizarra. Let us write the exercises on the blackboard.

2. The second person singular and plural, used in forming the negative of the informal imperative (Article **63**):

No hables. Do not talk.
No escribáis en la pizarra. Do not write on the blackboard.

3. The third person singular and plural, usually introduced by **que**:

Que no venga. He must not come.
Que entren. (They may) come in.
¡Viva España! Long live Spain!

70. *The Object Pronoun with Commands.* 1. In affirmative commands, either formal or informal, personal-pronoun objects, including reflexives, follow the verb and are attached to it. In negative commands they precede the verb.

> **Hábleme Vd.** Speak to me.
> **No me hable Vd.** Do not speak to me.
> **Levántate.** Get up.
> **No te levantes.** Do not get up.

2. The first person plural drops its final -s when the pronoun -nos is attached. This occurs only with reflexive verbs.

> **Sentémonos.** Let us sit down.

But:

> **No nos sentemos.** Let us not sit down.

71. *Position of the Object Personal Pronouns: Summary.* The object personal pronouns precede the verb (Article **42**, 1), except with the infinitive (Article **42**, 2), with the present participle (Article **54**, 3), and in affirmative commands (Articles **65**, 1 and **70**, 1).

VOCABULARY

la campanilla little bell
el estudiante student
la frase sentence
abrir to open
asistir to be present; **asistir a una clase** to attend a class
dirigirse to turn (to), speak (to), go (toward)
pronunciar to pronounce
sonar to sound; **suena** (it) sounds, rings

terminar to finish
traducir to translate
siguiente following
aquí here; **aquí tiene(n) usted(es)** here is (are)
correctamente correctly
distintamente distinctly
todavía yet, still
detrás de behind

Sawders

Part of the Business District, Montevideo, Uruguay. Statue of the
Patriot Artigas in the Foreground

Indian Market at San Miguel, near Mexico City

EXERCISES

A

Asistamos a una clase de español en nuestra escuela. Suena una campanilla; es la hora de la clase. El maestro está detrás de su mesa, y los alumnos están en sus asientos. El maestro dice a unos alumnos: — Pasen Vds. a la pizarra. Aquí tienen Vds. unas frases en inglés. Escríbanlas Vds. en español; no las escriban en inglés. — Entonces el maestro se dirige a los alumnos que están todavía en sus asientos, y dice: — Abran Vds. los libros. Leamos el primer ejercicio. Juan, lea Vd. la primera frase. Léala distintamente. — Cuando Juan termina la lectura, el maestro dice: — Vd. pronuncia muy bien. — Otros alumnos leen frases y las traducen. Los estudiantes que han ido a la pizarra vuelven a sus asientos, y el maestro nota las faltas. Suena otra vez la campanilla. El maestro dice: — Estudien Vds. la lección siguiente para mañana. Escriban todos los ejercicios con pluma; no los escriban con lápiz.

B

1. ¿A qué vamos a asistir? 2. ¿Qué hay en la sala de clase? 3. ¿Tienen mesas los alumnos? 4. ¿Está el maestro en un asiento? 5. ¿Pasan todos los alumnos a la pizarra? 6. ¿En qué lengua están las frases? 7. ¿En qué lengua las escriben en la pizarra? 8. ¿Qué hacen los alumnos que están todavía en sus asientos? 9. ¿Qué leen? 10. ¿Qué lee Juan? 11. ¿Cómo la lee? 12. ¿Pronuncia bien? 13. ¿Qué lección estudiarán para mañana? 14. ¿Escribirán ejercicios? 15. ¿Con qué los escribirán?

C

Translate each of the following expressions, and indicate to what type of command (formal, informal, or hortatory) it belongs:

Pronuncien Vds. las frases.   Créanme Vds.
Escríbelo.   Prepáralo, Josefa.
Entrad.   Asistan Vds. a la clase.

Dame los libros.	Termínenlos Vds.
No lo compre Vd.	No lo pregunten Vds.
Volvamos pronto.	Pensemos.
No nos los vendas.	Venid temprano mañana.
Aprended las palabras.	Léanoslo Vd.
No las escribáis.	No nos lo lea Vd.
Está aquí mañana.	Bébelo.
Cómalo Vd.	No lo bebas.
Sentémonos.	No corráis.
Levantaos.	

D

Translate the following three groups of sentences, using **usted** for *you* wherever the second person is called for :

I. Use reflexive verbs : 1. Get up. 2. Let us not sit down. 3. Bathe. 4. Let us wake up early. 5. Do not get up yet. 6. Do not stop. 7. Let us sit down. 8. Let us bathe every day.

II. Consider that the antecedent of *it* is *sentence* (**frase**) : 1. Let us read it. 2. Do not write it. 3. Pronounce it distinctly. 4. They are translating it. 5. He does not pronounce it well. 6. Write it with [a] pencil. 7. Do not write it with [a] pen.

III. Consider that the antecedent of *them* is *shoes* (**zapatos**) : 1. He sells them to us. 2. Do not buy them. 3. I do not need them. 4. Sell them to me. 5. Let us take them home. 6. Do not sell them to us.

E

1. John and Charles attend a school near their house. 2. The teacher has a class in Spanish. 3. There are many pupils in the class. 4. The teacher speaks to them in Spanish. 5. He says: "John, pass to the board. 6. Here are some sentences. 7. Write them on the board; do not write them on paper." 8. John does not write them well. 9. The teacher says: "He has made many mistakes. 10. Let us notice them. 11. Then write the sentences on paper. 12. Write them correctly. 13. Then let us open the books and read the first exercise. 14. Pronounce it well. 15. Prepare the following lesson for tomorrow. 16. Study the exercises, and write them on paper."

LESSON XVIII

72. *Present Subjunctive of Some Irregular Verbs*

ser	estar	dar	ir	tener	haber	querer
sea	esté	dé	vaya	tenga	haya	quiera
seas	estés	des	vayas	tengas	hayas	quieras
sea	esté	dé	vaya	tenga	haya	quiera
seamos	estemos	demos	vayamos	tengamos	hayamos	queramos
seáis	estéis	deis	vayáis	tengáis	hayáis	queráis
sean	estén	den	vayan	tengan	hayan	quieran

VOCABULARY

la bondad kindness; tenga Vd.
  la bondad de please
la cuenta account, bill
el diccionario dictionary
el librero bookseller
el mozo waiter
la prisa haste; tener prisa to
  be in a hurry
la propina tip, gratuity; dar
  de propina to tip
arreglar to settle
costar to cost; cuesta (it)
  costs

deber to owe, be under obligation, ought
enseñar to teach, show
pagar to pay
partir to depart, leave
barato cheap
completo complete
tranquilo tranquil, quiet
diez ten
cincuenta fifty
demasiado too much, too many
en seguida at once
sólo only

EXERCISES

A

Hemos dejado a Carlos y a Enrique en el restaurante.
Están a una mesa cerca de la ventana. Enrique no quiere salir
en seguida, porque está cansado. Dice a Carlos: — Esté Vd.
tranquilo; hay tiempo para todo. — Carlos tiene prisa, porque

105

quiere hacer más compras. Dice a Enrique: — Arreglemos la
cuenta y partamos. ¿Cuánto debo dar de propina al mozo?
— Déle una peseta. — Pagan la cuenta y salen a la calle. Carlos
dice: — Entremos en esta librería. Busco un buen diccionario. —
El librero les pregunta: — ¿Qué desean Vds.? — Carlos contesta: — Tenga Vd. la bondad de enseñarme un buen diccionario
de la lengua española. — Aquí tiene Vd. un diccionario muy
completo; vale cincuenta pesetas. — Cuesta demasiado. En-
séñeme otro más barato. — Este diccionario pequeño es muy
bueno y vale sólo diez pesetas.

B

1. ¿Están en casa Carlos y Enrique? 2. ¿Dónde los hemos
dejado? 3. ¿Dónde está su mesa? 4. ¿Quiere salir Enrique?
5. ¿Por qué no? 6. ¿Qué arreglan antes de partir? 7. ¿Cuánto
le dan al mozo? 8. ¿En qué entran después de salir del restaurante? 9. ¿Qué se vende allí? 10. ¿Está allí el librero? 11. ¿Qué
desean Carlos y Enrique? 12. ¿Lo tiene el librero? 13. ¿Les
gusta el libro que les enseña? 14. ¿Por qué no? 15. ¿Tiene otro
el librero? 16. ¿Cuánto vale?

C

I. Translate the following sentences and give the infinitive of
each verb: 1. Déme Vd. los libros. 2. No me los dé Vd. 3. No
tenga Vd. prisa. 4. Ábranse las puertas. 5. No vaya Vd. a casa.
6. Tengan Vds. la bondad de entrar. 7. Estén Vds. tranquilos.
8. No sea Vd. malo. 9. Que me lo enseñe. 10. No tengamos
prisa. 11. Sed buenos, niños. 12. Ve a la ciudad. 13. Vayan Vds.
a casa. 14. Sentémonos y comamos. 15. Que haya sillas para
todos.

II. Choose the correct verb forms and translate:

1. Danos el libro; no lo (*venda, vende, vendas, vendes*).

2. No te (*ve, id, vayas, vayáis*) en seguida; espera un poco.

3. No (*ten, tiene, tenga, tengas*) Vd. prisa; hay mucho tiempo.

4. Arreglen Vds. la cuenta y (*da, dad, deis, den*) una propina
al mozo.

5. (*Está, esté, estás, estés*) tranquilo y bebe la leche.

6. (*Compra, compre, compras, compres*) Vd. el diccionario; (*es, sé, sea*) muy barato.

7. Levantaos de la mesa y (*arregla, arregle, arreglad, arregléis*) la cuenta.

8. (*Partimos, partamos*) pronto porque todos estamos cansados.

9. Que se (*bañe, baña, bañes, bañad*) Vd.

10. (*Ten, tienen, tened, tengan*) Vds. la bondad de esperar un poco.

D

I. Translate, using **usted** for *you*: 1. Don't be in a hurry. 2. Be quiet. 3. Don't go home. 4. Show us another dictionary. 5. Settle the bill. 6. Do not enter the bookstore. 7. Talk to them. 8. Do not talk to us. 9. Give me the book. 10. Do not give it to him.

II. Repeat the above exercise, using **ustedes** for *you*.

E

1. When Charles enters the restaurant, Mary and I are at a table. 2. We do not want to go out at once. 3. We have visited many stores and have made many purchases. 4. Mary is tired. 5. She does not want to get up from the chair. 6. Charles says: "Please go with me to buy some ties." 7. Mary says: "We are not in a hurry to go (*para salir*). 8. You buy the ties, and then we shall look for you." 9. When we get up from the table, Mary says to me: "Look! 10. Charles is there in the street. 11. Now he is going to a bookstore. 12. Let us enter also." 13. We enter the bookstore, and Mary says: "Have you a good dictionary of the Spanish language?" 14. The bookseller shows her one, but it is very small and cheap. 15. She does not like it. 16. Then he shows her a large dictionary, and she buys it at once.

LESSON XIX

73. *Complementary Infinitive.* It often happens, in Spanish as in English, that one verb is used as the complement of another, that is, to complete its meaning. In case both verbs have the same subject, the dependent verb is in the infinitive. A connecting preposition may or may not be required, depending upon the main verb. (See verb list, Article **171.**)

> **Quiero verle.** I wish to see him.
> **Aprende a leer el francés.** He is learning to read French.
> **Insisten en venir.** They insist on coming.
> **Ceso de leer.** I stop reading.

74. *Dependent Clauses.* When the main and dependent verbs have different subjects, a subordinate clause is required in Spanish, even though in many cases English still employs the infinitive. The same connective (see Article **73**) is required before a clause as before an infinitive.

With the exception of its use in commands (Lesson XVII) the subjunctive is used almost wholly in dependent clauses. But verbs in dependent clauses are in the subjunctive only under certain specific conditions. For the sake of clearness the dependent subjunctive is treated separately in *noun* clauses, *adjective* clauses, and *adverbial* clauses.

75. *The Subjunctive in Noun Clauses.* (A noun clause is one used as subject or object of a verb.) The subjunctive is used in noun clauses that are dependent on expressions of: 1. *Volition* (ordering, desiring, forbidding, etc.):

> **Manda que vengan en seguida.** He commands them to come at once.
> **Quiero que Vd. estudie la lección.** I want you to study the lesson.
> **Prohibe que escribamos en nuestros libros.** He forbids us to write in our books.

108

2. *Emotion* (rejoicing, sorrow, surprise, fear) :

Me alegro de que Vd. esté aquí. I am glad that you are here.

Siento que Vd. esté enfermo. I am sorry that you are sick.

Me sorprende que no haya llegado. I am surprised that he has not arrived.

Tememos que no vuelva. We are afraid that he will not return.

3. *Doubt, denial,* or *uncertainty.* To the group of verbs expressing doubt or denial belong verbs of believing when used negatively or interrogatively :

Dudo que sea verdad. I doubt that it is true.

Niega que su amigo esté aquí. He denies that his friend is here.

Es posible que lo tenga. It is possible that he has it.

No creo que sea americano. I do not think that he is an American.

¿Cree Vd. que él no lo sepa? Do you think that he does not know it?

4. *Necessity* (in impersonal constructions) :

Es preciso que estén aquí temprano. It is necessary for them to be here early.

Es necesario que Vds. estudien. It is necessary that you study.

Noun clauses depending upon other expressions than those mentioned above are regularly in the indicative :

Dice que se va mañana. He says that he is going tomorrow.

Creo que hay un Dios. I believe that there is a God.

No dudo que vendrá. I do not doubt that he will come.

Note that the verb in noun clauses is indicative or subjunctive, depending on the verb or verbal expression used in the main clause.

VOCABULARY

el **café** coffee; café

el **cuidado** care, worry; **tener cuidado** to be careful; (una cosa de cuidado a serious thing

el **encargo** errand, commission

la **farmacia** drug store

el **gusto** pleasure

el **médico** doctor

el **paseo** walk; **dar un paseo** to take a walk

la **taza** cup

el **vaso** glass

el **vino** wine

Jorge George

acercarse to approach

alegrarse (de) to rejoice, be glad

conocer to meet, be acquainted with, know (a person)

continuar to continue

dudar to doubt

mandar to order

negar to deny; **niego,** etc.

permitir to permit

poder to be able; **puedo,** etc.

presentar to introduce

saludar to salute, greet

sentir to feel, feel sorry; **siento mucho** I am very sorry

traer to bring

cierto certain

malo bad; sick

necesario necessary

preciso necessary

probable probable

EXERCISES

A

Después de hacer sus compras Carlos y Enrique salen de la librería. En la calle ven a Jorge Méndez, un buen amigo de Enrique. — ¿Desea usted invitarle a que nos acompañe? — dice Enrique. — Invítele usted — dice Carlos; — quiero conocerle. — Buenos días, Jorge — dice Enrique; — Carlos, permítame que le presente a mi amigo, Jorge Méndez. Carlos le saluda y dice: — Tengo mucho gusto en conocerle a usted. — Deseamos que usted nos acompañe — dice Enrique. — Siento mucho no poder hacerlo. Mi padre está enfermo. Es preciso que yo vaya a la farmacia. — Sentimos mucho que su padre esté enfermo. ¿Está muy malo? — El médico dice que no es cosa de cuidado. No duda que se levantará mañana. — Entonces los dos amigos dejan que Jorge vaya a hacer sus encargos. Enrique y Carlos continúan su paseo. Enrique quiere que Carlos vaya con él a un café. Entran y se sientan a una mesa. Un mozo se acerca a la mesa y les pregunta: — ¿Qué desean los señores? — Uno de ellos dice: — Tenga usted la bondad de traerme café. — El otro manda que le dé un vaso de vino.

B

1. ¿En qué tienda han estado Carlos y Enrique? 2. ¿Qué han hecho? 3. ¿Conoce Carlos a Jorge Méndez? 4. ¿Qué quiere hacer Enrique? 5. ¿Lo quiere también Carlos? 6. ¿Puede acompañarlos Jorge? 7. ¿A dónde es preciso que vaya Jorge? 8. ¿Por qué? 9. ¿Ha visitado el médico al padre de Jorge? 10. ¿Dice que está muy malo? 11. ¿A dónde van Enrique y Carlos? 12. ¿Con quién hablan? 13. ¿Qué desea uno de los muchachos? 14. ¿Lo desea también el otro? 15. ¿Qué le da el mozo al otro?

C

Choose either the infinitive, the indicative, or the subjunctive form in each sentence, and give the reason for your choice:

1. Es preciso (*estudiar, estudian, estudien*).
2. Juan quiere (*aprender, aprende, aprenda*).
3. Quiero que él (*aprender, aprende, aprenda*).
4. Siento no (*poder, puedo, pueda*) ir.
5. Dudo que Juan (*estar, está, esté*) aquí.
6. Siente que nosotros no (*poder, podemos, podamos*) ir.
7. Es necesario que Vds. (*ir, van, vayan*).
8. Mande Vd. que (*pronunciar, pronuncian, pronuncien*) correctamente.
9. Quiero que me lo (*dar, da, dé*).
10. Me alegro de (*encontrar, encuentro, encuentre*) a su amigo.
11. El maestro manda que (*escuchar, escuchamos, escuchemos*).
12. Es preciso que nosotros (*tener, tenemos, tengamos*) cuidado.
13. No creemos que (*poder, pueden, puedan*) llegar mañana.
14. Dice que (*ir, va, vaya*) a estudiar.
15. Creemos que él (*ser, es, sea*) norteamericano.

16. No quieren que José le (*saludar, saluda, salude*).

17. Permitan Vds. que yo (*preguntar, pregunto, pregunte*) cuánto valen.

18. No dudo que (*haber, hay, haya*) un Dios.

19. Negamos que (*ser, es, sea*) necesario.

20. Creo que él (*estar, está, esté*) allí.

21. No creen que la casa (*ser, es, sea*) nueva.

22. Queremos que Juan (*estudiar, estudia, estudie*) para médico.

23. Es cierto que él no (*haya, ha, han*) llegado.

24. El médico dice que (*ser, es, sea*) cosa de cuidado.

D

I. Replace the English words in parentheses with the proper Spanish expressions, and translate:

1. Quiero (*go*) con ellos.

2. Queremos (*him to write*) la carta.

3. El mozo quiere (*us to give him*) una propina.

4. Es preciso (*for me to settle*) la cuenta.

5. Enrique desea (*buy*) un diccionario.

6. Es preciso (*that we prepare*) bien las lecciones.

7. Mandan (*us to give them*) la carta.

8. Desean (*go with me*) a la librería.

9. No queremos (*him to be*) malo.

10. Es preciso (*study*) mucho para aprender el español.

II. Translate: 1. I doubt that the dictionary is complete. 2. It is certain that he has the book. 3. We are sorry that you (*sing.*) are sick. 4. He says that the necktie is cheap. 5. We notice that John pronounces well. 6. It is probable that he will spend a week with us. 7. I desire that you give him the pen. 8. It is necessary that you (*pl.*) be here tomorrow.

E

1. I want to meet your friend. 2. We want him to accompany us. 3. He is sorry not to do it. 4. It is necessary for him to go to the drug store. 5. He says that his mother is sick. 6. The doctor says that it is serious. 7. He doubts that she will get up tomorrow. 8. We are sorry that she is sick. 9. We wish her to be well. 10. Charles and I continue our walk. 11. Charles wants me to go with him to a café. 12. We enter, and a waiter approaches. 13. Charles says: " Waiter, please bring me a glass of wine. 14. My friend wishes coffee. 15. I wish to settle the bill. 16. Do not give it to him."

LESSON XX

76. *The Subjunctive in Adjective Clauses.* An adjective clause modifies a noun or a pronoun and is introduced regularly by a relative pronoun. If the antecedent of the relative pronoun is definite, the verb is in the indicative; if it is indefinite, the verb is in the subjunctive. A definite antecedent is one which refers to a person or thing actually known to the speaker; an indefinite antecedent is one which refers to a person or thing which the speaker thinks of merely as a possibility or as having certain characteristics.

This use of the subjunctive is common when the antecedent is an indefinite pronoun, especially when it stands in a negative or interrogative clause, since in such a case the antecedent refers to an unknown person or thing.

Busco un hombre que hable español. I am looking for a man who speaks Spanish.

But: **Conozco a un hombre que habla español.** I know a man who speaks Spanish.

Deseo una casa que esté cerca del río. I want a house that is near the river.

But: **Vivo en una casa que está cerca del río.** I live in a house that is near the river.

No conozco a nadie que pueda hacerlo. I do not know anyone who can do it.

¿Conoce Vd. a alguien que pueda hacerlo? Do you know anyone who can do it?

Note that the verb in adjective clauses is indicative or subjunctive, depending on whether the clause modifies a definite or an indefinite antecedent.

77. *The Subjunctive in Adverbial Clauses.* An adverbial clause is one which modifies a verb. It is introduced by a subordinating conjunction, usually a compound of which **que** is the last element.

114

1. The subjunctive is used in temporal clauses that refer to future time, since future time is not yet an accomplished fact. (Temporal clauses that refer to present or past time are in the indicative.)

No me acostaré hasta que mi padre vuelva a casa. I shall not go to bed until my father comes home.

But: **No me acuesto hasta que mi padre vuelve a casa.** I do not go to bed until my father comes home.

Estará allí cuando yo llegue. He will be there when I arrive.

But: **Estaba allí cuando llegué.** He was there when I arrived.

2. The subjunctive is regularly used in clauses introduced by conjunctions that express purpose, concession, proviso, and the like, since such clauses imply uncertainty, indefiniteness, or non-accomplishment. The most common are

para que in order that **con tal que** provided

de modo que so that **sin que** without

aunque although

The indicative is used after some of the above expressions, notably **aunque**, when what is referred to is obviously a fact:

Habla lentamente para que le comprendan. He speaks slowly in order that they may understand him.

Iré con Vd. con tal que tenga tiempo. I shall go with you provided I have time.

Lo haremos sin que lo sepan. We shall do it without their knowing it.

Lo compraré aunque me cueste mucho. I shall buy it although it may cost me a great deal.

But: **Lo compré aunque me costó mucho.** I bought it although it cost me a great deal.

Note that, in general, the verb in adverbial clauses is subjunctive or indicative, depending, in the case of temporal clauses, on the tense and, in the case of certain other clauses, on the conjunction.

VOCABULARY

la **dificultad** difficulty
el **estudio** study
la **historia** history
el **profesor** professor
la **universidad** university
comprender to understand
explicar to explain
suplicar to entreat, request
venir to come; **viene** (he) comes
amable likable, obliging
joven young; **un joven** a young
  man

algo something
nadie no one, (not) anyone
quien, quienes who, whom
lentamente slowly
aunque although
con tal que provided
de modo que so that
hasta que until
para que in order that
sin (*prep.*) without; **sin que**
  (*conj.*) without

EXERCISES

A

(El profesor de historia habla :) — Busco un hombre que hable
y lea el español. Este joven tiene una carta para mí, y no puedo
leerla. (Un estudiante de español :) — Yo, señor, leo el español.
Tenga Vd. la bondad de enseñarme la carta. — Usted es muy
amable. Aquí la tiene usted. — La carta es de un profesor de la
universidad de Méjico. Dice que este joven, que se llama José
Gómez, viene a los Estados Unidos para estudiar la historia de
nuestro país. El profesor le suplica a usted que ayude al joven
mejicano. Dice que lee el inglés muy bien, pero que lo habla y
lo comprende muy poco. ¿Desea usted que yo le acompañe a ver
a los otros profesores? No perderé el tiempo, porque yo apren-
deré algo también. Iré con él a ver a los profesores con quienes
quiere estudiar. Les explicaré las dificultades del estudiante
mejicano. Les suplicaré que hablen lentamente hasta que aprenda
mejor el inglés.

B

1. ¿A quién busca el profesor de historia? 2. ¿Quién tiene una carta para él? 3. ¿Puede leerla el profesor? 4. ¿En qué lengua está la carta? 5. ¿Quién lee el español? 6. ¿De quién es la carta? 7. ¿Cómo se llama el joven mejicano? 8. ¿Por qué ha venido a los Estados Unidos? 9. ¿Qué desea el profesor mejicano? 10. ¿Lee bien el inglés José Gómez? 11. ¿Lo habla y lo comprende también? 12. ¿Qué hace el estudiante para ayudarle? 13. ¿Perderá todo el tiempo que pase con él? 14. ¿Por qué no? 15. ¿Con quiénes van a hablar?

C

Choose the correct verb form in each sentence and give a reason for your choice:

1. Esperaré hasta que Vd. (*irá, va, vaya*).
2. Esperó hasta que (*llegarían, lleguen, llegaron*).
3. Iré a donde me (*mandarán, mandan, manden*).
4. Aquí está el señor que (*veo, vea, vi*) ayer.
5. Aquí está la casa en que (*vivimos, vivamos, vivíamos*) ahora.
6. No hay nadie aquí que (*deseará, desea, desee*) ayudarnos.
7. Se lo diré cuando (*bajarán, bajan, bajen*) del tren.
8. ¿No pueden Vds. esperar hasta que yo (*terminaré, termina, termine*) el libro?
9. Seré su amigo mientras (*vivirá, vive, viva*).
10. Se lo daré con tal que (*vendrá, viene, venga*) mañana.
11. Cuando (*veremos, vemos, veamos*) a Jorge, le hablaremos.
12. Aunque lo (*desearán, desean, deseen*), no se lo daré.
13. Sin amigos no hay cosa que le (*gustará, gusta, guste*).
14. Carlos tiene un libro de lectura que (*es, sea*) muy interesante.
15. Vd. debe trabajar aunque su padre (*es, sea*) rico.
16. Podemos ir a casa con tal que (*terminaremos, terminamos, terminemos*) nuestras lecciones.

17. Podemos <u>salir de casa</u> sin que nos (*ven*, *vean*).

18. ¿Conoce Vd. ♠ un estudiante que (*lee*, *lea*) el español?

19. No hay diccionario que (*es*, *sea*) completo.

20. Escríbalo Vd. bien para que lo (*leeremos*, *leemos*, *leamos*) sin dificultad.

D

I. Substitute for the infinitives in parentheses the proper form of the indicative or subjunctive, as the case may require. Give reasons for your decision, and translate:

1. Tengo un hermano que (*hablar*) español.
2. Deseo un libro de lectura que (*ser*) muy fácil.
3. No hay nadie aquí que (*leer*) el español.
4. Hay muchos diccionarios que (*ser*) más baratos.
5. ¿Conoce Vd. alumnos que (*ser*) más inteligentes?
6. Cuando Vd. (*escribir*) a Juan, invítele a que nos (*visitar*).
7. Siempre hablo con Enrique cuando le (*ver*).
8. Voy a explicárselo para que lo (*aprender*) bien.
9. Traduciré la frase con tal que Vd. la (*leer*) lentamente.
10. Quiero entrar sin que ellos me (*ver*).

II. Translate: 1. We want a dictionary that is complete. 2. He has a dictionary that is very complete. 3. We have an uncle who lives in the country. 4. Have you friends who live in the country? 5. He will buy the book provided it is cheap. 6. I shall go with him to the station when he leaves. 7. I went with him to the station when he left. 8. Give him the book in order that he may read the exercise.

E

1. Charles has gone to the University of Mexico to study. 2. His professor of history has given him a letter to a Mexican professor. 3. The letter is (*está*) in English. 4. The professor does not read English. 5. He does not understand Charles when

he talks with him. 6. He is looking for a man who speaks and reads English. 7. A student of English at the university reads the letter. 8. He says: "This young man does not speak Spanish. 9. How do you wish me to help him?" 10. The professor says: "There is no one here who speaks English. 11. I wish you to go with him to talk with his other professors. 12. Help him until he learns Spanish well. 13. Please explain to them his difficulties. 14. I wish them to speak slowly, so that he may understand. 15. He will learn rapidly, provided he attends all the classes."

If a negative word follows the verb, "no" is used before the verb.

LESSON XXI

78. *Forms of the Imperfect Subjunctive.* Compared with the indicative, the subjunctive has very few forms. There are only two simple tenses in common use, the present and the imperfect, and two compound, the present perfect and the pluperfect. There are, however, two distinct sets of forms for the imperfect subjunctive, known as the -ra and -se forms. In most constructions either may be used.

The stem for the imperfect subjunctive of all verbs, regular and irregular, may be found by dropping -ron from the third person plural of the preterit indicative. To this stem the following endings are added:

-ra	-ras	-ra	-ramos	-rais	-ran
-se	-ses	-se	-semos	-seis	-sen
hablara	aprendiese	fuera	tuviese
hablaras	aprendieses	fueras	tuvieses
hablara	aprendiese	fuera	tuviese
habláramos	aprendiésemos	fuéramos	tuviésemos
hablarais	aprendieseis	fuerais	tuvieseis
hablaran	aprendiesen	fueran	tuviesen

In the same manner:

hablase	fuese	escribiese	estuviera
aprendiera	tuviera	diese	hubiera, etc.

In verb drills the imperfect subjunctive may be conveniently translated *might* (**hablara**, I might speak, etc.). Its translation in any given sentence depends on the construction.

79. *The Present Perfect Subjunctive.* The present perfect subjunctive is formed by adding the past participle of the main verb to the present-subjunctive forms of **haber** (Article **72**):

haya hablado   **hayas hablado, etc.**

120

80. *The Pluperfect Subjunctive.* The pluperfect subjunctive is formed by adding the past participle of the main verb to the forms of either of the imperfect subjunctives of **haber** (Article **78**):

> **hubiera hablado, hubieras hablado,** etc.
> **hubiese hablado, hubieses hablado,** etc.

I might have spoken

81. *Sequence of Tenses* (relation between the tenses of main and dependent verbs). 1. In dependent clauses that require the subjunctive, the present subjunctive is normally used if the main verb is in the imperative, the present indicative, or the future indicative.

> **Dígale que venga.** Tell him to come.
> **Temo que esté enfermo.** I fear he is sick.
> **Le escribiré cuando llegue.** I shall write him when I arrive.

2. The imperfect subjunctive is used if the main verb is in the imperfect, preterit, or conditional.

> **Deseaba que yo le acompañase.** He wanted me to accompany him.
> **Mandó que abriéramos la puerta.** He ordered us to open the door.
> **Preferiría que Vd. hablase más lentamente.** I should prefer that you speak more slowly.

3. The above rules apply equally to the compound tenses, the auxiliary being considered as the verb.

> **Siento que haya venido tan tarde.** I am sorry he has come so late.
> **Le he dicho que venga en seguida.** I have told him to come at once.
> **Habrá partido antes de que Vd. llegue.** He will have started before you arrive.
> **Dudaba que hubiesen venido.** He doubted that they had come.
> **Me habría gustado que estudiase más.** I should have liked to have him study more.

N. B.

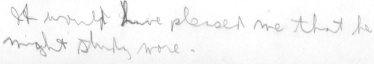

It would have pleased me that he might study more.

VOCABULARY

el **cinematógrafo** or el **cine**
  moving-picture theater *or*
  show; "movie"
el **edificio** building
el **teatro** theater
la **vez** time; **otra vez** again
admirar to admire
mostrarse to show oneself; **me
  muestro,** etc.

pedir to ask (a favor)
prometer to promise
posible possible
simpático likable
agradablemente agreeably
tan so, such
como since
siempre que whenever
dije I said

EXERCISES

A

Paso mucho tiempo con mi amigo mejicano. Es un joven muy
simpático. Ayer por la mañana quería que yo le acompañase a
ver a sus profesores. Fuí con él, y le presenté a todos. Les dije
que él no entendía bien el inglés. Les pedí que hablasen lentamente para que él los entendiese. Todos se mostraron muy
amables. Prometieron ayudarle siempre que fuese posible. Por
la tarde mi amigo quería ver la ciudad. Como no conocía las
calles, fué preciso que yo le acompañase otra vez. Tomamos un
tranvía, que nos llevó al centro de la ciudad. Él admiró mucho
los altos edificios. Pero dijo que las casas mejicanas le parecían
más hermosas. Quería que yo fuese con él a un cinematógrafo,
o cine, como se llama muchas veces. Entramos en un hermoso
teatro y pasamos dos horas muy agradablemente.

B

1. ¿Es norteamericano mi amigo? 2. ¿A dónde quería que
fuese con él? 3. ¿A quiénes le presenté? 4. ¿Qué les dije?
5. ¿Qué les pedí? 6. ¿Qué prometieron los profesores? 7. ¿Qué
quería hacer por la tarde? 8. ¿Por qué era preciso que yo le
acompañase? 9. ¿Tomamos un automóvil para ir al centro de la
ciudad? 10. ¿Qué tomamos? 11. ¿Eran pequeños los edificios?

12. ¿Eran más hermosos que las casas mejicanas? 13. ¿Cómo se llama muchas veces un cinematógrafo? 14. ¿Cree usted que haya buenos cines en Méjico? 15. ¿Era hermoso el teatro? 16. ¿Cuánto tiempo pasamos allí?

C

I. Give the mood, tense, person, and number of each verb form. In each case, what is the infinitive?

fuera	fuesen	habláramos
estuvieran	sea Vd.	lavemos
tuvieron	tuviera	fueron
estemos	tenga	mandasen
vivamos	estén	diera
diese	aprendiéramos	hubiésemos permitido
vayan Vds.	dé	haya pedido
diésemos	fuerais	hubiera admirado
	pronunciara	

II. Choose the correct verb form in each sentence and give the reason for your choice:

1. Deseábamos (*acompañar, acompañamos, acompañemos, acompañásemos*) a nuestros amigos.

2. Juan deseaba que le (*acompañan, acompañen, acompañaron, acompañaran*) a casa.

3. Le pedí que me lo (*da, dé, daba, diese*).

4. Se alegra de que su familia (*haber, ha, haya*) venido.

5. Dudaba que (*es, sea, era, fuese*) un buen libro.

6. No dudaba que (*es, sea, era, fuese*) un buen libro.

7. Salió de la casa sin que nadie le (*ve, vea, vió, viera*).

8. Niegan que él (*ha, haya*) estado aquí.

9. No creemos que (*han, hayan, hubieron, hubieran*) perdido las cartas.

10. Era probable que no las (*recibe, recibo, recibió, recibiera*).

11. Cuando mis padres (*llegaron, llegasen*), yo estaba allí.

12. Nos dijo que nos lo pagaría cuando (*recibe, reciba, recibió, recibiese*) la cuenta.

13. Tomó otra calle, para que yo no le (*encuentro, encontré, encontrase*).

14. No lo creeríamos aunque lo (*dice, dijo, dijese*) muchas veces.

15. Le diré que no se vaya hasta que (*habrá, ha, haya*) hablado con Vd.

16. Suplicaron que (*comimos, comamos, comiésemos*) más.

17. Siento que Vd. (*haber, ha, haya*) estado enfermo.

D

I. In each sentence change the verb of the main clause to the imperfect or preterit and make whatever additional changes are necessary. Then translate the sentence: 1. Desea que le acompañemos. 2. Mandará que le den un vaso de agua. 3. Dudamos que sea mejicano. 4. Será preciso que vaya a la farmacia. 5. Sentimos que su padre esté malo. 6. Nos alegramos de que le guste el libro. 7. Dudan que tengamos prisa. 8. No creo que haya venido.

II. Replace each infinitive in parentheses with the proper form of the verb and translate the sentence:

1. No conocíamos a nadie que (*hablar*) español.
2. Era preciso que él lo (*pagar*).
3. Les pedí que me (*dar*) el libro.
4. No creía que ellos (*vivir*) en el campo.
5. Sentían que nosotros (*haber*) llegado tarde.
6. Mandó que nosotros (*salir*) en seguida.
7. Querían una casa que (*estar*) cerca de la escuela.
8. No creíamos que ellos (*haber*) venido.

E

no repeated

1. Charles is now at the University of Mexico. 2. The Mexican student has helped him a great deal. 3. Yesterday Charles wished him to accompany him. 4. He wanted to talk with his professors. 5. His friend introduced him to all [of them]. 6. He

wanted them to help Charles. 7. He wanted them to speak slowly in the classroom. 8. They promised to speak slowly, so that he might understand. 9. It was necessary that he learn Spanish at once. 10. In the afternoon Charles wished his friend to accompany him again. 11. He wished to see the beautiful buildings of the city. 12. They went downtown in an automobile. 13. They went to a theater to see a moving-picture show. 14. Charles admired it [very] much. 15. He had not believed that the "movies" of Mexico were so good. 16. Then they went in their automobile through the interesting streets of the city.

[Handwritten notes:]

to ask
- inquire - preguntar
  - preguntar una cosa a una persona
  - preguntar + a direct or indirect question, which is in the subjunctive
- request - pedir
  - pedir una cosa a una persona (ask something for someone)
  - pedir + an indirect command, which is in the subjunctive

REVIEW LESSON IV

[Lessons XVII–XXI]

A

I. Give the mood, tense, person, and number of each of the following verb forms. In each case what is the infinitive?

hablé	pensemos	fueron
escriba	pierda	hubo
tome	estuviera	haya vivido
piensen	me siente	cuente
vuelva	se levantasen	estén
di	hubiesen aprendido	tuviéramos
haya perdido	vuelven	querría
vayan	hayamos contado	se sentasen
fuera	aprenda	demos
seamos	tengan	aprendamos

II. Place the words in each of the following groups in the correct order, and translate:

1. lo, dió, me
2. Vd., lo, dé, me
3. lo, dando, me
4. lo, que, quiero, dé, me
5. no, lo, Vd., dé, me
6. lo, quiere, me, dar
7. a, va, me, dar, lo
8. lo, él, da, me
9. me, quería, diese, que, lo
10. escribía, las, me
11. las, me, escribas, no
12. las, me, escribe (tú)
13. lo, se, dando
14. escribamos, no, las
15. lo, me, dando, está

III. Translate the following sentences and explain in each case why the dependent verb is in the infinitive, indicative, or subjunctive: 1. Quiere ir conmigo. 2. Quiere que yo vaya con él. 3. Estaré allí cuando él vuelva. 4. Estaba allí cuando él volvió. 5. Él quiere que yo esté allí cuando vuelva. 6. Busco un diccionario que sea más barato. 7. No dudo que está aquí. 8. En el campo es preciso levantarse temprano. 9. Cuando estoy en el campo, es preciso que me levante temprano. 10. No creo que esté aquí. 11. Lea Vd. distintamente, para que comprendamos. 12. Dice que Juan está aquí. 13. Mandan que volvamos en seguida. 14. No quiero estar enfermo. 15. Yo sentía que llegasen tarde.

IV. In each case choose the correct verb form, give the reason for your choice, and translate:

1. Mande Vd. que nos acompañ(-ar, -en, -an, -aran).
2. Mandó que nos acompañ(-ar, -en, -an, -asen).
3. Hablé con él cuando est(-ar, -é, -uvo, -uviera) aquí.
4. Hablaré con él cuando est(-ar, -é, -uvo, -uviese) aquí.
5. Si como demasiado, temo est(-é, -uviera, -ar) enfermo.
6. Temo que Juan no (*ha, hubiese, haya*) llegado.
7. Sentíamos que no (*habían, hayan, han, hubiesen*) llegado.
8. Habían mandado que yo los acompañ(-ar, -e, -ase, -o).
9. Siempre había querido viv(-a, -e, -ir, -iera) en Méjico.
10. Buscaba un hombre que compr(-ar, -a, -ase, -e) su casa.
11. Dudo que est(-ar, -án, -én, -arán) aquí.
12. No dudo que él (*tenga, tener, tiene, tuviese*) mi libro.

B

I. Substitute for each infinitive in parentheses the correct form of the verb. Give the reason for your decision, and translate:

1. José cree que (*llover*) mañana.
2. Todo se puede hacer sin que Vd. (*perder*) tiempo.
3. Yo dudaba que (*llover*).
4. Esperaré hasta que Vd. (*poder*) ir conmigo.

5. Era preciso que él (*volver*) en seguida.
6. Le pagaré el dinero cuando lo (*tener*).
7. Siento que Vd. (*haber*) tenido dificultades.
8. Déme Vd. su libro para que (*estudiar*) la lección.
9. Enrique dijo que (*ir*) conmigo.
10. Mi madre no tiene criada que la (*ayudar*).
11. Me dió el periódico que (*tener*).
12. Mi tío necesitaba un hombre que (*trabajar*) en la finca.

II. Translate: 1. On seeing me, he stopped. 2. Sleeping well is very necessary. 3. We do not wish you to be sick. 4. Give it to me; do not give it to him. 5. I wish to see them. 6. Let us get up. 7. I want them to sit down. 8. Losing it. 9. He is going to buy it. 10. The difficulties of writing Spanish. 11. Wait until the train stops. 12. I have no friends who live in the city.

C

Translate: 1. Writing well is very difficult. 2. He wanted me to give it to him. 3. Let us not stop. 4. It is necessary to be careful with this pen. 5. Provided he studies hard (much), his father will give him a car. 6. We are writing to Charles so that he may help you. 7. I did not believe that he had it. 8. It was necessary for him to get up early. 9. May you sleep well! 10. Although he may want it, do not give it to him. 11. He did not believe that they had arrived. 12. I will write you when I receive his letter. 13. We are glad that he has come so early. 14. They did not permit John to go with them.

LESSON XXII

82. *Conditional Sentences.* Conditional sentences are complex sentences consisting of two parts: the *condition*, introduced by **si** (*if*), and the *conclusion*. Either may come first.

1. Only *unreal conditions* may take the subjunctive. Under unreal conditions are included both conditions impossible of fulfillment and conditions contrary to fact:

If I were you, I should study more.

If I had the money (*but I have not*), I should go to Mexico.

In unreal conditions either imperfect subjunctive may be used in the **si**-clause, and either the conditional or the **-ra** imperfect subjunctive in the conclusion. This rule applies to the auxiliary verb in compound tenses.

Si fuera hombre, mi hermana iría a la guerra. If she were a man (*but she is not*), my sister would go to war.

Si fuese él, lo hiciera. If I were he (*but that is impossible*), I should do it.

Si hubiese estado aquí, habríamos ido al teatro. If he had been here (*but he was not*), we should have gone to the theater.

Si fuera mía esta casa, la vendiera. If this house were mine (*but it is not*), I should sell it.

2. In most other cases the indicative is used. Present or past conditions (present or past tenses in both clauses) express simple fact.

If the weather is good, I walk to my classes.

Future conditions, which denote mild uncertainty, take the present indicative in the **si**-clause and the future in the conclusion.

If you wish it, I will accompany you.

Si llueve, me quedo en casa. If it rains, I stay at home.
Si llovía, me quedaba en casa. If it rained, I stayed at home.
Si tengo tiempo, iré con Vd. If I have time, I will go with you.

83. *Conditional or Subjunctive in Mild Statements.* The conditional or the -ra imperfect subjunctive is used frequently in a softened statement or mild command.

Quisiera que Vd. me acompañase. I should like to have you go with me.

Me gustaría hacerlo. I should like to do it.

Juan debiera estudiar más. John ought to study more.

84. *Stem-Changing Verbs, Class A.* Many verbs of the first and second conjugations change **e** of the last syllable of the stem to **ie** or **o** to **ue**, when accented. Some preliminary discussion of this type of change has been given in Lesson VIII. The forms affected are all three persons of the singular and the third person plural of the present indicative and present subjunctive, and the singular of the informal imperative — nine forms in all. In the paradigms given below they are printed in bold-faced type.

Verbs of this class will be indicated henceforth in the vocabularies as follows:

perder (ie), contar (ue)

Keep in mind that in verbs of Class A the change is always from a vowel (**e** or **o**) to a diphthong (**ie** or **ue**).

The personal endings of all stem-changing verbs are exactly the same as those of regular verbs of the same conjugation.

perder to lose			
PRESENT INDICATIVE		IMPERATIVE	PRESENT SUBJUNCTIVE
pierdo perdemos			**pierda** perdamos
pierdes perdéis	**pierde** perded		**pierdas** perdáis
pierde **pierden**			**pierda** **pierdan**
contar to count, relate			
PRESENT INDICATIVE		IMPERATIVE	PRESENT SUBJUNCTIVE
cuento contamos			**cuente** contemos
cuentas contáis	**cuenta** contad		**cuentes** contéis
cuenta **cuentan**			**cuente** **cuenten**

VOCABULARY

el almuerzo lunch
el éxito success; **tener éxito**
to succeed
la gana desire; **tener ganas de**
to want to, feel like
la noche night
la nota grade
la novela novel
cansarse to tire oneself, get
tired
interesar to interest
retirarse to retire, withdraw
sacar to take out, get out

nueve nine; **a las nueve** at
nine o'clock
en efecto in fact
en vez de instead of
debiera (*impf. subj. of* **deber**)
ought
leyendo (*pres. part. of* **leer**)
reading
pudiera (*impf. subj. of* **poder**)
could, might
quisiera (*impf. subj. of* **querer**)
(I) should like

EXERCISES

A

Cuando llegó la noche, Juan estaba muy cansado. Se acostó a las nueve. Al retirarse a su cuarto dijo : — Si no llueve mañana, me levantaré temprano. Quisiera hacer algunas lecturas en la biblioteca. — En efecto se levantó muy temprano. Después del desayuno fué en seguida a la biblioteca, porque tenía muchas ganas de trabajar. Entró en la sala de lectura y sacó una historia de España. Pero como el libro no le interesaba mucho, se cansó pronto. Si el libro le hubiese interesado, hubiera continuado la lectura. Entonces tomó una novela nueva. Le gustaba mucho, y pasó toda la mañana leyéndola. Cuando llegó la hora del almuerzo, Juan había leído poco que pudiera ayudarle en sus estudios. Debiera estudiar más, porque a veces recibe malas notas. Le gustaría leer novelas siempre en vez de estudiar. Si pierde así el tiempo, no tendrá éxito en sus estudios. Si estudiase un poco más, recibiría buenas notas.

B

1. ¿A qué hora se acostó Juan? 2. ¿Por qué se acostó tan temprano? 3. ¿A qué hora deseaba levantarse? 4. ¿Qué deseaba hacer? 5. ¿A qué hora se levantó en efecto? 6. ¿A dónde fué después del desayuno? 7. ¿En qué sala entró? 8. ¿Qué librc sacó primero? 9. ¿Por qué se cansó pronto? 10. ¿Qué libro sacó entonces? 11. ¿Le interesaba más que el otro? 12. ¿Cuánto tiempo pasó leyéndolo? 13. ¿Le ayudó mucho en sus estudios? 14. ¿Recibe siempre buenas notas? 15. ¿Qué debiera hacer?

C

I. Indicate the correct spelling in the following verb forms:

1. Los enc(-o-, -ue-)ntramos en el cine.
2. Siempre me desp(-e-, -ie-)rto muy temprano.
3. No p(-e-, -ie-)rdan Vds. el libro.
4. Hable Vd. distintamente; no le ent(-e-, -ie-)ndo bien.
5. C(-o-, -ue-)ntemos los libros; debe haber cincuenta.
6. El muchacho v(-o-, -ue-)lvió a casa muy tarde.
7. ¿Qué p(-e-, -ie-)nsan Vds. de la novela?
8. T(-e-, -ie-)nen ganas de comer algo.
9. En efecto le enc(-o-, -ue-)ntro muchas veces.
10. Se ac(-o-, -ue-)staba a las nueve de la noche.

II. Choose the correct verb forms: 1. Si yo (*estoy, esté*) bueno, (*iré, vaya*) con Vd. 2. Si Juan (*estaba, estuviera*) malo, no (*iría, fuese*). 3. Si María (*tiene, tenga*) el libro, me lo (*dará, dé*). 4. Si él (*estaba, estuviese*) aquí, se lo (*contaría, contase*). 5. (*Hubiese, Hubiera*) ido al Canadá si (*habría, hubiese, había*) sido posible. 6. Si (*tiene, tenga*) éxito en sus negocios, (*compra, compre, comprará*) un automóvil. 7. Si yo (*era, fuera*) Vd., (*iba, iría*) a Méjico durante el verano. 8. (*Habría, Hubiese*) venido a verme si (*habría, hubiese*) tenido más tiempo. 9. Si Vd. me (*ayuda, ayudará, ayude*) mañana, lo (*terminemos, terminaremos*) pronto. 10. Si Juan (*hubo, hubiese*) estudiado más, (*hubiera, hubiese*) recibido buenas notas.

III. Translate: 1. Él podría hacerlo si quisiera. 2. Quisiera ir con ellos. 3. Debiéramos pagar la cuenta. 4. Nos gustaría ir a Méjico. 5. ¿Quisieran Vds. conocerle?

D

I. Replace the infinitives in parentheses with the proper form of the verb, and translate:

1. Si llueve mañana, Juan (*levantarse*) tarde.
2. Si lo tiene, me lo (*dar*).
3. Si yo tuviera una novela, la (*leer*).
4. Si Juan estuviera aquí, me (*ayudar*).
5. Le daré el libro si lo (*encontrar*).
6. Yo le acompañaría si (*tener*) tiempo.
7. Si hubiera llegado más temprano, yo le (*haber*) acompañado.

II. Translate: 1. If he comes we shall lunch early. 2. I should like to go to a moving-picture show. 3. If I had it I should give it to you. 4. If he is sick we shall go to see him. 5. If we had an automobile we should go to the country. 6. We should like to see some shirts. 7. If I were not tired I should accompany them. 8. If I have time I shall write to him.

E

1. We work a great deal during the day. 2. If we are tired we shall go to bed early. 3. We shall get up early tomorrow. 4. John does not work much. 5. If he worked more he would learn more. 6. If he learned more he would receive good grades. 7. He does not read books that help him in his studies. 8. He ought not to read novels. 9. He ought to read the history of Spain. 10. If he studies he will always receive good grades. 11. If he had not read the novel he would have studied. 12. We do not read books that do not interest us. 13. If we read novels we shall not succeed in our studies. 14. Students always want interesting books. 15. If the books are not interesting they will study little.

LESSON XXIII

85. *Stem-Changing Verbs, Class B.* Certain verbs of the third conjugation show the following changes from **e** or **o** of the last syllable of the stem: 1. **e** accented becomes **ie**, and **o** accented becomes **ue**, as in Class A.

2. **e** unaccented becomes **i**, and **o** unaccented becomes **u**, when followed in the next syllable by **a**, **ie**, or **io**.

The forms affected by these changes are printed below in bold-faced type.

sentir to feel		**dormir** to sleep	
PRESENT PARTICIPLE			
sintiendo		durmiendo	
PRESENT INDICATIVE			
siento	sentimos	**duermo**	dormimos
sientes	sentís	**duermes**	dormís
siente	sienten	**duerme**	**duermen**
IMPERATIVE			
siente	sentid	**duerme**	dormid
PRESENT SUBJUNCTIVE			
sienta	sintamos	**duerma**	**durmamos**
sientas	sintáis	**duermas**	**durmáis**
sienta	sientan	**duerma**	**duerman**
PRETERIT INDICATIVE			
sentí	sentimos	dormí	dormimos
sentiste	sentisteis	dormiste	dormisteis
sintió	**sintieron**	**durmió**	**durmieron**
IMPERFECT SUBJUNCTIVES			
sintiera etc.		**durmiera** etc.	
sintiese etc.		**durmiese** etc.	

134

5

James Sawders

Statue of George Washington (near the Paseo de la Reforma),
Mexico City

Entrance to Avenida de Mayo, Buenos Aires

Subway Entrance, Downtown, Buenos Aires

As far as changes from vowel to diphthong (**e** to **ie** or **o** to **ue**) are concerned, Class B is like Class A (nine changes: in present indicative, present subjunctive, and singular informal imperative). In addition, Class B has seventeen changes from one vowel to another vowel (**e** to **i** and **o** to **u**): in the present participle, third person singular and plural preterit, first and second person plural present subjunctive, and throughout both forms of the imperfect subjunctive. In the vocabularies, verbs of this class will be indicated as follows:

sentir (ie-i), dormir (ue-u)

VOCABULARY

el **brazo** arm
la **cabeza** head
la **cama** bed
el **cuerpo** body
el **dolor** pain, grief
la **enfermedad** sickness
anunciar to announce
consolar (ue) (de) to console (for)
decir to say; **se dice** it is said, the saying is
describir to describe
divertir(se) (ie-i) to amuse (oneself)
morir(se) (ue-u) to die
olvidar to forget

quedar(se) to remain
sentirse (bien) (mal) to feel (well) (badly)
triste sad
último last
viejo old; **un viejo** an old man
anoche last night
así thus
común: por lo común ordinarily
mal (*adv.*) badly
mejor better
menos less
ni nor; **ni . . . ni** neither . . . nor

EXERCISES

A

Hoy por la mañana fuí a ver a Carlos. Yo quería llevarle conmigo a dar un paseo. Le encontré enfermo. Se había despertado sintiéndose muy mal. Por lo común duerme muy bien; anoche durmió mal. No tiene ganas de comer ni de trabajar.

Lo siente mucho, porque no puede ni estudiar en la biblioteca ni divertirse en leer o en ir al cine. Se siente muy cansado. Su madre llama al médico, que llega pronto. — ¿Cómo se siente Vd.? — pregunta el médico. — Descríbame su enfermedad. — Me siento muy mal — contesta Carlos. — Duermo mal, como mal, siento dolores en la cabeza, en los brazos, por todo el cuerpo. ¿Cree Vd. que me voy a morir? — No, señor; esté tranquilo — dice el médico. — Uno no se muere por tan poco. Es preciso que se quede en cama dos o tres días hasta que se sienta mejor. Entonces quiero que se acueste temprano todas las noches, y que tenga mucho cuidado en comer. — Carlos está un poco triste. Por lo común se divierte mucho, y no le gusta pasar mucho tiempo en casa. Pero, como se dice, así es la vida, y se consuela pensando que su enfermedad no es cosa de cuidado, y que muy pronto se sentirá bien otra vez.

B

1. ¿A quién fuí a ver? 2. ¿Cuándo fuí a verle? 3. ¿Cómo durmió Carlos anoche? 4. ¿Cómo duerme por lo común? 5. ¿Tiene ganas de trabajar? 6. ¿Dónde estudia por lo común? 7. ¿Cómo se divierte? 8. ¿A quién llama su madre? 9. ¿Qué pregunta el médico? 10. ¿Dónde siente dolores Carlos? 11. ¿Es cosa de cuidado su enfermedad? 12. ¿Qué manda el médico? 13. ¿Por qué está triste Carlos? 14. ¿Qué no le gusta hacer? 15. ¿Cómo se consuela?

C

I. Give the mood, tense, person, and number of the following verb forms. In each case, what is the infinitive?

sintieron	se sentía	me divertí	sintáis
dormí	durmiesen	divierten	divirtieron
nos divertimos	muriera	muramos	consolé
muera	consuelan	dormimos	siente
consuelo	murió	duermes	morí

II. Choose the correct spelling in the following verb forms:

1. Carlos cree que se m(-o-, -ue-, -u-)re.

2. Los médicos quieren que nosotros d(-o-, -ue-, -u-)rmamos mucho.

3. Los muchachos se cons(-o-, -ue-, -u-)lan pronto de los dolores de la vida.

4. La madre de Carlos manda que él se ac(-o-, -ue-, -u-)ste temprano y que d(-o-, -ue-, -u-)rma muchas horas.

5. Nos s(-e-, -ie-, -i-)ntimos mal cuando nos levantamos ayer.

6. No queremos que Vd. se s(-e-, -ie-, -i-)nta mal mañana

7. ¡Que se div(-e-, -ie-, -i-)rtan Vds.!

8. Queríamos que María se div(-e-, -ie-, -i-)rtiese en Méjico.

9. Se alegraba de que yo me s(-e-, -ie-, -i-)ntiese tan bien.

10. Se ac(-o-, -ue-, -u-)stó temprano y d(-o-, -ue-, -u-)rmió bien.

11. El médico dudaba que Carlos se m(-o-, -ue-, -u-)riera.

12. ¿No desea Vd. que nos div(-e-, -ie-, -i-)rtamos?

D

I. Translate: 1. They die. 2. Amuse yourselves! 3. I sleep. 4. We amused ourselves. 5. He died. 6. They felt. 7. They might die. 8. I amused myself. 9. We feel. 10. Sleep! (*sing.*) 11. Let us amuse ourselves. 12. He might sleep. 13. He feels. 14. I felt. 15. Let us sleep.

II. Translate: 1. He cannot forget his grief. 2. They did not sleep last night. 3. Let us take a walk with him. 4. He always amuses me [very] much. 5. How do you feel today? 6. They announced that the old man was dying. 7. It is necessary that we all die sooner or later (late or early). 8. The last time she wrote she said that she did not feel well. 9. How do you amuse yourself generally? 10. His head, his arms, and his whole body ache (He feels pains in . . .).

E

1. Charles wishes me to go to the library. 2. I am very sorry, but I cannot go. 3. Yesterday we received a very sad letter. 4. It announced to us that my good aunt died last week. 5. It was very sad that she died so young. 6. If she were old we should be less sorry (we should feel it less). 7. The last time I visited her it did not seem possible that she would die. 8. She told me that she was feeling very well. 9. She amused herself [by] going with me to a moving-picture show. 10. She was sorry that my cousin did not go. 11. She slept well during the night. 12. I woke up very early, and she was sorry that I had slept so badly 13. She said that ordinarily boys sleep well. 14. I answered that at times they have too good a time (amuse themselves too well), and then they sleep badly. 15. My aunt always interested herself in (*por*) young people. 16. I cannot console myself for (*de*) her death (that she died).

LESSON XXIV

86. *Stem-Changing Verbs, Class C.* Certain verbs of the third conjugation show the following changes from **e** in the last syllable of the stem:

1. **e** accented becomes **i**.

2. **e** unaccented becomes **i** if followed in the next syllable by **a, ie,** or **io**.

The forms affected by these changes are printed below in bold-faced type.

pedir to ask for, request					
PRESENT PARTICIPLE					
pidiendo					
PRESENT INDICATIVE					
pido	**pides**	**pide**	pedimos	pedís	**piden**
IMPERATIVE					
pide			pedid		
PRESENT SUBJUNCTIVE					
pida	**pidas**	**pida**	**pidamos**	**pidáis**	**pidan**
PRETERIT INDICATIVE					
pedí	pediste	**pidió**	pedimos	pedisteis	**pidieron**
IMPERFECT SUBJUNCTIVES					
pidiera etc.			**pidiese** etc.		

In Class C the number and distribution of the forms affected by the stem change are exactly the same as in Class B. There is, however, only one type of change: that from **e** to **i**. In the vocabularies Class C verbs are indicated thus:

pedir (i-i)

87. *Additional Notes on the Definite Article* (see Article **52**).
1. The definite article has a neuter form **lo**, which is found before an adjective used in a general or abstract sense :

> **lo bueno** what is good, everything good

2. **El** is used instead of **la** before feminine nouns that begin with stressed **a** or **ha** :

> **el agua** the water   **el hacha** the ax
> But : **la acción** the action

3. The definite article is used before titles, except in direct address :

> **El señor Gómez está aquí.** Mr. Gómez is here.
> **Conozco al doctor Sánchez.** I know Dr. Sánchez.
> But : **Señor Gómez, este caballero quiere hablarle.** Mr. Gómez, this gentleman wishes to speak to you.

4. The definite article is normally used instead of the possessive adjective (Article **38**) in referring to parts of the body or to articles in personal use. Possession is expressed when desirable by the indirect object. When each individual of a group possesses one of the objects in question, the expression is in the singular.

> **Abrió los ojos.** He opened his eyes.
> **Levantó la cabeza.** He raised his head.
> **Me pongo el sombrero.** I put on my hat.
> **Nos limpió los zapatos.** He cleaned our shoes.
> **Siento dolores en los brazos y la cabeza.** I feel pains in my arms and in my head.
> **Los muchachos se lavan las manos y la cara.** The boys wash their hands and faces.

A variant of this usage is found in constructions following **tener** (to have), in which English uses the indefinite article or the possessive adjective :

> **Tiene la cabeza muy grande.** He has a very large head.
> **Tiene la boca ancha.** He has a wide mouth.

Tengo los ojos cansados. My eyes are tired.

Vd. tiene los ojos muy pequeños. Your eyes are very small.

5. In expressions of rate Spanish uses the definite article where English uses the indefinite:

Las naranjas valen dos pesetas la docena. Oranges cost two pesetas a dozen.

Vende pan a diez centavos el kilo. He sells bread at ten cents a kilogram.

6. The definite article is always used with certain geographical names — for example,

el Perú   **el Canadá**   **la Habana**

With others it is not used — for example,

Méjico   **España**   **Cuba**

Each case must be learned by observation. When modified, geographical names regularly take the article:

la América central Central America

la Guayana holandesa Dutch Guiana

los Estados Unidos the United States

la Europa occidental western Europe

VOCABULARY

el agua (*f.*) water	**el puerto** port
el alma (*f.*) soul, spirit	**la raza** race
el año year	**la señora** Mrs., lady
el castillo castle	**la tierra** earth, land
el coche carriage, cab	**el vapor** steam, steamship
el ferrocarril railway	**Cayo Hueso** Key West
el fin end; **al fin** finally	**la Habana** Havana
la naturaleza nature	**Morro: Castillo del Morro**
la oportunidad opportunity	Morro Castle
la plaza public square	**Nueva York** New York
la pregunta question	**Santa Clara** a city in Cuba

abundar to abound
repetir (i-i) to repeat
servir (i-i) to serve; servirse
  to be kind enough to, please
cubano Cuban
extranjero foreign

famoso famous
pintoresco picturesque
propio own
delante de in front of
desde since (~~Tune~~)
enfrente opposite, in front

EXERCISES

A

Una vez mi maestro de español me dijo : — Para comprender el alma de una raza extranjera es preciso visitar el país. — Desde entonces siempre he deseado visitar un país de lengua española. Al fin llegó la oportunidad. Un amigo de mi padre, el señor Gómez, vive en Cuba. El año pasado nos invitó a pasar unas semanas con su familia en Santa Clara. Mi madre y mi hermana no podían ir, pero mis hermanos y yo salimos con nuestro padre para nuestra primera visita a un país extranjero. Nos hubiera gustado hacer el viaje en vapor de Nueva York a la Habana, pero teníamos sólo dos semanas, y para no perder tiempo fuimos a Cayo Hueso en automóvil. Allí tomamos el vapor para la Habana. En unas horas vimos delante de nosotros la tierra cubana, donde abunda lo hermoso y lo pintoresco en la naturaleza. Al entrar en el puerto pasamos cerca del famoso Castillo del Morro. Al llegar a tierra mi padre se dirigió a un cubano que estaba cerca y le dijo : — Sírvase Vd. decirme dónde puedo encontrar un coche que nos lleve a la estación del ferrocarril. — Como lo dijo en inglés, el cubano no le comprendió. Entonces repitió la misma pregunta en español. El hombre contestó que encontraría un coche en la plaza de enfrente.

B

1. ¿Quién es el señor Gómez? 2. ¿En qué ciudad vive? 3. ¿En qué país está la ciudad? 4. ¿Fué toda la familia a visitar al señor Gómez? 5. ¿Cuántas hermanas tengo? 6. ¿Cómo se puede hacer el viaje de Nueva York a la Habana? 7. ¿Cuántas

semanas podíamos pasar en Cuba? 8. ¿Cómo fuimos de Cayo
Hueso a la Habana? 9. ¿Cuánto tiempo necesitamos para
hacer el viaje? 10. ¿Qué es el Morro? 11. ¿Dónde está? 12. ¿A
quién habló mi padre? 13. ¿Qué le preguntó? 14. ¿En qué
lengua habló primero? 15. ¿Comprendió el hombre? 16. ¿Dónde
estaban los coches?

C

I. Give the mood, tense, person, and number of the following
verb forms. In each case, what is the infinitive?

repitamos	murió	pienso	volvemos
puedo	me sentí	nos sentamos	se muestran
nos acostamos	perdieron	encuentran	quiere
consuelan	contásemos	sirvieron	cuesten
pidiésemos	se divierta	pidiese	llueve
sirva	sirviéramos	nos despertamos	durmamos
duermes	vuelven	repito	pedí

II. Decide which, if any, of the words in parentheses should be
used in the following sentences. Give the reason for your decision.

1. Levanté (*mi, la*) cabeza cuando me habló.
2. Nos gusta hablar (*el*) español.
3. Así es (*la*) vida.
4. (*Los*) médicos están siempre muy ocupados.
5. (*El, la*) agua no es buena.
6. ¿Quisiera Vd. ir (*a, al*) Perú, (*a, al*) Méjico, o (*a, al*)
Canadá para pasar el verano?
7. ¿Conoce Vd. (*a, al*) señor García?
8. (*La*) Habana es una ciudad de (*la*) Cuba.
9. (*Las*) flores son hermosas.
10. Es difícil comprender (*el, la*) alma de un país.
11. Tiene (*la, una*) cabeza muy pequeña.
12. Me gusta vivir en (*los*) Estados Unidos.
13. (*El*) señor Gómez, tenga Vd. la bondad de sentarse aquí.
14. (*Las*) vacas son útiles.
15. (*Las*) peras cuestan dos pesetas (*la, una*) docena.
16. (*El, lo*) barato no es siempre (*el, lo*) bueno.

D

I. Replace the infinitives in parentheses with the proper forms of the verb:

1. Dice que la criada le (*servir*) bien.
2. El profesor desea que nosotros (*repetir*) la frase.
3. Su padre (*morir*) ayer.
4. Ellos (*pedir*) que los visitemos.
5. María (*vestirse*) ahora en su cuarto.
6. Él (*repetir*) la palabra, porque no la comprendimos.
7. Sentimos que Carlos no (*vestirse*) bien.
8. Se acostaron temprano, y (*dormir*) mucho tiempo.
9. El médico sentía que Carlos (*dormir*) tan mal.
10. Queríamos que ellos (*divertirse*).
11. No me iré hasta que Vd. (*sentirse*) mejor.
12. (*Pedir*) que yo le acompañara.
13. No queríamos que los pájaros (*morir*) durante el invierno.
14. No quiero que el hombre me (*pedir*) dinero.

II. Translate: 1. The soul. 2. Mrs. García is young. 3. The English are tall. 4. We admire what is beautiful. 5. Havana is in Cuba. 6. Good day, Mrs. Méndez. 7. Water is useful. 8. Canada is near the United States. 9. Nature is always interesting. 10. He always wants what is new.

E

1. John and Henry Moreno were two Cuban boys. 2. Once (One time) they had spent some weeks in New York. 3. There they had met the White family (the family White): Charles, Mary, and their mother. 4. After returning to Cuba, John and Henry wished their American friends to visit them. 5. They requested their parents to invite them. 6. Mrs. White and her family went to Havana by (*en*) steamer. 7. Charles and Mary had wanted to go to Key West by automobile, in order to go more rapidly. 8. But Mrs. White said that the trip by steamer would be more interesting.

9. On entering the port of Havana the travelers noticed a great castle near the city. 10. They turned to a man and asked in Spanish what castle it was. 11. The man did not understand. 12. Then Charles repeated the same question in English. 13. The man replied: " It is Morro Castle. 14. But why do you speak to me in Spanish? 15. I am an American. 16. I do not understand Spanish well."

LESSON XXV

88. *Spelling Changes in Verbs.*[1] In verbs of the following types, certain changes in spelling are necessary in order that the final consonant of the stem may be pronounced throughout the conjugation as it is in the infinitive. (For a discussion of the sounds involved see Introduction, Article **7**.)

1. When the infinitive ends in **-car**, **c** becomes **qu** before **e**.

sacar to take out		
PRETERIT INDICATIVE	saqué sacaste sacó	sacamos sacasteis sacaron
PRESENT SUBJUNCTIVE	saque saques saque	saquemos saquéis saquen

2. When the infinitive ends in **-gar**, **g** becomes **gu** before **e**.

llegar to arrive		
PRETERIT INDICATIVE	llegué llegaste llegó	llegamos llegasteis llegaron
PRESENT SUBJUNCTIVE	llegue llegues llegue	lleguemos lleguéis lleguen

---

[1] The following general observations may be made regarding all orthographic changes discussed in this lesson (except Article **89**, 2) :

1. The change always occurs *throughout* the present subjunctive.

2. It also occurs, in verbs of the first conjugation, in the first person singular preterit ; and in those of the second and third conjugations, in the first person singular present indicative.

3. When the infinitive ends in **-zar**, **z** becomes **c** before **e**.

almorzar (ue) to lunch		
PRETERIT INDICATIVE	almorcé	almorzamos
	almorzaste	almorzasteis
	almorzó	almorzaron
PRESENT SUBJUNCTIVE	almuerce	almorcemos
	almuerces	almorcéis
	almuerce	almuercen

4. When the infinitive ends in **-guir**, **gu** becomes **g** before **a** and **o**.

seguir (i-i) to follow		
PRESENT INDICATIVE	sigo	seguimos
	sigues	seguís
	sigue	siguen
PRESENT SUBJUNCTIVE	siga	sigamos
	sigas	sigáis
	siga	sigan

5. When the infinitive ends in **-ger** or **-gir**, **g** becomes **j** before **a** and **o**.

dirigir to direct		
PRESENT INDICATIVE	dirijo	dirigimos
	diriges	dirigís
	dirige	dirigen
PRESENT SUBJUNCTIVE	dirija	dirijamos
	dirijas	dirijáis
	dirija	dirijan

6. When the infinitive ends in **-cer** or **-cir** preceded by a consonant, **c** becomes **z** before **a** and **o**.

vencer to conquer		
PRESENT INDICATIVE	venzo	vencemos
	vences	vencéis
	vence	vencen
PRESENT SUBJUNCTIVE	venza	venzamos
	venzas	venzáis
	venza	venzan

89. In certain other types of spelling change the general principle stated in Article **88** is not involved, and the forms must be committed to memory.

1. When the infinitive ends in **-cer** or **-cir** preceded by a vowel, **z** is inserted before **c** when the latter is followed by **o** or **a**.

conocer to know		
PRESENT INDICATIVE	conozco	conocemos
	conoces	conocéis
	conoce	conocen
PRESENT SUBJUNCTIVE	conozca	conozcamos
	conozcas	conozcáis
	conozca	conozcan

2. Between vowels **y** always replaces unstressed **i**. This affects all **-er** and **-ir** verbs with stem ending in a vowel.

leer: leyendo, leyó, leyeron, leyese, etc. But : **leía, leído**

90. *The Comparative of Adjectives and Adverbs.* 1. To form the comparative, **más** (more) or **menos** (less) is placed before the positive form of an adjective or an adverb. *Than* is translated by **que**

Juan es más rico que yo. John is richer than I.
Yo soy menos rico que él. I am less rich than he.
Habla más rápidamente que yo. He talks more rapidly than I.

2. Adjectives that are compared irregularly are:

POSITIVE	COMPARATIVE
mucho much	**más** more
poco little	**menos** less
bueno good	**mejor** better
malo bad	**peor** worse
grande large	**más grande** larger *and* **mayor** older, larger
pequeño small	**más pequeño** smaller *and* **menor** younger, smaller

When referring to persons **mayor** and **menor** denote age, not size.

Mi hermano menor es más grande que yo. My younger brother is larger than I.

3. Adverbs that are compared irregularly are:

POSITIVE	COMPARATIVE
mucho much	**más** more
poco little	**menos** less
bien well	**mejor** better
mal badly	**peor** worse

4. To express an equal degree or quantity use **tan** (as) or **tanto -a** (as much), **tantos -as** (as many) . . . **como** (as). **Tan** precedes an adjective or an adverb and **tanto, -a** (**tantos, -as**) precedes a noun.

Es tan pobre como yo. He is as poor as I.
Canta tan bien como su hermana. She sings as well as her sister.
Juan tiene tanto dinero como José. John has as much money as Joseph.
Tiene tantos libros como yo. He has as many books as I.

91. *The Superlative of Comparison*. 1. Spanish lacks a true superlative degree. That is, Spanish does not distinguish between such expressions as *the better people* and *the best people, the younger* and *the youngest, faster* and *fastest*. In almost every case, however, the context makes clear the meaning intended.

¿**Quién es más alto?** Who is the taller (*or* tallest)?

¿**Dónde corre más rápidamente el río?** Where does the river run faster (*or* fastest)?

mi mejor amigo my best friend

el más fuerte de los dos the stronger of the two

Los que hablan más alto saben menos. Those who talk loudest know least.

2. The neuter article **lo** precedes an adverbial superlative followed by an expression of possibility :

Iré lo más pronto posible. I will go as soon as possible (the soonest possible).

Strictly speaking, this is not a superlative of comparison but an *absolute superlative* (see Article **92**).

3. After a superlative adjective, English *in* is translated by **de** :

el hombre más rico de la ciudad the richest man in the city

el alumno más inteligente de la clase the most intelligent student in the class

92. *The Absolute Superlative*. A high degree without comparison may be expressed by adding **-ísimo** to the adjective or adverb. When the suffix is added, the final vowel is dropped and occasionally other changes in spelling are made :

rapidísimo very (extremely, exceedingly) rapid

poquísimo very little

importantísimo very important

VOCABULARY

el **azúcar** sugar
la **caña** cane; **caña de azúcar** sugar cane
el **cochero** coachman
el **comerciante** merchant
el **minuto** minute
el **momento** moment
la **nota** note, trait
el **ojo** eye
el **paisaje** landscape
la **palma** palm
el **punto** point; **a punto de** on the point of
el **tabaco** tobacco
Colón Columbus
Europa Europe
coger to catch, gather
distinguir to distinguish
enviar to send
hallar to find; **hallarse** to find oneself, be

seguir to follow, continue
vencer to conquer, overcome
bello beautiful
característico characteristic
chico small
inmenso immense
mayor larger, older
menor smaller, younger
pobre poor
poquísimo very little
rico rich
tanto as much, so much, as many, so many
tropical tropical·
casi almost, nearly
lejos far
dentro de within
veíamos (*impf. ind. of* **ver**) we were seeing
visto (*past part. of* **ver**) seen

EXERCISES

A

Mi padre me envió a buscar un coche. Me acerqué a un coche y dije al cochero: — Es preciso que lleguemos a la estación del ferrocarril dentro de diez minutos. — No está lejos — contestó. — En un momento los llevaré allí. — Al llegar a la estación yo pagué al cochero. Mi padre entró en la estación y pidió billetes para todos. Poco después nos hallábamos en un tren que estaba a punto de salir para Santa Clara. Colón dijo que Cuba era el país más hermoso que ojos habían visto. En efecto, nosotros, que veíamos por primera vez un país tropical, lo hallábamos hermosísimo. Los inmensos campos de caña de azúcar y de tabaco interesaban más a mi hermano mayor, que estudia para comerciante. Pero mi hermano menor, que es todavía chico, hallaba más interesantes las pintorescas casas de los campesinos. Las bellísimas palmas que dan la nota característica del paisaje cubano nos interesaban a todos. Creo que un viaje a Cuba es casi tan interesante como un viaje a Europa.

B

1. ¿A dónde era preciso ir? 2. ¿Cuántos minutos teníamos para llegar allí? 3. ¿Fuimos en automóvil? 4. ¿Estaba lejos la estación? 5. ¿Quién pagó al cochero? 6. ¿Dónde pidió billetes mi padre? 7. ¿Salió pronto el tren? 8. ¿Ha visto Vd. un país tropical? 9. ¿Cree Vd. que Cuba es tan hermosa como los Estados Unidos? 10. ¿Cómo la hallaron nuestros viajeros? 11. ¿Qué vieron en los campos? 12. ¿Para qué estudia el hermano mayor? 13. ¿Es grande el hermano menor? 14. ¿Qué le interesa a él?

C

I. Choose the correct spelling of the following verb forms, and give the mood, tense, person, and number of each. In each case what is the infinitive?

1. pare(-c-, -z-, -zc-)emos
2. supli(-c-, -qu-)é
3. expli(-c-, -qu-)an
4. cono(-c-, -z-, -zc-)a
5. pa(-g-, -gu-)amos
6. co(-g-, -j-)ieron
7. se acer(-c-, -qu-)ó
8. tradu(-c-, -z-, -zc-)o
9. si(-g-, -gu-, -j-)an

10. se diri(-g-, -gu-, -j-)e
11. cre(-i-, -y-)ese
12. almor(-c-, -z-)é
13. lle(-g-, -gu-, -j-)an
14. bus(-c-, -qu-)emos
15. le(-í-, -y-)an
16. co(-g-, -gu-, -j-)o
17. distin(-g-, -gu-, -j-)en
18. pa(-g-, -gu-)e

II. *a.* Decide whether the following are comparisons of equality or inequality and translate: 1. Tiene tantos años como yo, pero es menos grande que yo. 2. Su hermana es más hermosa que inteligente. 3. Él ha tenido tantas oportunidades de viajar como Vd. 4. Nos gusta menos ir por tren que por automóvil. 5. Mi hermano es tan alto como Vd.

b. Decide whether the following are comparative or superlative and translate: 1. Lo más característico de Cuba son las palmas. 2. Juan tiene menos libros que yo. 3. Su mejor amigo vive ahora en Méjico. 4. Está más enfermo hoy que ayer. 5. Viajó lo más rápidamente posible. 6. María tiene una hermana mayor.

III. *a.* Choose the correct form and translate:

1. Sus hermanas no eran (*tan, tantas, tantos*) diligentes como ella.

2. El muchacho pequeño escribe el español (*tan, tanto*) bien como yo.

3. Hay (*tan, tantos, tantas*) muchachas bonitas en España como en nuestro país.

4. ¿Bebe Vd. (*tan, tanto, tanta*) leche como nosotros?

5. Hay pocos estudiantes que sean (*tan, tantos, tantas*) inteligentes como Vds.

b. Tell in each case whether the italicized word is an adjective or an adverb, give its form in the positive degree, and translate:

1. Yo soy *menos* diligente que él.

2. Es la *peor* cosa que he visto.

3. Una pluma es *mejor* que un lápiz.

4. Escribe el español *mejor* que yo.

5. Las peras cuestan *muchísimo.*

D

I. In each of the following sentences replace the infinitive in parentheses with a proper form of the verb and translate:

1. El maestro quiere que nosotros (*traducir*) las frases.

2. Dudo que él se (*dirigir*) a su casa.

3. Ayer Juan no (*leer*) el periódico.

4. ¡(*Pagar*) Vds. la cuenta!

5. Dudo que (*llegar*) sus padres hoy.

6. Yo (*almorzar*) muy temprano ayer.

7. ¿Es preciso que él nos (*seguir*)?

8. Manda que nosotros (*buscar*) el libro que perdimos.

9. Estaba (*leer*) el periódico cuando entré.

10. Yo (*conocer*) a un hombre que sabe mucho de azúcar.

II. Translate: 1. Henry is my older brother. 2. I am as large as he. 3. There are as many girls as boys in the class. 4. Charles is my best friend. 5. He writes better than I. 6. Our house is smaller than the schoolhouse. 7. It is the smallest house on our street. 8. His younger sister is more diligent than he. 9. I am a poor (bad) student; John is worse, but Henry is worst of all. 10. He is the most famous man in the city. 11. Their house is extremely beautiful. 12. The living room is the largest room in the house.

E

1. There are very many (see Article **92**) automobiles in Havana. 2. At times we saw cabs also. 3. The automobiles go more rapidly than the cabs, but are less cheap. 4. We like the cabs because we have more time to see (the) interesting things. 5. The houses interested us very much. 6. They are larger than our house, and are closer to the street. 7. There were many shops of all kinds. 8. Some tropical fruits interested us, and we wanted the coachman to buy them. 9. He was sorry not to do it. 10. If we had more time, he would stop. 11. But it was necessary that we be in the station within ten minutes. 12. The railroad station in Havana is very beautiful. 13. It is larger than the station in our city. 14. All the railroads of Cuba go out from there. 15. The trains were not so large as those (*los*) which we had seen in our [own] country.

93. *The Possessive Adjective.* 1. In addition to the forms of the possessive adjective given in Article **38**, Spanish has a set of forms which are fully inflected; that is, each may end in -o, -a, -os, or -as:

mío	mía	míos	mías	my, of mine
tuyo	tuya	tuyos	tuyas	thy, of thine
suyo	suya	suyos	suyas	his, her, its, your (*formal*), of his, of hers, of its, of yours (*formal*)
nuestro	nuestra	nuestros	nuestras	ours, of ours
vuestro	vuestra	vuestros	vuestras	your, of yours (*familiar plural*)
suyo	suya	suyos	suyas	their, your (*formal plural*), of theirs, of yours (*formal plural*)

2. The possessive adjective agrees in gender and number with the thing possessed.

3. The above forms are used whenever the possessive adjective follows its noun, as occurs regularly in the following cases:

a. In direct address:

> **amigo mío** my friend
> **Padre Nuestro** Our Father

Letters begin:

> **Muy señor mío** My dear Sir
> **Querido amigo mío** My dear Friend, etc.

b. When another limiting word precedes the noun:

> **una hija suya** one of his daughters
> **algunos libros nuestros** several books of **ours**

94. *The Possessive Pronoun.* 1. In form the possessive pronoun is the longer form of the possessive adjective, regularly preceded by the definite article.

Tengo mi libro y el suyo. I have my book and his.
Juan tiene su pluma y la mía. John has his pen and mine.

2. Owing to the many possible meanings of **suyo** (his, hers, its, theirs, yours) it is often well to avoid it, for the sake of clearness, by substituting the article followed by **de** plus the appropriate personal pronoun. (Compare Articles **39**, 2, and **99**.) This construction is not used in the first and second persons, as the meaning is clear without it.

Tengo mi libro y el de Vd. I have my book and yours.
mi hermana y la de él my sister and his
But : **tu hermana y la mía** your sister and mine

95.

hacer to do, make				
PRES. PART.	haciendo		PAST PART.	hecho
PRES. IND.	hago haces hace	hacemos hacéis hacen		
IMPF. IND.	hacía			
PRET. IND.	hice hiciste hizo	hicimos hicisteis hicieron		
FUT. IND.	haré		CONDITIONAL	haría
IMPERATIVE	haz	haced		
PRES. SUBJ.	haga		IMPF. SUBJ.	hiciera hiciese

96. *Idiomatic Uses of* **hacer** *and* **tener.** 1. **Hacer** is used impersonally in certain expressions of time. (*a*) Action or state begun in the past and still continuing in the present is expressed in Spanish by **hace . . . que** and the present tense; it is not expressed by the present perfect tense, as in English:

Hace dos meses que estamos aquí. We have been here two months. (It makes two months that we are here.)

Hace un año que estudiamos el español. We have been studying Spanish for a year.

(*b*) Similarly, action or state begun in the past and continuing up to a point in the more recent past is expressed by **hacía . . . que** and the imperfect tense; not by the past perfect tense, as in English:

Hacía dos meses que estábamos aquí cuando Vd. llegó. We had been here for two months when you arrived. (It made two months that we were here, etc.)

Hacía seis meses que estudiaba el español cuando caí enfermo. I had been studying Spanish for six months when I became ill.

2. *Ago* is expressed by **hace** and the preterit tense:

Hace dos días que llegó, or **Llegó hace dos días.** He arrived two days ago.

Le escribí hace una semana. I wrote him a week ago.

3. In expressions of weather, Spanish uses **hacer** impersonally with a noun object, whereas English uses *to be* impersonally with a predicate adjective:

Hace frío. It is cold.
Ayer hacía calor. Yesterday it was hot.

Since **frío, calor,** etc. are nouns, Spanish uses the adjective **mucho** for the English adverb *very*:

Hace mucho calor. It is very hot.

4. In certain expressions referring to physical or mental states of persons or other living things, Spanish uses **tener** with a noun object, whereas English uses *to be* with an adjective:

Tenemos calor. We are (too) warm.
Tiene frío. He is cold.
Su perro tiene hambre. Your dog is hungry.
Los pájaros tienen miedo de los muchachos. The birds are afraid of the boys.
Tengo sueño. I am sleepy.

As in paragraph 3, above, **mucho** translates English *very*:

Tiene mucho sueño. He is very sleepy.

VOCABULARY

el aire air
el calor heat
el fresco coolness, cool weather
el frío cold
la habitación room
el hambre (*f.*) hunger
el hijo son
la hoja leaf
el miedo fear
el patio court, patio
la planta plant
el recuerdo remembrance, souvenir; **recuerdos** regards
el suelo ground, floor
el sueño sleep
la vuelta turn, return
ancho wide, broad
cariñoso affectionate
cerrado closed
fresco cool, fresh
querido dear
alrededor de around

EXERCISES

A

Muy amigo mío:

Hace dos días que llegamos a la bellísima ciudad de Santa Clara. Hace sólo una semana que salimos de casa. El señor Gómez y un hijo suyo nos esperaban en la estación. Nos llevaron en seguida en automóvil a su casa de campo, que está cerca de la ciudad. Su casa es más grande que la nuestra. Las habitaciones son grandes y altas con ventanas anchas que bajan al suelo.

Como hace mucho calor aquí, las ventanas están cerradas durante el día. Cuando viene la noche las abren para que entre el aire fresco. En el centro de la casa hay un patio lleno de plantas y flores. En el jardín alrededor de la casa, hay árboles tropicales y muchas plantas con hojas anchas que no había visto antes de venir aquí. A mi vuelta dentro de un par de semanas, tendré mucho que contarle.

Muy cariñosos recuerdos a su familia.

Enrique

B

1. ¿Cuántos días hace que llegó Enrique a Santa Clara? 2. ¿Cuánto tiempo hace que salieron de casa? 3. ¿Dónde bajaron del tren? 4. ¿Dónde está la casa del señor Gómez? 5. ¿Cómo fueron allí? 6. ¿Es pequeña la casa del señor Gómez? 7. ¿Es más pequeña que la de Enrique? 8. ¿Cómo son las ventanas? 9. ¿Hace frío durante el día? 10. ¿Por qué abren las ventanas durante la noche? 11. ¿Dónde está el patio? 12. ¿Qué hay en el patio? 13. ¿Dónde está el jardín? 14. ¿Qué hay en él? 15. ¿Había visto Enrique todas las plantas que hay en el jardín? 16. ¿Cuándo volverá a los Estados Unidos?

C

I. *a*. Choose the correct form of the possessive adjective, and place it before or after the noun, as required. (Do not write in this book.)

1. Ella esperaba a _ _?_ _ hermano _ _?_ _ (*su, suyo, suya*).
2. Un _ _?_ _ hermano _ _?_ _ estaba con ella ayer (*su, suyo, suya*).
3. El señor Gómez llegó con un _ _?_ _ hijo _ _?_ _ (*su, suyo, suya*).
4. _ _?_ _ casa _ _?_ _ es muy pequeña (*su, suyo, suya*).
5. Visité a un _ _?_ _ amigo _ _?_ _ (*mi, mío, mía*).
6. Querida _ _?_ _ madre _ _?_ _ (*mi, mío, mía*).

¿Qué hora es?

7. Hemos vendido __?__ casa __?__ (*nuestro, nuestra, el nuestro, la nuestra*); la compró un __?__ primo __?__ (*mi, mío, mía*).

8. Muy __?__ señores __?__ (*nuestros, nuestras, los nuestros, las nuestras*).

9. José y Dorotea son unos __?__ amigos __?__ (*nuestros, nuestras, los nuestros, las nuestras*).

10. __?__ jardín __?__ está muy cerca de aquí (*mi, mío, mía*).

b. Translate the following sentences and tell what form of the possessive is used in each : 1. Su libro de ella y el mío están en la mesa. El de él y el de Vd. están aquí. 2. — ¿De quién es la pluma? — Es la mía. 3. Mi hermana y la de ella fueron a Cuba. 4. Nuestros amigos y los de Vds. nos visitaron ayer. 5. Busco el sombrero de ella, no el de Vd. 6. Mi casa es pequeña, pero la de Vd. es grande. 7. El padre de Enrique y el mío son hermanos. 8. El automóvil del Sr. Gómez es más nuevo que el nuestro.

II. *a*. Translate the following sentences and explain the various uses of **hacer** : 1. Hace una semana que está enfermo. 2. Estuve en la Habana hace dos años. 3. Cuando los visité, hacía un mes que vivían allí. 4. Hizo mal tiempo ayer, pero hace más calor hoy. 5. — ¿Es nuevo su automóvil? — No, lo compramos hace mucho tiempo. 6. Hace unos días que hace mucho frío. 7. Me desayuné hace una hora. 8. Hacía tres meses que no le veía a Vd. cuando le encontré en la calle.

b. Choose the correct form :

1. — ¿Qué tiempo (*es, está, hace*)? — Está lloviendo.
2. (*Soy, estoy, tengo*) sueño. No dormí mucho anoche.
3. Siempre (*somos, estamos, tenemos*) hambre cuando almorzamos tan tarde.
4. (*Hace, hacía*) dos días que llegó Vd.
5. Me gusta más cuando (*es, está, hace*) frío que cuando (*es, está, hace*) calor.
6. Hace dos semanas que (*está, ha estado*) en el campo.

7. Creo que (*será, estará, hará*) fresco mañana.

8. Nos gustaría más (*ser, estar, tener*) frío que (*ser, estar, tener*) calor.

D

I. Translate: 1. My pen and hers. 2. Gentlemen: 3. Several friends of ours. 4. Dear Mother: 5. His pencil and mine. 6. A cousin of mine. 7. Our house and yours (*sing.*). 8. Dear Friends: 9. A brother of his. 10. His book and ours.

II. Translate: 1. It is cold today. 2. They have been here two days. 3. They had been here two days when we arrived. 4. He gave me the book a week ago. 5. He had had the book a week, when he lost it. 6. It was very hot yesterday. 7. It will be hot tomorrow. 8. We were cold and hungry. 9. He has had the pencil two weeks. 10. I am sorry it is cold. 11. We don't want him to be cold. 12. I wrote to him four days ago. 13. It has always been hot in Cuba. 14. We have been in Cuba a week. 15. It was not necessary for them to be hungry.

E

1. Henry and his family left home ten days ago. 2. It was very hot when they arrived in (at) Cuba. 3. It is hot there every day. 4. We have known Mr. Gómez for ten years. 5. His house was extremely large. 6. The family gave them the coolest rooms in the house. 7. They did it in order that they might sleep well. 8. They did not want to sleep near the window. 9. It was cool in Henry's room. 10. The Cubans want it to be cool in their houses. 11. For that reason (*Por eso*) they have a patio in the center of the house. 12. A patio is not so large as (less large than) a garden, because it is within the house. 13. Many houses have gardens also. 14. Tropical plants and flowers are exceedingly beautiful. 15. I should like to live in Cuba (for) always. 16. If I were rich I should do it.

para siempre — for ever (always)

REVIEW LESSON V

[Lessons XXII–XXVI]

A

I. Give the mood, tense, person, and number of each of the following stem-changing verb forms. Also tell what the infinitive is and to what classification the verb belongs:

vuelva	piensen	repitamos	sirvan
sirvamos	acuesto	muramos	muriésemos
sintieron	niega	almuerzan	repito
durmiésemos	divirtamos	pidamos	pide
cuesta	pidieran	pierde	duermen
mueren	niego	consuelo	muestro
llueva	suena	durmamos	piense
	muestren	siente	

II. Identify as in I, above, the following forms of spelling-changing verbs:

dirija	lleguen	dirijo	dirijan	saqué
venza	saquen	almuercen	conozca	almorcé
conozcan	sigamos	saquemos	creyeron	siga
leyéramos	llegué	conozco	lleguemos	venzamos

III. Translate the following sentences, give the mood and tense of each verb, and explain why that form is used: 1. Si tuviera más tiempo, iría con Vd. 2. Quisiera ver unas corbatas. 3. Si tenemos tiempo, vamos a casa para almorzar. 4. Si hacía buen tiempo, dábamos un paseo todos los días. 5. Lo haría si fuera posible. 6. Dice que irá conmigo, si voy temprano. 7. Me gustaría que Vd. lo hiciese lo más pronto posible. 8. Si no estoy ocupado, leo durante la tarde. 9. Le daré el libro si lo necesita. 10. Si fuese Vd., vendería la casa. 11. Si tenía éxito en sus negocios, compraba un automóvil nuevo todos los años. 12. Si llueve, se levantarán tarde.

IV. In the following sentences distinguish between (a) adjectives and adverbs, (b) comparative and superlative degrees of comparison, and (c) the types of comparison (superiority, inferiority, equality) : 1. Enrique es tan grande como yo. 2. Nueva York es la ciudad más grande de los Estados Unidos. 3. Mi hermana es menos hermosa que la de él. 4. Es el libro más interesante que he leído. 5. José es mi mejor amigo. 6. Trabaja más que yo. 7. María estudia tanto como su hermano. 8. Carlos estudia poco y comprende menos. 9. Enrique es mayor que yo, pero menos alto. 10. Ha tenido tanto éxito como yo. 11. Jorge es el menor de la familia. 12. Vd. escribe bien sus ejercicios, pero puede escribirlos mejor todavía. 13. Su casa tiene tantas habitaciones como la nuestra. 14. María es la más pequeña de los estudiantes, y también la más inteligente. 15. Leo tan rápidamente como él, pero pronuncio menos distintamente. 16. Hay pocos coches en la plaza, pero en la calle hay menos todavía.

V. Translate the following sentences and explain each example of (a) special uses of the definite article, (b) possessive adjectives and pronouns, (c) idiomatic uses of **hacer** and **tener** : 1. Hace más frío en Nueva York que en la Habana. 2. Hija mía, no tengas miedo. 3. El Sr. Blanco tiene la cabeza muy grande. 4. Hace mucho tiempo que no comemos, y tenemos hambre. 5. Hace dos años que mi padre está en la América central. 6. Cuando mi amigo abrió los ojos, tuvo mucho miedo. 7. Cuando mi tío volvió del Perú, hacía mucho tiempo que no le veía. 8. Los panecillos cuestan dos pesetas la docena. 9. No es posible siempre distinguir lo malo de lo bueno. 10. El agua está fresca. 11. — ¿ Tiene Vd. calor, Señora Blanco? En el jardín hace más fresco. 12. Mi hermana Dorotea tiene los ojos azules. 13. Siempre compra lo barato en vez de lo bueno. 14. El hombre tenía todavía el sombrero en la cabeza. 15. Unos amigos nuestros están ahora en el Canadá. Partieron hace dos semanas. 16. En el verano tenemos calor, pero en el invierno tenemos frío.

B

I. Translate: 1. If he had it, he would give it to you. 2. I should like to talk with you tomorrow. 3. If it is cold we stay at home. 4. If we were in Cuba we should not be cold. 5. If they reach the station in time (*a tiempo*) they will take the train. 6. He ought not to do it. 7. If my aunt had things to sell she went to the village every day. 8. I will help you if you wish.

II. Translate: 1. Continue (*seguir*) reading. 2. I am sorry that you do not know Mr. Gómez. 3. He requested that I amuse him. 4. They are sorry it is raining. 5. Overcome (*vencer*) your fear; you are not dying. 6. He was sorry that his books cost him so much. 7. They requested him to repeat his question. 8. They hoped that I would sleep well, and that I would have a good time (*divertirse*) the following day.

III. Replace the English words in parentheses with the correct Spanish expressions:

1. Volvió (*a year ago*).
2. Ya no tenía (*his*) sombrero en (*his*) cabeza.
3. (*Dear Father:*)
4. (*Mrs. Blanco*) estuvo aquí ayer.
5. (*Central America*) está cerca de Méjico.
6. No puede distinguir entre (*what is good*) y (*what is bad*).
7. Las peras cuestan una peseta (*a*) kilo, y las naranjas dos pesetas (*a*) docena.
8. (*Water*) no cuesta tanto como (*wine*).

C

Translate: 1. When we were in Havana it was always hot during the day. 2. At Mr. Gómez's house we were sometimes cold during the night. 3. Mrs. Gómez said that she wanted us to sleep well, but that she did not want us to die of cold. 4. She always gave us the best that she had. 5. She used to say: " If you are hungry when you wake up, ask the servant to serve (the) breakfast at once. 6. [Have] lunch here too, because (the) meals are served better here than in the restaurants. 7. Don't be afraid that (*de que*) the servants will work too much. 8. They always feel well, and they have a good time (*divertirse*) when they are not working." 9. In fact, Cuban servants work better than ours. 10. They are always carrying things in (*entre*) their arms or on their heads. 11. If it is hot, they do not seem to be as warm as we [are]. 12. They are not as much in a hurry as we [are]. 13. Ordinarily the Cubans seem to have what is good and avoid what is bad. 14. What [a] life theirs [is]! 15. Ours is often much worse. 16. If Mr. Gómez had invited me, I would have spent a year in Santa Clara.

LESSON XXVII

97.   *The Demonstrative Adjective*

Singular		Plural		
Masculine	Feminine	Masculine	Feminine	
este	esta	estos	estas	this, these
ese	esa	esos	esas	that, those (of yours, near you)
aquel	aquella	aquellos	aquellas	that, those (distant)

In Spanish there are two demonstratives that translate the English word *that*. **Ese** refers to something near or relating to the person addressed; **aquel** indicates something distant from both speaker and person spoken to.

> **Esta carne es muy buena.** This meat (that I am eating) is very good.
> **¿Qué es ese libro?** What is that book (which you have)?
> **Aquel árbol es muy alto.** That tree (yonder) is very tall.

98. *The Demonstrative Pronoun.* 1. The forms given in Article **97** may all be used as pronouns. In that case they always bear a written accent to distinguish them from the corresponding adjectives.

> **esta pluma y aquélla** this pen and that one
> **¡Qué rosa tan bonita es ésa!** What a pretty rose that (which you have) is!
> **Éste es mi sombrero.** This is my hat.

2. **Éste** is used for *the latter, the last mentioned*; and **aquél** for *the former*. When both occur in the same sentence, **éste** precedes **aquél**, the reverse of the English order.

> **María y Carlos son amigos míos; éste es cubano, aquélla mejicana.** Mary and Charles are friends of mine; the former is a Mexican, the latter a Cuban.

166

The " Central," or Mill, of a Cuban Sugar Plantation

This Important Business Street in Havana Is Only Eleven Feet Wide

Vaqueros (Cowboys), Central Valley of Chile

Cattle Market, Buenos Aires, Argentina

**Mi madre y la criada salieron de la casa al mismo tiempo;
ésta iba al mercado, aquélla a la biblioteca.** My mother and
the servant left the house at the same time; the former was
going to the library, the latter to the market.

3. **Esto, eso**, and **aquello** are neuter demonstrative pronouns,
which have the same respective meanings as their non-neuter
counterparts. They have no accent because there are no corresponding adjectives. They refer to something to which gender
cannot logically be ascribed, such as an idea or an object not yet
identified.

> **¿ Qué es esto?** What is this thing?
> **Eso es verdad.** That (which you said) is true.

99. *The Definite Article Used Demonstratively.* 1. The definite
article is frequently used as a demonstrative pronoun before a **de**
phrase. (See Articles **39**, 2, and **94**, 2.)

Tengo mis libros y los de Juan. I have my books and John's
(those of John).

Es mi amigo y también el de mi padre. He is my friend and
also my father's.

2. It has a similar use before a relative clause (Article **102**, 3).

100. *Some Expressions of Necessity or Obligation.* 1. **Tener
que** (to have to, be obliged to). When a noun object comes between **tener** and **que,** the idea of obligation is somewhat weakened.

Tengo que estudiar. I have to study.

Tendré que estudiar mi lección. I shall have to study my
lesson.

Tengo una lección que estudiar. I have a lesson to study.

2. **Haber de** (to be [expected] to). This expression denotes a
weaker obligation than **tener que** — hardly more than future
probability :

He de ir mañana. I am to go tomorrow (that is my present
intention).

Hemos de almorzar con ellos. We are to lunch with them.

3. **Haber que** (to be necessary to). The idea of obligation in this expression is as strong as in **tener que**, but the expression is impersonal.

Hay que estudiar para aprender. It is necessary to study in order to learn.

En aquella escuela había que trabajar. In that school it was necessary to work.

101.

saber to know				
PRES. PART.	sabiendo		PAST PART.	sabido
PRES. IND.	sé sabemos			
	sabes sabéis			
	sabe saben			
IMPF. IND.	sabía			
PRET. IND.	supe supimos			
	supiste supisteis			
	supo supieron			
FUT. IND.	sabré		CONDITIONAL	sabría
IMPERATIVE	sabe sabed			
PRES. SUBJ.	sepa		IMPF. SUBJ.	supiera
				supiese

VOCABULARY

la **conversación** conversation
el **empleado** employee, official, agent
la **forma** form
el **idioma** language
la **página** page
un **rato** a short time
la **regla** rule
el **verbo** verb

observar to observe
saber to know (a fact)
bastante enough, fairly, numerous
claro clear, evident
poco little, few
varios various, several
escrito written

EXERCISES

A

Estamos otra vez en la sala de clase. María, Juan y Carlos han de escribir los ejercicios en la pizarra. El profesor les dice: — En estos papeles hay varias frases en inglés que ustedes tienen que escribir en español. Pasen ustedes a la pizarra. Mientras Vds. escriben, tendremos un rato de conversación. Todos tenemos libros. ¿Qué hay en este libro? — Ése es un libro de lectura. En ese libro hay cuentos fáciles en español. — ¿Qué tiene usted, Juan? — Este libro es una gramática de español. — ¿Para qué sirve ese libro? — En la gramática aprendo muchas cosas útiles, como las formas de los verbos, y las reglas que hay que observar para hablar y escribir bien. — Ahora leamos los ejercicios que están en la pizarra. Juan, su ejercicio es bueno. Vd. sabe bien su lección. ¿Quién ha escrito este ejercicio? — Yo lo he escrito — contesta Carlos. — Usted ha hecho bastantes faltas. Está claro que no sabe bien las reglas. Para aprender un idioma extranjero hay que estudiar mucho. María ha escrito aquellas frases que están en la otra pizarra, y ha hecho pocas faltas. Eso es todo para hoy. Para mañana Vds. tienen que aprender todas las formas del verbo *saber*, y leer tres páginas más en el libro de lectura.

B

1. ¿Estamos ahora en Cuba? 2. ¿Qué hay en los papeles? 3. ¿Qué han de hacer unos alumnos? 4. Juan, ¿qué libro es ése? 5. ¿Qué es aquél que está cerca de la ventana? 6. ¿Qué es éste que tengo yo? 7. ¿Qué hay que aprender en la gramática? 8. ¿Qué hay que observar? 9. ¿Qué han escrito en la pizarra María, Juan y Carlos? 10. ¿Qué han de hacer ahora los otros alumnos? 11. ¿Es bueno el ejercicio de Juan? 12. ¿Qué hay que hacer para aprender un idioma? 13. ¿Es bueno también el ejercicio de Carlos? 14. ¿Hay faltas en el de María? 15 ¿Qué tienen que hacer para mañana?

C

I. Choose the correct word from each group of words in parentheses, and translate the sentence:

1. (*Ese, Esa, Aquel, Aquella*) señora es la madre de Carlos.

2. Hemos comprado una casa. Está cerca de (*el, la, los, las*) de Vd.

3. (*Este, Esta, Esto*) jardín es el nuestro.

4. ¿Dónde está mi sombrero? Sólo están aquí (*el, la, los, las*) de Juan y María.

5. Yo sé mi nota, pero no sé (*los, las*) de mis amigos.

6. Me gusta mucho (*esa, aquella*) corbata. ¿Cuándo la compró Vd.?

7. Nos acompañaron mi hermana y (*el, la, los, las*) de Enrique.

8. ¿Qué piensa Vd. de todo (*éste, esto*)?

9. Murió la madre de mi amigo cuando (*éste, ésta, esto*) tenía sólo dos años.

10. Mis padres son viejos, pero (*el, la, los, las*) de Dorotea son bastante jóvenes.

11. Shakespeare y Cervantes fueron muy famosos. (*Éste, Aquél*) escribió en español, (*éste, aquél*) en inglés.

12. Estas habitaciones son pequeñas, pero (*el, la, los, las*) de nuestra casa son grandes.

13. ¿Qué es (*ese, aquel*) libro que Vd. tiene?

14. (*Aquel, Aquello*) libro está escrito en inglés, pero (*éste, ésta, esto*) está en español.

15. ¿Qué es (*eso, aquello*) que Vd. me dijo? No lo comprendí bien.

16. ¡Cuántas peras hay en (*ese, aquel*) árbol!

17. La hermana de María se va mañana, pero (*ésta, aquélla*) se queda.

18. Tengo su libro y (*el, la, los, las*) de ella también.

II. Choose the correct expressions of necessity and translate:

1. En esta universidad (*he de, hay que*) estudiar mucho.

2. (*Tenemos, Hemos*) muchas cosas que hacer antes de salir para Méjico.

3. (*Tiene que, Ha de, Hay que*) almorzar conmigo.

4. (*Tengo que, He de, Hay que*) estudiar mi lección esta noche.

5. (*Tienen que, Han de, Hay que*) visitarnos esta semana.

6. (*Tendremos que, Habremos de*) salir pronto para tomar el tren.

7. Cuando estábamos en el campo (*teníamos que, habíamos de*) levantarnos temprano todas las mañanas.

8. Enrique (*tenía que, había de, había que*) volver la semana pasada, pero no ha llegado todavía.

9. Después de su enfermedad, Carlos (*tuvo que, hubo de, hubo que*) quedarse en casa varios días.

10. (*Hemos de, Hay que*) ir a la escuela durante el invierno.

11. (*Tengo, He*) una lección que estudiar.

12. (*Ha de, Hay que*) estudiar para aprender.

D

I. Substitute the correct Spanish forms for the English words in parentheses, and translate:

1. Mi hermana y (*John's*).

2. ¿Qué es (*that*) allí en la calle?

3. (*These*) zapatos y (*my friend's*).

4. María, ¿qué lee Vd. en (*that*) libro?

5. (*This*) pluma es barata, pero (*the teacher's*) vale mucho.

6. (*That*) sombrero y (*Mary's*).

7. ¿Qué gramática es (*this*)?

8. (*These*) casas son pequeñas, pero (*those*) son más grandes.

9. (*That*) cuaderno que Vd. tiene es (*Henry's*).

10. (*Those*) campos son (*my uncle's*).

II. Translate: 1. We are to spend a week in the country. 2. In the country it is necessary to get up early. 3. We shall have to get up early. 4. John has much to do. 5. Charles is to visit us this week. 6. In our city it is necessary to go by (in) cab. 7. Mary has had to work hard this year. 8. They are to come today. 9. They will have to study this afternoon. 10. In Cuba it was necessary to speak Spanish.

E

1. We have left our friends in Cuba. 2. Now we are to attend a class in Spanish in our university. 3. There are many students in the class. 4. They want to learn Spanish because they would like to take a trip to Mexico or (to) Cuba. 5. In order that a trip to a foreign country may be interesting, it is necessary to understand the language that is spoken there. 6. When we were in Cuba we had to read the newspapers in Spanish. 7. We had to speak Spanish in order to eat in a restaurant. 8. In the markets we always had to speak Spanish, because the venders did not speak [any] other language. 9. In the streets there were many venders with carts full of fruit and vegetables. 10. We always had to speak Spanish with these [people]. 11. In the large stores it was not necessary (to do it) because there were employees who spoke English. 12. There is a girl in our class who wishes to learn Spanish very well. 13. Her father is extremely rich. 14. He has immense fields of sugar cane and tobacco in Cuba and (in) Mexico. 15. At the end of the year Mary is to go with him to those countries. 16. It is necessary to speak Spanish there, and she already speaks it fairly well.

102. *The Relative Pronoun.* 1. The invariable relative pronoun **que** (who, whom, which, that) is used both as subject and as object of a verb to refer both to persons and to things. After a preposition, **que** can refer only to things. The relative pronoun is never omitted in Spanish, as is frequently the case in English.

El hombre que viene es mi padre. The man who is coming is my father.

El libro que está sobre la mesa es una gramática. The book that is on the table is a grammar.

La persona que veo es un amigo mío. The person (whom) I see is a friend of mine.

La cosa que tengo es una piedra. The thing (which) I have is a stone.

La lección de que hablo es fácil. The lesson (which) I am talking about is easy.

2. The relative pronoun **quien** (*plural*, **quienes**) (who, whom) is used after prepositions to refer to persons. It is used also in nonrestrictive clauses as subject or object of a verb referring to persons. (A nonrestrictive clause is one which forms a supplementary statement not needed to identify the antecedent, as in the second and third examples below.) As object of a verb **quien** requires the personal **a**.

El hombre de quien Vd. habla es español. The man you are speaking of is Spanish.

Quiere ver a su padre, quien está malo. He wishes to see his father, who is sick.

El señor Gómez, a quien Vd. conoce, viaja ahora por Méjico. Mr. Gómez, whom you know, is traveling now in Mexico.

Quien may include its antecedent. In this use it is equivalent to English *he who, the one who, anyone who,* etc.

Quien eso dice, miente. He who says that, lies.

3. **El que, la que, los que, las que, lo que.** The definite article followed by **que** translates English *he who, the one who, that which,*

173

etc. The neuter construction **lo que** (that which, what) is very frequent.

> **Los que vienen son amigos míos.** Those who are coming are friends of mine.
>
> **El profesor desea mi libro y el que Vd. tiene.** The teacher wants my book and the one you have.
>
> **Yo sé lo que Vd. tiene.** I know what you have.

103.

poder to be able				
PRES. PART.	pudiendo		PAST PART.	podido
PRES. IND.	puedo puedes puede	podemos podéis pueden		
IMPF. IND.	podía			
PRET. IND.	pude pudiste pudo	pudimos pudisteis pudieron		
FUT. IND.	podré		CONDITIONAL	podría
PRES. SUBJ.	pueda puedas pueda	podamos podáis puedan		
IMPF. SUBJ.	pudiera, pudiese			

104. *Distinctions in Meaning between* **conocer, saber,** *and* **poder. 1. Conocer** means *to meet* (*become acquainted with*) a person, or *to know* (*be acquainted with*) a person or thing. Its object is always a noun or pronoun, never a clause.

> **Le conocí en Madrid.** I met him in Madrid.
>
> **Conocemos al doctor Gómez.** We know Dr. Gómez.
>
> **Mi hermano conoce muy bien a París.** My brother knows Paris very well.

2. **Saber** means *to know* in the sense of *to have knowledge concerning*. It is often followed by a clause. When followed by a dependent infinitive, it means *can* in the sense of *know how to*:

¿Sabe Vd. que Enrique no está aquí? Do you know that Henry is not here?

Yo sé por qué no ha venido María. I know why Mary has not come.

Sabe a fondo las matemáticas. He knows mathematics thoroughly.

¿Sabe Vd. conducir un automóvil? Can you (do you know how to) drive a car?

3. **Poder,** as distinguished from **saber,** means *can* in the sense of being physically able (to do a thing). It also means *may,* in the sense of asking or granting permission:

No puede leer sin gafas. He cannot read without glasses.

But: **No sabe leer el francés.** He cannot read French.

No puedo levantar este baúl. I cannot lift this trunk.

¿Se puede entrar? May I come in?

impersonal (*May one come in?*)

VOCABULARY

la **altura** height	el **pie** foot; **ir a pie** to walk
la **central** sugar mill	el **producto** product
la **estación** season	el **valor** value
la **excursión** excursion	**crecer** to grow
la **fábrica** factory, refinery	**cargado** loaded
la **isla** island	**importante** important
el **lugar** place	**seis** six

EXERCISES

A

Estoy todavía en Santa Clara donde ustedes me han dejado hace unos días. Ayer hicimos una excursión al campo en automóvil. El señor Gómez no pudo acompañarnos, pero envió a su hijo, quien conocía muy bien todos los lugares interesantes. Como es la estación de la cosecha de la caña de azúcar, vimos muchos carros grandes cargados de caña. La llevaban a la fábrica o central, como se llama aquí, donde sacan el azúcar. Hicimos una visita a una central, y nos explicaron cómo se prepara el azúcar. No puedo explicárselo a ustedes, porque yo no lo comprendí muy bien. El azúcar es el producto más importante de la isla. El famoso tabaco cubano es de menos valor que el azúcar. Lo que yo quería ver era cómo crecía el tabaco. Me llevaron a un campo donde lo cultivaban. Es una planta de hojas anchas que tiene una altura de unos seis pies.

B

1. ¿En qué ciudad de Cuba estamos hoy? 2. ¿A dónde fuimos ayer? 3. ¿Hicimos la excursión a caballo? 4. ¿Quién nos acompañó? 5. ¿Por qué nos podía ayudar mucho este señor? 6. ¿Qué cosecha hacían? 7. ¿De qué estaban cargados los carros? 8. ¿Dónde sacan el azúcar? 9. ¿Qué se dice en Cuba: " fábrica " o " central "? 10. ¿Qué nos explicaron? 11. ¿Por qué no puedo explicárselo a ustedes? 12. ¿Es más importante el tabaco que el azúcar? 13. ¿Es bueno el tabaco cubano? 14. ¿Crece el tabaco en un árbol? 15. ¿Qué forma tienen las hojas? 16. ¿Qué altura tiene la planta?

C

I. *a*. Give the meaning of **que** in the following sentences: 1. El hombre que entró era un amigo mío. 2. ¿Cuándo llegó la carta que Vd. recibió? 3. La fábrica en que trabaja aquel hombre está muy lejos de su casa. 4. Comí toda la fruta que mi amigo me dió. 5. El amigo mío que va a visitarme debe llegar esta mañana.

b. Choose the correct relative pronoun and translate:

1. Éste es el señor con (*que, quien*) viajé en España.
2. Es (*que, lo que*) yo pensaba.
3. Esta casa es (*que, el que, la que*) más me gusta.
4. La ciudad en (*que, quien*) vivía no era muy grande.
5. Colón no halló la tierra (*que, la que, a quien*) buscaba.

6. ¿Quién es el muchacho de (*que, quien*) Vd. hablaba?

7. Mi madre, quien sabía (*que, lo que*) yo había hecho, me ayudó.

8. No encontramos al vendedor a (*que, quien*) buscábamos, ni (*a que, al que, quien*) nos vendió la fruta.

9. (*Que, Quienes, Los que*) vienen son amigos suyos.

10. Me gustan más estos libros que (*lo que, los que*) Vds. tienen.

II. Choose the correct verb and translate:

1. (*Conocemos, Sabemos*) muy bien a sus tíos de Vd. Los (*conocimos, supimos*) el año pasado.

2. ¿(*Conoce, Sabe*) Vd. su lección para hoy?

3. Cuando llegó a este país, no (*sabía, podía*) hablar una palabra de inglés.

4. Me gusta mucho (*conocerle, saberle*) a Vd.

5. Quiero que Vd. (*conozca, sepa*) lo que ha pasado.

6. ¿(*Conoce, Sabe*) Vd. dónde está la estación?

7. (*Conocí, Supe*) que él había venido.

8. (*Conocen, Saben*) muy bien a muchos españoles, pero no (*conocen, saben*) su idioma.

9. (*Sé, Puedo*) montar a caballo, pero lo hago muy poco.

10. ¿(*Conoce, Sabe*) Vd. un hombre que (*sepa, pueda*) traducir esta carta?

D

I. Fill each blank with the proper form of the relative pronoun. (Do not write in this book.)

1. El muchacho _ _ ? _ _ estaba con Vd.

2. Los señores de _ _ ? _ _ (yo) le hablaba.

3. La pluma _ _ ? _ _ compré ayer.

4. El amigo con _ _ ? _ _ yo viajaba.

5. Éste es el señor a _ _ ? _ _ (yo) debía dar la carta.

6. Tengo dos pesetas con _ _ ? _ _ puedo pagar al cochero.

7. Es el señor con _ _ ? _ _ hablé.

8. Las alumnas _ _ ? _ _ asistían a la clase.

9. He visto a Enrique, _ _ ? _ _ me lo explicó.

10. La señora _ _ ? _ _ vi ayer es la madre de Carlos.

II. Translate into Spanish the English words in parentheses:

1. Me dió (*what*) yo deseaba.
2. (*Anyone who*) no lo sabe no es inteligente.
3. Estas casas y (*those which*) vimos ayer.
4. Carlos fué (*the one who*) lo hizo.
5. Recibimos su carta y (*the one which*) nos escribió Carlos.
6. No comprendí (*what*) Vd. dijo.
7. Estos libros y (*those which*) compré ayer.
8. El lápiz de Enrique y (*the one which*) me dió.

III. Translate into Spanish the English words in parentheses:

1. Vd. (*cannot*) ver su casa desde aquí.
2. Mi padre (*knows*) muy bien el inglés.
3. Los (*we met*) hace muchos años.
4. ¿(*Do you know*) por qué vendió su casa?
5. Juan (*can*) hablar y escribir el español.
6. Mi madre dice que (*we may*) ir al cine esta tarde.
7. (*We know*) muy poco al Sr. Blanco.
8. María (*cannot*) abrir esta puerta.

E

1. The plants which grow in tropical countries are very interesting. 2. There are many plants that we do not see in the United States. 3. If you were in Cuba you would see fields of sugar cane. 4. It is a tall plant with broad leaves. 5. It grows rapidly during the summer, when it is very hot. 6. They do not do the harvesting during the summer. 7. It is easier to do it during the winter. 8. The fields are drier, and it is cooler. 9. The cane is taken to the mills on great carts. 10. In the mill the sugar is extracted from the cane. 11. A large part of the Cuban sugar is eaten in the United States. 12. Another Cuban product which is very important is tobacco. 13. The tobacco which grows in this country is not so good as the tobacco of Cuba. 14. It is cultivated there in immense fields. 15. When the plants reach (use *llegar*) a height of six feet the harvesting is done. 16. The dry leaves are taken to the factories of Havana.

LESSON XXIX

105. *Interrogatives.* 1. The interrogative pronoun **quién** (*plural*, **quiénes**) (who, whom) refers to persons only. The phrase **de quién** may be translated either *of whom* or *whose*.

¿Quiénes vienen? Who are coming?
¿De quién habla Vd.? Of whom are you speaking?
¿De quién es este libro? Whose book is this?
No me dijo a quién hablaba. He did not tell me to whom he
    was speaking.

2. **Qué** (*invariable*) (what) is used as a pronoun to refer to things, and as an adjective to refer to both persons and things.

¿Qué tiene Vd.? What have you?
¿De qué habla Vd.? What are you talking about? *identification*
¿Qué libro tiene Vd.? What book have you?
¿Qué mozo le sirvió? What waiter served you?

3. The interrogative pronoun **cuál** (*plural*, **cuáles**) (which [one], what [one]) is commonly used before the verb **ser** and the preposition **de**. It may refer to both persons and things.

¿Cuál de los muchachos es su hijo? Which of the boys is
    your son? *identification*
¿Cuáles son las dificultades que Vd. encuentra? What are
    the difficulties that you meet?

When a definition is called for, however, *what* is translated **qué**:

    ¿Qué es la vida? What is life?

4. **Cuánto** (**cuánta**) (how much), **cuántos** (**cuántas**) (how many), is used as an interrogative adjective:

¿Cuánta agua hay en el vaso? How much water is there in
    the glass?
¿Cuántos hermanos tiene Vd.? How many brothers (and
    sisters) have you?

179

With "son" and a demonstrative, "cuál" is used instead of "qué".

5. **Dónde** (where), **cuándo** (when), **cómo** (how), **por qué** (why), are the common interrogative adverbs. Unlike English, Spanish differentiates clearly between **dónde** (where), **de dónde** ([from] where, whence), and **a dónde** ([to] where, whither).

> **¿Dónde está mi libro?** Where is my book?
> **¿De dónde viene Vd.?** Where do you come from?
> **Me preguntó a dónde iba.** He asked me where I was going.
> **¿Cuándo llegó?** When did he arrive?
> **No sé cómo ha pasado el día.** I do not know how he spent the day.
> **¿Por qué vino Enrique con Vds.?** Why did Henry come with you?

Note that interrogative adjectives, pronouns, and adverbs require a written accent in both direct and indirect questions.

106. *Exclamations.* Exclamations are similar to questions in regard to order of words, use of accents, etc. The following usages should be observed: 1. **Qué** before an adverb, or before an adjective not accompanying a noun, means *how*:

> **¡Qué fácilmente lo hace!** How easily he does it!
> **¡Qué rico es!** How rich he is!

2. **Qué** followed by a noun means *what* or *what a*. When the noun is itself followed by an adjective, **tan** or **más** is normally placed between them:

> **¡Qué éxito!** What success!
> **¡Qué ciudad!** What a city!
> **¡Qué biblioteca tan** (or **más**) **grande!** What a large library!

3. **Cuánto(s)** is used before nouns and verbs in the sense of *how much* (with plural of nouns, *how many*):

> **¡Cuánto dinero gasta!** How much money he spends!
> **¡Cuántos libros tiene!** How many books he has!
> **¡Cuánto trabaja!** How much he works!

107.

decir to say				
PRES. PART.	diciendo		PAST PART.	dicho
PRES. IND.	digo dices dice	decimos decís dicen		
IMPF. IND.	decía			
PRET. IND.	dije dijiste dijo	dijimos dijisteis dijeron		
FUT. IND.	diré		CONDITIONAL	diría
IMPERATIVE	di	decid		
PRES. SUBJ.	diga		IMPF. SUBJ.	dijera dijese

VOCABULARY

el baúl trunk
el dinero money
la maleta valise
el nombre name
la ropa clothing
despedirse (de) (i-i) to take
  leave (of)

llamar to call
meter to put within
preferir (ie-i) to prefer
rápido fast
las tres, las diez three o'clock,
  ten o'clock
salgo (from salir) I go out

EXERCISES

A

Nos hemos levantado muy temprano esta mañana porque
tenemos que volver en seguida a los Estados Unidos. Primero
meto mi ropa en la maleta. Ahora todo está listo. — ¿Quién
ha visto mi sombrero? Es preciso que tome los billetes de ferro-

carril. — Hallo mi sombrero, y salgo a la calle. Espero un coche que pueda llevarme a la estación. Pronto pasa un coche. Llamo al cochero y le digo: — ¿Puede Vd. llevarme a la estación del ferrocarril? — Sí, señor — contesta el cochero. Pasamos rápidamente por las calles de la ciudad, y llegamos a la estación. Entro, me acerco a un empleado, y le digo: — Tenga usted la bondad de decirme a qué hora sale el tren para la Habana. — Hay un tren a las diez de la mañana y otro a las tres de la tarde. — ¿Cuál es más rápido? — El de las tres es tren rápido; el de las diez se para en todas las estaciones. — Tomo los billetes y vuelvo a casa. Después del almuerzo nos despedimos de nuestros buenos amigos cubanos. Nos preguntan: — ¿Les ha gustado Cuba? ¿Cuándo volverán a visitarnos? — Los invitamos a visitarnos en los Estados Unidos.

B

1. ¿Por qué tenemos que levantarnos muy temprano? 2. ¿Dónde tengo que meter mi ropa? 3. ¿Cuál es más grande: una maleta o un baúl? 4. ¿A dónde hay que ir para tomar los billetes? 5. ¿Cómo voy? 6. ¿A quién me acerco después de entrar en la estación? 7. ¿Qué le pregunto? 8. ¿Lo sabe el hombre? 9. ¿Cuántos trenes hay todos los días para la Habana? 10. ¿A qué horas salen los trenes? 11. ¿Se para en todas las estaciones el tren de las tres? 12. ¿A dónde vuelvo al salir de la estación? 13. ¿De quiénes nos despedimos? 14. ¿A qué hora? 15. ¿Qué nos preguntan nuestros amigos? 16. ¿Qué deseamos que hagan ellos?

C

I. Choose the correct form of the interrogative and translate:

1. ¿Sabe Vd. con (*qué, quién*) hablábamos?
2. ¿(*Qué, Cuál*) es esto?
3. ¿(*Dónde, De dónde, A dónde*) está la casa de Vd.?
4. ¿De (*qué, cuál*) le hablaron?
5. ¿De (*qué, cuál*) color son los ojos de Vd.?
6. ¿(*Qué, Cuál, Quién*) de los dos hermanos prefiere Vd.?
7. ¿(*Qué, Quién*) es la muchacha con quien le vi ayer?

8. ¿(*Dónde, De dónde, A dónde*) fueron Enrique y José?

9. ¿(*Qué, Cuál, Quién*) de estos muchachos es su primo?

10. ¿Con (*qué, cuál*) escribe Vd.?

11. ¿(*Qué, Cuál, Quién*) de los alumnos es el más inteligente?

12. ¿(*Cuánto, Cuántos, Cuántas*) páginas hay en el libro?

13. No sé (*dónde, de dónde, a dónde*) vino este señor.

14. ¿(*Cuánto, Cuántos, Cuántas*) pesetas quiere Vd. pagarme por el automóvil?

II. Translate **qué** and **cuánto** (-a, -os, -as) in the following exclamations: 1. ¡Qué hermosa es Cuba! 2. ¡Cuántas cartas recibe Vd.! 3. ¡Qué día más hermoso! 4. ¡Qué viejo era el hombre! 5. ¡Cuánto estudia Jorge! 6. ¡Qué hombre tan amable! 7. ¡Cuánta bondad me ha mostrado! 8. ¡Qué estudiante más inteligente es éste! 9. ¡Qué rápidamente va este tren! 10. ¡Cuánto ayuda Carlos a su tío! 11. ¡Qué comida! 12. ¡Qué mal escribe Vd.!

D

I. Fill the following blanks with either **qué** or **cuál**, as the construction requires. (Do not write in this book.)

1. ¿ _ _ ? _ _ es el nombre de su amigo?

2. ¿ _ _ ? _ _ de Vds. vive aquí?

3. ¿ _ _ ? _ _ ha hecho Vd.?

4. ¿ _ _ ? _ _ libro quiere Vd.?

5. ¿ _ _ ? _ _ de los libros prefiere Vd.?

6. ¿ _ _ ? _ _ son los libros que Vd. prefiere?

7. ¿ _ _ ? _ _ hombre entró en la casa?

8. ¿ _ _ ? _ _ de los hombres entró en la casa?

II. Substitute the proper Spanish expressions for the English words in parentheses, and translate:

1. ¿(*Whom*) ha visto Vd.?

2. ¡(*How many*) muchachas hay en la clase!

3. ¡(*How much*) habla!

4. ¿Para (*whom*) es la carta?

5. ¡(*How*) hermosa es!

6. ¿En (*what*) país está la Habana?
7. ¿(*Whence*) viene el tabaco?
8. ¿Con (*what*) escribe Vd. en la pizarra?
9. ¿(*Who*) le dió el dinero?
10. ¿(*Where*) llevan la caña?
11. ¿(*When*) volverá su amigo?
12. ¿(*Why*) no escribe Vd. con pluma?

E

1. We are returning to the United States. 2. My father wishes me to get the railroad tickets. 3. Now everything is ready, and I am going to the station. 4. When I go out into the street it is still cool. 5. I prefer to walk. 6. I ask a man, " Where is the railroad station? Is it far? " 7. He says, " Which of the stations are you looking for? 8. To what city are you going? " 9. I tell him that we are going to Havana. 10. He says the station is not far away. 11. When I enter the station I say to myself, " What a beautiful building! 12. How many travelers are getting tickets! " 13. I ask the agent, " How many trains for Havana are there every day? " 14. He says, " There are many. At what time do you prefer to go? " 15. I tell him that we prefer the afternoon. 16. He says there is a good train at three, and I get the tickets.

The following pronouns are always preceded by the personal " a " when used as direct object of verb:

quién (interrogative)
alguien
nadie
quien (relative) — But, *not* relative pronoun

The following pronouns are always preceded by personal " a " when they refer to persons not things and when used as the direct object of the verb:
cuál
alguno   ninguno

108. *Some Indefinite Adjectives and Pronouns*

alguien (*invariable pron.*) someone, somebody, anyone, anybody

nadie (*invariable pron.*) no one, nobody, not anyone

alguno, -a, -os, -as (*adj. and pron.*) some, any, someone, anyone, several

ninguno, -a, -os, -as (*adj. and pron.*) no, none, no one, not any ~~not often used in the plural~~

Alguno becomes **algún** and **ninguno** becomes **ningún** before a masculine singular noun (compare Article **30**, 1).

Alguno and **ninguno** as pronouns refer to persons already thought of or mentioned; **alguien** and **nadie**, to persons unknown or hitherto not spoken of. When used as direct objects referring to persons, all are preceded by the preposition **a** (compare Article **34**, 5).

> **algo** (*invariable pron.*) something, anything
> **nada** (*invariable pron.*) nothing
> **cada** (*invariable adj.*) each, every
> **otro, -a, -os, -as** (*adj. and pron.*) other, another

Neither the indefinite article nor any word corresponding to English *some* or *any* is used before **otro**.

Alguien me ha robado el reloj. Someone has stolen my watch.

¿Busca Vd. a alguien? Are you looking for someone?

Alguna de ellas vendrá. Some one of them will come.

algunos libros míos several of my books, ~~a few books of mine~~

—¿Han venido nuestros amigos? —Ningunos. "Have our friends come?" "None of them."

Tiene algo que hacer. He has something to do.

Cada uno me visita cada día. Each one visits me each day.

Vuelva Vd. otro día. Come back some other day.

Alguien, alguno, and **algo** are used only in affirmative sentences: for example, the English sentence "I don't see anything" is not

135

to be translated **No veo algo** but **No veo nada**, as you will see below.

109. *Compound Negatives.* The negative indefinites **nadie, ninguno,** and **nada** and the negative adverbs **ni . . . ni, nunca,** and **jamás** require a verb in the negative (that is, preceded by **no**) when they follow the verb. If they precede the verb or stand alone, **no** is not employed. The former construction is the more common.

No veo nada or **Nada veo.** I see nothing.
No conozco a nadie. I know nobody.
No he dicho nada a nadie. I have not said anything to anyone.
No tengo ni lápiz ni pluma. I have neither pencil nor pen.
No lo he creído jamás. I have never believed it.
Nunca he visto tal cosa. I have never seen such a thing.
Ninguno de ellos ha venido. None of them has come.
—¿**Qué tiene Vd.?**—**Nada.** "What have you?" "Nothing."

110

poner to put, place				
PRES. PART.	poniendo		PAST PART.	**puesto**
PRES. IND.	**pongo** ponemos pones ponéis pone ponen			
IMPF. IND.	ponía			
PRET. IND.	puse pusimos pusiste pusisteis puso pusieron			
FUT. IND.	pondré		CONDITIONAL	pondría
IMPERATIVE	pon poned			
PRES. SUBJ.	ponga		IMPF. SUBJ.	pusiera pusiese

VOCABULARY

el **acento** accent
la **costumbre** custom
la **diferencia** difference
el **hielo** ice
la **nieve** snow
el **palacio** palace
la **pregunta** question; **hacer una pregunta** to ask a question
el **presidente** president
el **pueblo** people, race, town
la **salida** departure
el **tiempo** weather
la **verdad** truth; **es verdad** it is true

acostumbrarse to become accustomed
entender (ie) ~~to hear~~, understand
recorrer to go through, roam about
agradable agreeable
desagradable unpleasant
distinto different
excesivo excessive
húmedo humid
principal principal
tal such, such a
nunca never
acerca de concerning

EXERCISES

A

Al llegar a la Habana tuvimos que esperar algunas horas antes de la salida del vapor que iba a llevarnos a Nueva York. Visitamos el hermoso palacio en que vive el presidente de Cuba. Recorrimos los paseos y las plazas principales. Entramos en varias tiendas donde compramos algunos recuerdos para nuestros amigos. Mi padre se cansó al fin y todos fuimos al vapor. Una hora después salimos del puerto, y en cuatro días llegamos a la ciudad de Nueva York. Ahora estoy otra vez en casa. Mis amigos me hacen muchas preguntas acerca del viaje. — ¿Qué tiempo hace en Cuba? — No hace frío nunca; en el invierno hace un tiempo muy agradable. No hace calor excesivo en ninguna estación, pero el verano es bastante húmedo y desagradable. — ¿Hay mucha diferencia entre sus costumbres y las nuestras? — Cada pueblo tiene sus propias costumbres. La vida cubana es muy distinta de la nuestra. No puedo describírsela toda, pero Vds. deben visitar a Cuba algún día. — ¿Podía Vd. entender y contestar a los cubanos cuando le hablaban en español? — Los primeros días no podía comprender casi nada, pero pronto me acostumbré a su acento.

B

1. ¿Cómo fuimos de la Habana a Nueva York? 2. Al llegar a la Habana, ¿entramos en seguida en el vapor? 3. ¿Dónde vive el presidente de Cuba? 4. ¿Qué visitamos en la ciudad? 5. ¿En qué entramos? 6. ¿Qué compramos? 7. ¿Cuándo llegamos a Nueva York? 8. ¿Hace mucho calor en Cuba? 9. ¿Es seco el verano? 10. ¿Cuál de las estaciones es más agradable? 11. ¿Qué estación es húmeda? 12. ¿Sería fácil describir todas las costumbres cubanas? 13. ¿Qué hay que hacer para comprenderlas? 14. ¿Podíamos comprender en seguida el español que hablan los cubanos? 15. ¿Por qué no?

C

I. Choose the correct form and translate :

1. (*Ningún, Ninguno, Nadie*) de ellos lo hizo.

2. — ¿Conoce Vd. a (*algún, alguno, alguien*) aquí? — No conozco a (*ningún, ninguno, nadie*).

3. — ¿Va (*alguno, alguna, alguien*) de sus amigas a Cuba con Vd.? — No, (*ninguno, ninguna, nadie*) de ellas irá.

4. No tengo (*ningún, ninguno*) libro de lectura.

5. — ¿Hay (*algo, alguien*) que puedo hacer? — No, no hay (*nadie, nada*).

6. ¿Quisiera Vd. hacer (*un otro, una otra, otro, otra*) pregunta?

7. (*Alguno, Alguien*) me ha escrito una carta.

8. ¿Hay (*algo, alguno, alguien*) que pudiera ayudarle a Vd.?

9. ¿No tienen Vds. (*algo, nada*) que hacer?

10. ¿No hay (*alguien, nadie, alguno, ninguno*) aquí que sepa hacerlo?

II. Translate the negative expressions into good English : 1. ¿No halló ninguna casa su amigo? 2. ¿Por qué no dijeron Vds. nada a nadie? 3. Nadie le visitó ayer. 4. Ella no podía ni

entrar ni salir. 5. No le he conocido jamás. 6. Nunca viene a
verme. 7. Dice que no tiene ni dinero ni amigos. 8. Jamás lo
hemos dicho. 9. No se puede ver nada. Llueve demasiado.
10. — ¿Quién salió? — Nadie. 11. Nunca he visto a nadie más
desagradable que él. 12. No tiene nunca bastante dinero para
pagar lo que debe. 13. No había nadie allí que quisiese ir con él.
14. Ninguno de ellos puede acompañarnos.

D

I. Substitute the correct Spanish expressions for the English
words in parentheses, and translate :

1. — ¿Ha visto Vd. (*anyone*) hoy ?
2. — No, señor, (*no one*) ha venido ; no he visto (*anyone*).
3. — ¿Ha llegado (*any*) carta ?
4. — No ha llegado (*nothing*).
5. — No lo comprendo ; (*some*) de mis amigos iban a visitarme
hoy. Me visitan (*each*) verano.
6. — Sin duda vendrán (*some other*) día.
7. — Es verdad, pero debieron escribirme (*something*). (*Never*)
han hecho tal cosa.

II. Translate each of the following sentences in two ways :
(*a*) with negative indefinite or negative adverb only ; (*b*) with
no plus negative indefinite or negative adverb : 1. He says nothing. 2. Neither he nor she knows it. 3. None of my friends is
here. 4. I have never been in Cuba. 5. No one knows it. 6. We
have nothing. 7. No one has arrived. 8. None of us has it.

E

1. Do you know anyone who has been in Cuba? 2. Yes, **sir** ;
some of my (Article **93**, 3) friends have been there. 3. They spent
last winter in Havana. 4. They spend some time each year in
foreign countries. 5. When they returned from their trip I asked
them many questions about Cuba. 6. I have never been there,
and know nothing of Cuban customs. 7. Some Americans be-

tendency to omit article after a negative

lieve that it is hot there, because Cuba is a tropical country. 8. My friends said that often it is hotter in Chicago than in Havana. 9. In the United States it is hot one day, and another day it is cool. 10. In tropical countries the heat is less excessive, but there are no cool days in the summer. 11. In the winter it is cool, but never cold. 12. There is neither ice nor snow. 13. You ought to learn Spanish well before going to Cuba. 14. Some of the Cubans speak English, but not many. 15. When they speak Spanish their accent is quite different from that (*del*) of Spain. 16. They also use many words which are heard only in Cuba.

LESSON XXXI

111.   *Cardinal Numbers*

0	cero	31	treinta y un(o)
1	un(o), una	40	cuarenta
2	dos	50	cincuenta
3	tres	60	sesenta
4	cuatro	70	setenta
5	cinco	80	ochenta
6	seis	90	noventa
7	siete	100	cien(to)
8	ocho	105	ciento cinco
9	nueve	122	ciento veinte y dos
10	diez	200	doscientos -as
11	once	300	trescientos -as
12	doce	400	cuatrocientos -as
13	trece	500	quinientos -as
14	catorce	600	seiscientos -as
15	quince	700	setecientos -as
16	diez y seis	800	ochocientos -as
17	diez y siete	900	novecientos -as
18	diez y ocho	1000	mil
19	diez y nueve	1942	mil novecientos cuarenta y dos
20	veinte	2000	dos mil
21	veinte y un(o)	100,000	cien mil
22	veinte y dos	1,000,000	un millón
30	treinta		

112. *Peculiarities of the Cardinals.* 1. All the cardinals are invariable except **uno** and **ciento** and its compounds.

a. **Uno** becomes **un** before a masculine noun :

un caballo a horse   **veinte y un hombres** twenty-one men

191

b. **Ciento** becomes **cien** before a noun or a larger number which it multiplies: *[when it directly precedes a word that is multiplied]*

> **cien libros** a hundred books
> **cien mil pesos** one hundred thousand pesos

But:

> **ciento treinta y dos días** one hundred and thirty-two days

c. The multiples of **ciento** agree in gender with the following noun even when they are followed by another numeral:

doscientos hombres two hundred men
quinientas veinte mujeres five hundred and twenty women
doscientas mil pesetas two hundred thousand pesetas

Quinientos (five hundred), **setecientos** (seven hundred), and **novecientos** (nine hundred), are irregular.

2. **Un** is omitted before **cien(to)** and **mil**:

> **ciento** one hundred
> **mil soldados** one thousand soldiers

3. **Millón** is considered a noun. It therefore takes the indefinite article and is followed by **de**:

> **un millón de libros** a million books

4. The conjunction **y** is used only between tens and units (numbers less than ten):

diez y seis sixteen
veinte y un(o) twenty-one
ochocientos cuarenta y cinco eight hundred and forty-five

Frequently the tens and the units are written as one word. In that case **y** becomes **i**, and the final **e** of **veinte** is dropped:

> **dieciséis, veintiun(o)**

5. Counting by hundreds is not carried beyond nine hundred. In numerals of one thousand or more, **mil** is used:

tres mil quinientos pesos thirty-five hundred pesos
mil novecientos cuarenta y dos nineteen forty-two

113.   *The Months*

enero January	**julio** July
febrero February	**agosto** August
marzo March	**septiembre** September
abril April	**octubre** October
mayo May	**noviembre** November
junio June	**diciembre** December

The names of the months are masculine and are regularly used without the definite article. In general they are not capitalized, although usage varies.

114.   *The Seasons*

la primavera spring	**el otoño** autumn
el verano summer	**el invierno** winter

The definite article is usually required before the names of the seasons.

VOCABULARY

el abuelo grandfather; **los abuelos** grandparents
la edad age
el mes month
el soldado soldier
el viento wind; **hacer viento** to be windy
la América del Sur South America

dividirse to be divided
empezar (ie) to begin
nacer to be born
los demás the others, the rest
algo somewhat
por consiguiente consequently

EXERCISES

A

Hay trescientos sesenta y cinco días en el año. El año se divide también en estaciones, meses y semanas. Hay cuatro estaciones, doce meses, y cincuenta y dos semanas en el año. En cada estación hay tres meses. Los meses del invierno son diciembre, enero y febrero. En el invierno hace mucho frío. Los meses de la primavera son marzo, abril y mayo. En marzo hace mucho viento; en abril llueve mucho; pero en el mes de mayo hace un tiempo muy hermoso. Me gusta el verano, aunque hace calor muchas veces. En esta estación no hay clases y hay tantas cosas que hacer. Febrero es el mes más corto de todos; no tiene más que veinte y ocho días. Los meses de abril, junio, septiembre y noviembre tienen treinta días; los demás tienen treinta y uno. Nací en el año 1926. Ahora tengo diez y seis años. Mi padre nació en 1895, por consiguiente tiene cuarenta y siete años. Su padre, mi abuelo, murió el año pasado a la edad de setenta y nueve. Hace muchos años que murió la madre de mi padre. Mi madre es algo más joven que mi padre, y sus padres viven todavía. Visito a mis abuelos de vez en cuando.

B

1. ¿Cuáles son las estaciones del año? 2. ¿Cuáles son los meses de cada estación? 3. ¿En cuáles de los meses del año hace calor? ¿frío? ¿fresco? 4. ¿En qué estación hay nieve? 5. ¿En qué meses llueve más? 6. ¿En qué estación hay más frutas? 7. ¿En qué estación hay más flores? 8. ¿En qué mes hace más viento? 9. ¿Cuál de las estaciones le gusta más? 10. ¿Por qué? 11. ¿En qué meses no hay clases? 12. ¿Qué meses tienen treinta y un días? 13. ¿Cuáles tienen treinta días? 14. ¿En qué año y qué mes nació Vd.? 15. ¿En qué día del mes? 16. ¿Qué edad tiene Vd.?

C

I. Choose from within each set of parentheses what is needed for a correct reading, and translate:

1. Quinient(-os, -as) veinte y (*uno, un*) hombres.

2. (*Cien, Ciento, Cientos, Cientas*) casas.

3. — ¿Cuántas familias viven en esta aldea? — (*Cien, Ciento, Cientos, Cientas*).

4. Hay (*millón, un millón, un millón de*) libros en esta biblioteca.

5. Han salido (*mil, un mil, un mil de*) soldados de este puerto.

6. (*Un, Uno*) mes del año tiene (*veinte ocho, veinteiocho, veintiocho*) días.

7. — ¿Tiene Vd. dos caballos? — No, señor, tengo sólo (*un, uno*).

8. Hay (*cien veinte, cien y veinte, ciento veinte, ciento y veinte*) alumnos en esta escuela.

9. (*Cien, Ciento, Cientos, Cientas*) mil pesetas.

10. Cuatrocient(-os, -as) mil mujeres.

11. (*Otoño, El otoño*) empieza en (*septiembre, el septiembre, la septiembre*).

12. Colón descubrió a América en (*catorcecientos, mil cuatrocientos*) noventa y dos.

13. Hay (*dieziseis, dieciseis, dieciséis*) alumnos en esta clase.

14. (*Veinte una, Veinte y una, Veinte y un*) pesetas.

II. Translate into English : 1. Cuarenta y tres. 2. Ochenta y seis. 3. Noventa y cuatro. 4. Ciento uno. 5. Ciento quince. 6. Doscientos diez y seis. 7. Quinientos treinta y nueve. 8. Mil novecientos diez y ocho. 9. Doce mil cincuenta y cinco. 10. Cien mil trescientos veintiuno. 11. Trescientos sesenta y cuatro mil seiscientos trece. 12. Setecientos setenta y nueve mil cuatrocientos noventa y cinco. 13. Hay cuarenta y ocho estados (*states*) en los Estados Unidos. 14. Este país tiene más de ciento veinte millones de habitantes (*inhabitants*). 15. El mes de febrero tiene veintiocho días. Los demás tienen treinta o treinta y un días. 16. El año mil setecientos setenta y seis fué muy importante en la historia de los Estados Unidos. 17. Colón nació en el año mil cuatrocientos cincuenta y uno y murió a la edad de cincuenta y cinco años en mil quinientos seis.

D

Read in Spanish :

| 24 | 47 | 65 | 86 | 104 | 296 | 578 | 821 | 3798 | 168,435 |
| 38 | 52 | 79 | 93 | 127 | 364 | 644 | 1087 | 100,679 | 239,866 |

1 libro	847 muchachos	el año 1257
71 alumnos	1000 hombres	el año 1846
100 casas	100,000 soldados	el año 1942
300 alumnas	600,000 pesetas	

E

1. There are four seasons in the year: spring, summer, autumn, and winter. 2. In the United States the months of summer are June, July, and August. 3. In these months it is hot, and there is no school (classes). 4. In South America the summer months are December, January, and February. 5. In Buenos Aires it is hotter in January than in July. 6. Spring begins in September in Argentina and Chile. 7. In July and August it is cold, and they have snow. 8. I like spring very much, because it is cool, and there are many flowers. 9. I do not like summer because it is very hot. 10. There are fewer flowers than in the spring. 11. In the autumn there are many fruits and vegetables. 12. I am the oldest of our family. 13. I was born in 1923, and am nineteen years old. 14. My youngest brother was born in 1933. 15. My parents are of the same age. 16. They were born in 1897, and are forty-five years old.

115. *Ordinal Numbers*

primer(o) first	**sexto** sixth
segundo second	**séptimo** seventh
tercer(o) third	**octavo** eighth
cuarto fourth	**noveno** or **nono** ninth
quinto fifth	**décimo** tenth

116. *Agreement and Uses of the Ordinals.* 1. The ordinal numbers agree in gender and number with the nouns they modify. Except in titles (see next paragraph), they usually precede the noun:

las primeras casas de la calle the first houses on the street
el segundo capítulo the second chapter

2. Ordinals are normally used only up to the tenth, cardinals being substituted for them beyond that point. This is specifically true in titles of sovereigns and Popes and numbers of centuries. In these cases both types of numerals follow the noun. Observe the omission of the definite article in titles:

Carlos Tercero Charles the Third
Luis Quince Louis the Fifteenth
Pío Once Pius the Eleventh
el siglo veinte the twentieth century

3. With pages, chapters, volumes, etc. either ordinals or cardinals are used through 10:

la tercera página or **página tres** the third page

After 10, only cardinals are employed.

4. **Primero** and **tercero** drop the final **-o** before masculine singular nouns:

el primer tomo the first volume
el tercer capítulo the third chapter

197

(Compare Articles **30**, 1, and **108**.)

5. The days of the month, except the first, are expressed by the cardinals. Except in dating letters, the definite article precedes the numeral, which is usually connected with the month and year by the preposition **de**:

> el primero de julio de **1880** July 1, 1880
> el trece de agosto de **1900** August 13, 1900

6. From fourths to tenths, inclusive, fractions are read as in English, numerators being expressed by the cardinals, and denominators by the ordinals. Irregular forms are **medio** (half) and **tercio** (third). Above **décimo**, the denominators are regu· larly formed by adding **-avo** to the cardinal and dropping a final vowel:

un medio $\frac{1}{2}$	seis onzavos $\frac{6}{11}$
dos tercios $\frac{2}{3}$	diez trezavos $\frac{10}{13}$
cuatro quintos $\frac{4}{5}$	siete treintavos $\frac{7}{30}$
cinco séptimos $\frac{5}{7}$	

117. *Days of the Week*

domingo Sunday	**jueves** Thursday
lunes Monday	**viernes** Friday
martes Tuesday	**sábado** Saturday
miércoles Wednesday	

The names of the days of the week are masculine. In most cases they are accompanied by the definite article. They are not capitalized. No equivalent of the English word *on* is used in such expressions as the following:

Llegué el lunes. I arrived (on) Monday.
No hay clases los sábados. There is no school (on) Saturdays.

118. *Date Idioms*

¿A cuántos estamos (del mes)? What day of the month is it?
Estamos a (or Hoy es el) quince de marzo. It is the fifteenth of March.
Estamos en (or Hoy es) domingo. Today is Sunday.

119.   *Hours of the Day*

¿ **Qué hora es?** What time is it?

Es la una y media. It is half past one.

Son las dos menos cuarto. It is a quarter to two.

Son las cinco y diez (minutos). It is ten minutes past five.

a las ocho de la mañana at eight A.M.

a las tres de la tarde at three P.M.

a las diez de la noche at ten P.M.

1. Note that in the third and fourth examples above, the plural of the verb is used to agree with **horas** understood.

2. **La una, las dos, tres,** etc. and the adjective **media** are feminine to agree with **hora** and **horas** understood. **Cuarto** is a noun, and is equivalent to **un cuarto de hora**.

VOCABULARY

la **abuela** grandmother	**Fernando** Ferdinand
el **autor** author	**Isabel** Isabella, Elizabeth
la **batalla** battle	**descansar** to rest
el **capítulo** chapter	**descubrir** to discover
la **hija** daughter	**publicar** to publish; **publi-**
la **iglesia** church	**carse** to be published
el **mundo** world	**reinar** to reign
el **niño** child	**reunirse** to reunite, meet
la **reina** queen	**católico** Catholic
el **reinado** reign	**reciente** recent
el **rey** king	**entre** between, among
el **siglo** century	

EXERCISES

A

I. La semana se divide en siete días. El día tiene 24 horas, y la hora tiene 60 minutos. El domingo es el primer día de la semana. El domingo descansamos y vamos a la iglesia. Los demás días tenemos que trabajar. Nos levantamos a las siete o a las siete y media. Mi padre va a su oficina, y los niños van a la escuela. Nos reunimos otra vez a las seis de la tarde para comer. — ¿Qué día es hoy? — Hoy es martes. — ¿A cuántos estamos del mes? — Estamos a 10 de enero.

II. La mejor reina de España fué Isabel la Católica. Mandó a la ciudad de Palos que diese a Colón el dinero para su primer viaje. Colón descubrió el Nuevo Mundo el 12 de octubre de 1492. Miguel de Cervantes es el más famoso autor español. Nació en 1547. La primera parte de *Don Quijote* se publicó en 1605, la segunda en 1615. Cervantes murió el 23 de abril de 1616.

B

1. ¿Cuál es el primer día de la semana? 2. ¿El tercero? 3. ¿El quinto? 4. ¿El segundo? 5. ¿El séptimo? 6. ¿El sexto? 7. ¿A qué hora se desayuna? 8. ¿A qué hora almorzamos? 9. ¿A qué hora tenemos clase de español? 10. ¿A qué hora se va a la iglesia los domingos? 11. ¿Qué hora es en este momento? 12. ¿A cuántos estamos del mes? 13. ¿Cuándo nació Wáshington? 14. ¿Lincoln? 15. ¿Cuándo murió Lincoln? 16. ¿Cuándo empezó la primera Guerra Mundial (*World War*)?

C

I. Translate into English: 1. Nos reunimos los sábados a las dos de la tarde. 2. Estamos en la página ciento cinco. 3. Llegó el miércoles, once de diciembre de mil novecientos treinta y nueve, a las once y cuarto de la noche. 4. El martes es el tercer día de la semana y el jueves es el quinto. 5. Las primeras clases de la mañana empiezan a las ocho. 6. Las primeras clases de la tarde empiezan a la una y diez. 7. Carlos Quinto fué rey de España de mil quinientos dieciséis a mil quinientos cincuenta y seis. 8. Alfonso Trece fué el último rey de España.

II. Choose the correct forms and translate:

1. — ¿Qué hora es? — (*Es, Son*) (*la, las*) una y (*cuarto,* *cuarta*).

2. Vamos a la escuela a (*la, las*) ocho (*en, por, de*) la mañana.

3. No me gusta el (*un, uno, primer, primero*) día del mes porque hay que pagar cuentas.

4. El sábado será el (*un, uno, primer, primero*) de marzo.

5. Tengo que leer (*cien, ciento*) diez páginas esta tarde.

6. Más de doscient(-*os*, -*as*) mujeres trabajan en aquella fábrica.

7. La historia del siglo (*nueve, noveno*) y del siglo (*diez, décimo*) de España es muy interesante.

8. El libro no empezó a interesarme hasta que llegué al (*seis, sexto*) o (*siete, séptimo*) capítulo.

D

I. Read in Spanish:

$$\frac{1}{3} \qquad \frac{3}{4} \qquad \frac{1}{5} \qquad \frac{5}{6} \qquad \frac{2}{7} \qquad \frac{5}{8}$$

$$\frac{2}{9} \qquad \frac{7}{10} \qquad \frac{2}{11} \qquad \frac{5}{12} \qquad \frac{9}{13} \qquad \frac{5}{14}$$

II. Render correctly into Spanish the English words in parentheses:

1. La (*tenth*) casa.
2. El (*third*) hombre.
3. Los (*first*) capítulos del libro.
4. El siglo (*seventeenth*).
5. Luis (*the Thirteenth*).
6. El (*first*) rey de España.
7. La (*first*) página.
8. Carlos (*the Sixth*).

III. Translate: 1. September 15, 1794. 2. February 1, 1916. 3. Wednesday, May 16, 1929. 4. He comes on Tuesdays. 5. At 4:10 P.M. 6. At a quarter to one. 7. It is 8:15 A.M. 8. They arrived on Thursday, August 7, 1941, at 11:30 A.M.

E

1. Our Spanish class (class of Spanish) meets at 2:10 P.M., Mondays, Wednesdays, and Fridays. 2. There is a second-year class at 7:45 A.M., Tuesdays, Thursdays, and Saturdays. 3. We

go to church at 10:30 A.M. on Sundays. 4. Sometimes we go at 8 P.M. 5. Many Spaniards get up very late. 6. They go to bed at twelve o'clock or later. 7. Charles I of Spain was born in 1500 and died in 1558. 8. Isabella I, his grandmother, reigned from 1474 to 1504. 9. Isabella II was the daughter of Ferdinand VII. 10. She was born in 1830 and reigned from 1833 to 1868. 11. Her son, Alfonso XII, began his reign in 1874 and died in 1885. 12. Cervantes lived during the reigns of Charles V, Philip II, and Philip III. 13. He took part in the battle of Lepanto, October 7, 1571. 14. Among the most famous kings of Spain were Ferdinand III and Alfonso X. 15. One of the worst was Ferdinand VII. 16. The most recent were Alfonso XII and Alfonso XIII.

REVIEW LESSON VI

[Lessons XXVII–XXXII]

A

I. Choose the correct expression from each group in parentheses and identify it (demonstrative adjective or pronoun, relative pronoun, etc.):

1. (*Este, Ese, Aquel*) libro (*que, quien, el que*) estoy leyendo es muy interesante.

2. (*Que, Quien*) entra aquí no puede salir.

3. (*Este, Ese, Aquel*) señor (*que, quien*) está subiendo al tren es mi primo.

4. El baúl de (*que, quien*) hablábamos era (*el, la, lo*) de Enrique.

5. El hombre (*que, quien*) encontré era muy viejo.

6. (*Esta, Esa, Aquella*) pluma con (*que, quien*) estoy escribiendo es muy mala.

7. (*Este, Ese, Aquel*) libro (*que, quien*) tiene Vd. es una gramática.

8. Me dijo (*que, lo que, el que*) quería.

9. (*Este, Ese, Aquel*) libro mío y (*que, lo que, el que*) tiene Vd. son grandes.

10. No me diga Vd. (*ése, eso, ésa*).

11. Los mejores amigos son (*que, el que, los que*) nos ayudan en nuestras dificultades.

12. Carlos y María llegaron ayer; (*ésta, ésa, aquélla*) viajó por ferrocarril, (*éste, ése, aquél*) en automóvil.

II. Choose the correct expression and identify it (interrogative adjective, pronoun, or adverb, indefinite adjective or pronoun. etc.):

1. ¿Hay (*alguien. nadie. alguno, ninguno*) aquí que me conozca?

2. (*Alguien, Nadie, Alguno. Ninguno*) de mis amigos ha venido todavía.

203

3. ¿(*Dónde, De dónde, A dónde*) va Vd.?

4. No conozco a (*alguien, nadie, alguno, ninguno*) aquí.

5. ¿(*Qué, Cuál*) de sus hermanos vive en la Habana?

6. No tengo (*alguien, nadie, algo, nada*) que hacer.

7. ¿(*Qué, Quién, Cuál*) es el libro que más le gusta?

8. ¿(*Qué, Quién, Cuál*) empleado le dió a Vd. los billetes?

9. ¿(*Dónde, De dónde, A dónde*) viene Vd.?

10. — ¿Busca Vd. a (*alguien, nadie, alguno, ninguno*)? — No, señor; no busco a (*alguien, nadie, algo, nada*).

11. — ¿Quiere Vd. comer (*alguien, nadie, algo, nada*)? — No, gracias; no quiero (*alguien, nadie, algo, nada*).

12. ¿(*Quién, Qué, Cuál*) viene?

III. Translate each expression of necessity and explain its use: 1. Han de venir mañana. 2. Hay que viajar mucho para llegar a la América del Sur. 3. Tengo mucho que hacer. 4. Tenemos que ir a Nueva York esta semana. 5. No hay que pensar en tal cosa. 6. Había que bajar una escalera para tomar el tren. 7. ¿Qué he de hacer? Todo está perdido. 8. No tienen que estudiar esta noche.

IV. Choose the correct expression from each group in parentheses, and translate:

1. Enrique no (*sabe, puede*) venir; está enfermo.

2. (*Conozco, Sé*) muy bien a este señor.

3. No (*sabe, puede*) leer el inglés.

4. ¿(*Sabemos, Podemos*) ir con Vds.?

5. (*Conocemos, Sabemos*) bien a Nueva York.

6. (*Conozco, Sé*) por qué Vd. lo dijo.

7. Mi padre es tan viejo que no (*sabe, puede*) trabajar.

8. El maestro dice que (*sabemos, podemos*) asistir a su clase.

9. Carlos no (*conoce, sabe*) bien la gramática.

10. (*Conozco, Sé*) que no han llegado todavía.

V. *a.* Read aloud and translate:

mil cuatrocientos noventa y dos
seiscientos ocho

doscientos mil seiscientos cincuenta y ocho
mil treinta y cinco
cuatrocientos diez y ocho
mil
dos mil
un millón
ciento
doscientos cuarenta
quinientos doce
cuatrocientos setenta y nueve
mil novecientos cuarenta y cinco
dos millones, setecientos treinta y tres mil, ciento treinta
quinientos once mil, cuatrocientos sesenta y uno
cuatrocientos siete
cincuenta mil, ciento ochenta y ocho
sesenta y cuatro mil, cuatrocientos cincuenta y cuatro
mil ciento cincuenta y tres
un tercio
dos quintos
cinco sextos
tres octavos
cinco novenos
nueve décimos
cinco onzavos
siete dozavos
cinco trezavos
siete dieciseisavos
nueve veintiunavos

b. Select the correct expression from each group in parentheses :

1. Tengo (*ciento, cien*) pesetas.
2. (*Doscientos, Doscientas*) mujeres.
3. (*Quinientos, Quinientas*) mil casas.
4. (*Catorcecientos, Mil cuatrocientos*) quince.
5. (*Ochenta y un, Ochenta y uno*) hombres.
6. Ciento (*uno, y uno*).
7. Cuarenta (*dos, y dos*).

8. El (*primero, uno*) de julio.
9. El (*segundo, dos*) de mayo.
10. Carlos (*Cuarto, Cuatro*).
11. Alfonso (*Octavo, Ocho*).
12. (*El, La, Los, Las*) una de la tarde.
13. (*El, La, Los, Las*) diez de la noche.
14. Le vi (*en, a, el, los*) sábado.
15. (*Cien, Ciento*) mil hombres.
16. (*Cien, Ciento*) cuarenta y dos hombres.
17. Cinco millones (*pesetas, de pesetas*).
18. Siete mil (*casas, de casas*).

B

I. Read in Spanish:

1468	1269	379,971	88,163	$\frac{3}{4}$	$\frac{11}{13}$
1005	86,379	14,042	1020	$\frac{3}{8}$	$\frac{9}{11}$
1507	46,838	1001	98,239	$\frac{4}{7}$	$\frac{2}{9}$
102,699	1303	2010	200,099,900	$\frac{5}{12}$	$\frac{13}{14}$

II. Translate into Spanish the English words in parentheses:

1. ¿Qué es (*that*) allí en la calle?
2. ¿(*Which*) de los muchachos es su hijo?
3. — ¿Quiere Vd. (*anything*)? — No, señor; no quiero (*anything*).
4. (*Nobody*) vive aquí; no he visto a (*anybody*) en la casa.
5. ¡(*How*) hermosa es María!
6. ¡(*How many*) automóviles hay en esta calle!
7. Quiere comprar (*this*) casa y (*mine*). No le gusta (*yours*).
8. No comprendo (*what*) Vd. dice.
9. (*Never*) la he visto; ¿(*where*) vive?
10. Tengo dos hermanos: (*this one*) y (*the one who*) vive en Nueva York.
11. (*Someone*) ha tomado mi pluma; ¿sabe Vd. (*who*) es?
12. (*He who*) sabe mucho, habla poco.

III. Translate the words in parentheses:

1. (*I know*) muy bien a este señor, pero (*I do not know*) dónde le vi primero.
2. El (*first*) rey de España.
3. (*We are to*) verle mañana.
4. ¿(*May we*) esperar aquí?
5. El (*third*) edificio.
6. (*He knows*) dónde vive José.
7. No hay clases (*on Sundays*).
8. (*Spring*) viene después de (*winter*).
9. Enrique (*can*) leer el español, pero (*he cannot*) hablarlo.
10. El (*fourth*) de julio.
11. (*One has to*) escuchar mucho para comprender lo que dice.
12. (*We do not have to*) estudiar esta noche.

C

Translate: 1. Until today we did not know that Henry was in Cuba this winter. 2. This was his first trip to a foreign country. 3. He had to go by train to (the) Florida. 4. He was to go by car, but he had to take the train because he was in a hurry. 5. One has to go one hundred miles (*millas*) by steamer from Florida to Havana. 6. That steamer is not the one which goes to New York. 7. It left Key West at ten minutes to nine in the morning and reached Havana at half past two in the afternoon. 8. On the steamer Henry had met a Cuban gentleman, Mr. Álvarez, who knew the city very well. 9. When they entered the port, Henry said, "What a beautiful city Havana is! 10. How many steamers there are in the port! 11. Where are they from, and where are they going?" 12. Mr. Álvarez replied, "You know that this one is from the United States. 13. That one is from Mexico, and that other one is from South America. 14. Some are from Europe, but none of these is from Spain. 15. Each day steamers arrive from all parts of the world. 16. No one knows how many steamers enter the port of Havana each year."

THE VERB AND ITS FORMS
REGULAR VERBS

120.   *Simple Tenses*

INFINITIVE

habl **ar** to speak   aprend **er** to learn   viv **ir** to live

PRESENT PARTICIPLE

habl **ando**   aprend **iendo**   viv **iendo**

PAST PARTICIPLE

habl **ado**   aprend **ido**   viv **ido**

INDICATIVE MOOD

Present

habl **o**	aprend **o**	viv **o**
habl **as**	aprend **es**	viv **es**
habl **a**	aprend **e**	viv **e**
habl **amos**	aprend **emos**	viv **imos**
habl **áis**	aprend **éis**	viv **ís**
habl **an**	aprend **en**	viv **en**

Imperfect

habl **aba**	aprend **ía**	viv **ía**
habl **abas**	aprend **ías**	viv **ías**
habl **aba**	aprend **ía**	viv **ía**
habl **ábamos**	aprend **íamos**	viv **íamos**
habl **abais**	aprend **íais**	viv **íais**
habl **aban**	aprend **ían**	viv **ían**

Preterit

habl **é**	aprend **í**	viv **í**
habl **aste**	aprend **iste**	viv **iste**
habl **ó**	aprend **ió**	viv **ió**
habl **amos**	aprend **imos**	viv **imos**
habl **asteis**	aprend **isteis**	viv **isteis**
habl **aron**	aprend **ieron**	viv **ieron**

209

Future

hablar é	aprender é	vivir é
hablar ás	aprender ás	vivir ás
hablar á	aprender á	vivir á
hablar emos	aprender emos	vivir emos
hablar éis	aprender éis	vivir éis
hablar án	aprender án	vivir án

Conditional

hablar ía	aprender ía	vivir ía
hablar ías	aprender ías	vivir ías
hablar ía	aprender ía	vivir ía
hablar íamos	aprender íamos	vivir íamos
hablar íais	aprender íais	vivir íais
hablar ían	aprender ían	vivir ían

IMPERATIVE MOOD

habl a	aprend e	viv e
habl ad	aprend ed	viv id

SUBJUNCTIVE MOOD

Present

habl e	aprend a	viv a
habl es	aprend as	viv as
habl e	aprend a	viv a
habl emos	aprend amos	viv amos
habl éis	aprend áis	viv áis
habl en	aprend an	viv an

Imperfect, -ra Form

habl ara	aprend iera	viv iera
habl aras	aprend ieras	viv ieras
habl ara	aprend iera	viv iera
habl áramos	aprend iéramos	viv iéramos
habl arais	aprend ierais	viv ierais
habl aran	aprend ieran	viv ieran

Imperfect, -se Form

habl ase	aprend iese	viv iese
habl ases	aprend ieses	viv ieses
habl ase	aprend iese	viv iese
habl ásemos	aprend iésemos	viv iésemos
habl aseis	aprend ieseis	viv ieseis
habl asen	aprend iesen	viv iesen

Future (little used)

habl are	aprend iere	viv iere
habl ares	aprend ieres	viv ieres
habl are	aprend iere	viv iere
habl áremos	aprend iéremos	viv iéremos
habl areis	aprend iereis	viv iereis
habl aren	aprend ieren	viv ieren

121.   *Perfect Tenses*

PERFECT INFINITIVE

haber hablado	haber aprendido	haber vivido

PERFECT PARTICIPLE

habiendo hablado	habiendo aprendido	habiendo vivido

INDICATIVE MOOD

Present Perfect

he hablado	he aprendido	he vivido
has hablado	has aprendido	has vivido
ha hablado	ha aprendido	ha vivido
hemos hablado	hemos aprendido	hemos vivido
habéis hablado	habéis aprendido	habéis vivido
han hablado	han aprendido	han vivido

Pluperfect

había hablado	había aprendido	había vivido
habías hablado, etc.	habías aprendido, etc.	habías vivido, **etc.**

Preterit Perfect

hube hablado, etc.	hube aprendido, etc.	hube vivido, etc.

Future Perfect

habré hablado, etc.	habré aprendido, etc.	habré vivido, etc.

Conditional Perfect

habría hablado, etc.	habría aprendido, etc.	habría vivido, etc.

SUBJUNCTIVE MOOD

Present Perfect

haya hablado, etc.	haya aprendido, etc.	haya vivido, etc.

Pluperfect, -ra Form

hubiera hablado, etc.	hubiera aprendido, etc.	hubiera vivido, etc.

Pluperfect, -se Form

hubiese hablado, etc.	hubiese aprendido, etc.	hubiese vivido, etc.

122. *Passive Voice.* The past participle of the main verb agrees in gender and number with the subject, but **sido** in the perfect tenses is invariable.

Infinitive	Perfect Infinitive
ser amado, -a, -os, -as to be loved	**haber sido amado** to have been loved

Present Participle	Present Perfect Participle
siendo amado	**habiendo sido amado**

Present Indicative	Present Perfect Indicative
soy amado	he sido amado
eres amado	has sido amado
es amado	ha sido amado
somos amados	hemos sido amados
sois amados	habéis sido amados
son amados	han sido amados

Imperfect Indicative
era amado, etc.

Pluperfect Indicative
había sido amado, etc.

Preterit Indicative
fuí amado

Preterit Perfect Indicative
hube sido amado

Future Indicative
seré amado

Future Perfect Indicative
habré sido amado

Conditional
sería amado

Conditional Perfect
habría sido amado

Imperative
sé amado
sed amados

Present Subjunctive
sea amado

Present Perfect Subjunctive
haya sido amado

Imperfect Subjunctive, -ra Form
fuera amado

Pluperfect Subjunctive, -ra Form
hubiera sido amado

Imperfect Subjunctive, -se Form
fuese amado

Pluperfect Subjunctive, -se Form
hubiese sido amado

PECULIARITIES IN CERTAIN GROUPS OF VERBS

123. *Spelling Changes in Verbs.* Many verbs that are regular in pronunciation require changes in spelling, either in order to retain the same sound for the final consonant of the stem or to conform to the conventional rules of orthography. Only tenses affected are mentioned below.

1. Verbs ending in **-car** change **c** to **qu** before **e**.

buscar to seek

PRET. IND. busqué, buscaste, buscó, buscamos, buscasteis, buscaron
PRES. SUBJ. busque, busques, busque, busquemos, busquéis, busquen

2. Verbs in **-gar** change **g** to **gu** before **e**.

llegar to arrive

PRET. IND. llegué, llegaste, llegó, llegamos, llegasteis, llegaron
PRES. SUBJ. llegue, llegues, llegue, lleguemos, lleguéis, lleguen

3. Verbs in **-guar** change **gu** to **gü** before **e**.

averiguar to investigate

PRET. IND. averigüé, averiguaste, averiguó, averiguamos, averiguasteis, averiguaron
PRES. SUBJ. averigüe, averigües, averigüe, averigüemos, averigüéis, averigüen

4. Verbs in **-zar** change **z** to **c** before **e**.

cruzar to cross

PRET. IND. crucé, cruzaste, cruzó, cruzamos, cruzasteis, cruzaron
PRES. SUBJ. cruce, cruces, cruce, crucemos, crucéis, crucen

5. Verbs ending in **-cer** or **-cir** preceded by a consonant change **c** to **z** before **a** and **o**.

vencer to conquer

PRES. IND. venzo, vences, vence, vencemos, vencéis, vencen
PRES. SUBJ. venza, venzas, venza, venzamos, venzáis, venzan

6. Verbs in **-ger** or **-gir** change **g** to **j** before **a** and **o**.

coger to catch

PRES. IND. cojo, coges, coge, cogemos, cogéis, cogen
PRES. SUBJ. coja, cojas, coja, cojamos, cojáis, cojan

7. Verbs in **-guir** change **gu** to **g** before **a** and **o**.

distinguir to distinguish

PRES. IND. distingo, distingues, distingue, distinguimos, distinguís, distinguen
PRES. SUBJ. distinga, distingas, distinga, distingamos, distingáis, distingan

8. Between vowels **y** always takes the place of unaccented **i**.

creer to believe

PRES. PART. creyendo   PAST PART. creído
PRET. IND. creí, creíste, creyó, creímos, creísteis, creyeron
IMPF. SUBJ., -ra FORM, creyera etc.   IMPF. SUBJ., -se FORM, creyese etc.

9. Verbs in **-llir**, **-ñer**, or **-ñir** drop the **i** of the diphthongs **ie** and **io**.

gruñir to grunt, growl

PRES. PART. gruñendo   PAST PART. gruñido
PRET. IND. gruñí, gruñiste, gruñó, gruñimos, gruñisteis, gruñeron
IMPF. SUBJ., -ra FORM, gruñera etc.   IMPF. SUBJ., -se FORM, gruñese etc.

124. *Verbs in* **-cer** *or* **-cir** *following a Vowel.* Verbs ending in **-cer** or **-cir** following a vowel insert **z** before the **c** in the first person singular of the present indicative and throughout the present subjunctive.

conocer to know

PRES. IND. conozco, conoces, conoce, conocemos, conocéis, conocen
PRES. SUBJ. conozca, conozcas, conozca, conozcamos, conozcáis, conozcan

All other forms are regular.

1. Exceptions to the rule just given are **cocer, cuezo** (Articles 128; 129); **mecer, mezo** (Article 123, 5); **hacer** (Article 149); **decir** (Article 145); and compounds of **-ducir** (Article 142).

125. *Verbs in* **-uir.** Verbs in **-uir** (including **-güir** but not **-guir**) insert **y** except before **i**, and change unaccented **i** between vowels to **y**.

huir to flee

PRES. IND. huyo, huyes, huye, huimos, huís, huyen
IMPF. IND. huía, huías, huía, huíamos, huíais, huían
PRET. IND. huí, huiste, huyó, huimos, huisteis, huyeron
FUT. IND. huiré, etc.   CONDITIONAL huiría, etc.
IMPERATIVE huye, huid
PRES. SUBJ. huya, huyas, huya, huyamos, huyáis, huyan
IMPF. SUBJ., -ra FORM, huyera etc.   IMPF. SUBJ., -se FORM, huyese etc.

126. *Verbs in* **-iar.** 1. Some verbs in **-iar** take a written accent on the **i** throughout the singular and in the third person plural in the present tenses. These verbs must be learned by observation.

confiar to confide

PRES. IND. confío, confías, confía, confiamos, confiáis, confían
IMPERATIVE confía, confiad
PRES. SUBJ. confíe, confíes, confíe, confiemos, confiéis, confíen

2. In other **-iar** verbs **ia** is always a diphthong, and the stress in the nine stem-accented forms falls on the preceding syllable.

cambiar to exchange

PRES. IND. cambio, cambias, cambia, cambiamos, cambiáis, cambian
IMPERATIVE cambia, cambiad
PRES. SUBJ. cambie, cambies, cambie, cambiemos, cambiéis, cambien

127. *Verbs in* **-uar.** Verbs in **-uar** (except **-guar**; see Article 123, 3) have a written accent on the **u** in the nine stem-accented forms.

continuar to continue

PRES. IND. continúo, continúas, continúa, continuamos, continuáis, continúan
IMPERATIVE continúa, continuad
PRES. SUBJ. continúe, continúes, continúe, continuemos, continuéis, continúen

128. *Stem-Changing Verbs, Class A.* Many verbs of the first and second conjugations change **e** in the last syllable of the stem to **ie**, and **o** to **ue**, when accented. This change affects all the singular and the third person plural of all present tenses, nine forms in all. Verbs of this class are indicated in vocabularies and verb lists by **ie** or **ue** in parentheses after the infinitive, thus:

perder (ie)   **contar (ue)**

pensar to think

PRES. IND. pienso, piensas, piensa, pensamos, penséis, **piensan**
IMPERATIVE piensa, pensad
PRES. SUBJ. piense, pienses, piense, pensemos, penséis, **piensen**

contar to tell

PRES. IND. cuento, cuentas, cuenta, contamos, contáis, **cuentan**
IMPERATIVE cuenta, contad
PRES. SUBJ. cuente, cuentes, cuente, contemos, contéis, **cuenten**

perder to lose

PRES. IND. pierdo, pierdes, pierde, perdemos, perdéis, **pierden**
IMPERATIVE pierde, perded
PRES. SUBJ. pierda, pierdas, pierda, perdamos, perdáis, **pierdan**

entender to understand

PRES. IND entiendo, entiendes, entiende, entendemos, entendéis, **entienden**
IMPERATIVE entiende, entended
PRES. SUBJ. entienda, entiendas, entienda, entendamos, entendáis, **entiendan**

All other tenses of Class-A verbs are regular.

129. *Spelling Changes in Class-A Verbs.* Class-A verbs ending in **-car, -gar, -zar, -cer** have also the spelling changes mentioned in Article 123. For example:

trocar to exchange

PRES. IND. trueco, truecas, trueca, trocamos, trocáis, **truecan**
PRET. IND. troqué, trocaste, trocó, trocamos, trocasteis, trocaron
IMPERATIVE trueca, trocad
PRES. SUBJ. trueque, truegues, trueque, troquemos, troquéis, **truequen**

130. *Other Changes in Class-A Verbs.* 1. **Jugar** changes **u** to **ue** in accented syllables, and **g** to **gu** before **e**.

jugar to play

PRES. IND. **juego, juegas, juega,** jugamos, jugáis, **juegan**
PRET. IND. **jugué,** jugaste, jugó, jugamos, jugasteis, jugaron
IMPERATIVE **juega,** jugad
PRES. SUBJ. **juegue, juegues, juegue, juguemos, juguéis, jueguen**

2. **Errar** takes **ye** for **ie**, since **ie** never begins a word in Spanish.

errar to err

PRES. IND. **yerro, yerras, yerra,** erramos, erráis, **yerran**
IMPERATIVE **yerra,** errad
PRES. SUBJ. **yerre, yerres, yerre,** erremos, erréis, **yerren**

3. **Oler (ue)** always takes **h** before **ue**.

oler to smell

PRES. IND. **huelo, hueles, huele,** olemos, oléis, **huelen**
IMPERATIVE **huele,** oled
PRES. SUBJ. **huela, huelas, huela,** olamos, oláis, **huelan**

4. Class-A verbs with **-go-** in the last syllable of the stem require the diæresis (··) wherever **ue** occurs.

degollar to behead

PRES. IND. **degüello, degüellas, degüella,** degollamos, degolláis, **degüellan**
IMPERATIVE **degüella,** degollad
PRES. SUBJ. **degüelle, degüelles, degüelle,** degollemos, degolléis, **degüellen**

5. **Volver (ue), solver (ue),** and their compounds have irregular past participles:

vuelto   **suelto**   **devuelto**   etc.

131. *Stem-Changing Verbs, Class B.* Certain verbs of the third conjugation show the following changes from **e** or **o** of the last syllable of the stem:

1. **e** accented becomes **ie**, and **o** accented becomes **ue**.

2. **e** unaccented becomes **i**, and **o** unaccented becomes **u**, when followed in the next syllable by **a**, **ie**, or **io**.

Verbs of this class are indicated in vocabularies and verb lists by **ie-i** or **ue-u** in parentheses after the infinitive, thus:

sentir (ie-i)   dormir (ue-u)

sentir to feel

PRES. PART. sintiendo   PAST PART. sentido

PRES. IND. siento, sientes, siente, sentimos, sentís, **sienten**

IMPF. IND. sentía

PRET. IND. sentí, sentiste, **sintió**, sentimos, sentisteis, **sintieron**

FUT. IND. sentiré   CONDITIONAL sentiría

IMPERATIVE **siente**, sentid

PRES. SUBJ. **sienta, sientas, sienta**, sintamos, sintáis, **sientan**

IMPF. SUBJ., –ra FORM, sintiera, sintieras, sintiera, sintiéramos, sintierais, sintieran

IMPF. SUBJ., –se FORM, sintiese, sintieses, sintiese, sintiésemos, sintieseis, sintiesen

dormir to sleep

PRES. PART. durmiendo   PAST PART. dormido

PRES. IND. **duermo, duermes, duerme**, dormimos, dormís, **duermen**

IMPF. IND. dormía

PRET. IND. dormí, dormiste, **durmió**, dormimos, dormisteis, **durmieron**

FUT. IND. dormiré   CONDITIONAL dormiría

IMPERATIVE **duerme**, dormid

PRES. SUBJ. **duerma, duermas, duerma**, durmamos, durmáis, **duerman**

IMPF. SUBJ., –ra FORM, durmiera, durmieras, durmiera, durmiéramos, durmierais, durmieran

IMPF. SUBJ., –se FORM, durmiese, durmieses, durmiese, durmiésemos, durmieseis, durmiesen

132. *Irregularities in Class-B Verbs.* **1. Morir** is inflected like **dormir**, except that the past participle is **muerto**.

2. **Adquirir** and **inquirir** change **i** in the last syllable of the stem to **ie** when accented. Otherwise these verbs are regular.

133. *Stem-Changing Verbs, Class C.* Certain verbs in the third conjugation have the following changes in the last syllable of the stem:

1. **e** accented becomes **i.**
2. **e** unaccented becomes **i** when followed by **a, ie,** or **io.**

pedir to ask for

PRES. PART. **pidiendo**   PAST PART. **pedido**
PRES. IND. **pido, pides, pide,** pedimos, pedís, **piden**
IMPF. IND. pedía
PRET. IND. pedí, pediste, **pidió,** pedimos, pedisteis, **pidieron**
FUT. IND. pediré   CONDITIONAL pediría
IMPERATIVE **pide,** pedid
PRES. SUBJ. **pida, pidas, pida, pidamos, pidáis, pidan**
IMPF. SUBJ., **-ra** FORM, **pidiera, pidieras, pidiera, pidiéramos, pidierais, pidieran**
IMPF. SUBJ., **-se** FORM, **pidiese, pidieses, pidiese, pidiésemos, pidieseis, pidiesen**

134. *Spelling Changes in Class-C Verbs.* Class-C verbs ending in **-gir, -guir, -ñir,** have also the spelling changes described in Article 123. For example:

seguir to follow

PRES. IND. **sigo, sigues, sigue,** seguimos, seguís, **siguen**
PRES. SUBJ. **siga, sigas, siga, sigamos, sigáis, sigan**

Other forms are like those of **pedir.**

135. *Irregularities in Class-C Verbs.* 1. **Erguir** (to erect) may be conjugated as a Class-C verb, **irgo, irgues,** etc., or according to Class B, with the change of **ie** to **ye** in stem-accented forms, **yergo, yergues,** etc.

2. **Reír** and **sonreír** belong to Class C, but when **i** in the stem would be followed by **ie** or **io** the two like vowels are reduced to one. Note that a written accent is necessary when the stress falls on **i.**

reír to laugh

PRES. PART. riendo　　　　　　PAST PART. reído

PRES. IND. río, ríes, ríe, reímos, reís, ríen

IMPF. IND. reía

PRET. IND. reí, reíste, rió, reímos, reísteis, rieron

FUT. IND. reiré　　　　　　CONDITIONAL reiría

IMPERATIVE ríe, reíd

PRES. SUBJ. ría, rías, ría, riamos, riáis, rían

IMPF. SUBJ., -ra FORM, riera, rieras, riera, riéramos, rierais, rieran

IMPF. SUBJ., -se FORM, riese, rieses, riese, riésemos, rieseis, riesen

3. **Freír** is conjugated like **reír**, except that the past participle is **frito**.

IRREGULAR VERBS

Verbs having irregularities that cannot be classified in the foregoing groups are given below in alphabetical order. When a single form only of a tense is given, the other forms are to be made regularly from the first form.

136. *Memory Aids for Learning Irregular Verbs.* As an aid to the memory in learning the forms of irregular verbs, several general observations may be of value.

1. Only three verbs in Spanish have irregular imperfect indicatives:

> ir (iba)   ser (era)   ver (veía)

2. Fourteen of the irregular verbs in the following alphabetical list have the same set of endings in the preterit, namely:

> -e   -iste   -o   -imos   -isteis   -ieron[1]

Those fourteen verbs are:

andar	decir	poder	tener
caber	estar	poner	traer
conducir	haber	querer	venir
	hacer	saber	

Except in the first and third persons singular these endings are the same as the preterit endings of regular verbs of the second and third conjugations. In order to learn the preterits of the verbs mentioned, memorize the single set of endings just given and the preterit stem of each of the verbs involved:

anduv-	dij-	pud-	tuv-
cup-	estuv-	pus-	traj-
conduj-	hub-	quis-	vin-
	hic- (third person sing. hiz-)	sup-	

---

[1] Following -j-, in the preterit of **conducir**, **decir**, and **traer**, -ieron becomes **eron**.

222

3. In memorizing the future and the conditional, remember that the personal endings of *all* verbs are regular in these tenses, and are as follows:

FUTURE	-é	-ás	-á	-emos	-éis	-án
CONDITIONAL	-ía	-ías	-ía	-íamos	-íais	-ían

Recall also that the future and the conditional of any given verb have the same stem, no matter how irregular that stem may be. The stems of the future and conditional of irregular verbs fall into the following classes: *a.* Those which drop the vowel of the infinitive ending:

cabr- (caber)	podr- (poder)	sabr- (saber)
habr- (haber)	querr- (querer)	

b. Those which drop two letters of the infinitive:

dir- (decir)   har- (hacer)

c. Those which change the vowel of the infinitive ending to **d**:

pondr- (poner)	tendr- (tener)	vendr- (venir)
saldr- (salir)	valdr- (valer)	

4. In a number of irregular verbs the stem of the present subjunctive is the same as that of the irregular first person singular of the present indicative. The verbs affected by this rule are:

asir (asgo, asga)	poner (pongo, ponga)
caber (quepo, quepa)	salir (salgo, salga)
caer (caigo, caiga)	tener (tengo, tenga)
conducir (conduzco, conduzca)	traer (traigo, traiga)
decir (digo, diga)	valer (valgo, valga)
hacer (hago, haga)	venir (vengo, venga)
ir (with change of vowel: voy, vaya)	ver (veo, vea)
oír (oigo, oiga)	yacer (yazco, yazca)

137.   **abrir** to open

PAST PART. abierto

(Other forms regular)

138. **andar** to go, walk

PRES. PART. andando   PAST PART. andado
PRES. IND. ando, andas, anda, andamos, andáis, andan
IMPF. IND. andaba
PRET. IND. **anduve, anduviste, anduvo, anduvimos, anduvisteis, anduvieron**
FUT. IND. andaré   CONDITIONAL andaría
IMPERATIVE anda, andad
PRES. SUBJ. ande, andes, ande, andemos, andéis, anden
IMPF. SUBJ., **-ra** FORM, **anduviera**   **-se** FORM, **anduviese**

139. **asir** to seize

PRES. IND. **asgo,** ases, ase, asimos, asís, asen
PRES. SUBJ. **asga, asgas, asga, asgamos, asgáis, asgan**
(Other forms regular)

140. **caber** to be contained, fit within

PRES. PART. cabiendo   PAST PART. cabido
PRES. IND. **quepo,** cabes, cabe, cabemos, cabéis, caben
IMPF. IND. cabía
PRET. IND. **cupe, cupiste, cupo, cupimos, cupisteis, cupieron**
FUT. IND. **cabré**   CONDITIONAL **cabría**
IMPERATIVE cabe, cabed
PRES. SUBJ. **quepa, quepas, quepa, quepamos, quepáis, quepan**
IMPF. SUBJ., **-ra** FORM, **cupiera**   **-se** FORM, cupiese

141. **caer** to fall

PRES. PART. **cayendo**   PAST PART. caído
PRES. IND. **caigo,** caes, cae, caemos, caéis, caen
IMPF. IND. caía
PRET. IND. caí, caíste, **cayó,** caímos, caísteis, **cayeron**
FUT. IND. caeré   CONDITIONAL caería
IMPERATIVE cae, caed
PRES. SUBJ. **caiga, caigas, caiga, caigamos, caigáis, caigan**
IMPF. SUBJ., **-ra** FORM, **cayera**   **-se** FORM, **cayese**

142. **conducir** to conduct

PRES. PART. conduciendo   PAST PART. conducido
PRES. IND. **conduzco,** conduces, conduce, conducimos, **conducís, con**
ducen

IMPF. IND. conducía
PRET. IND. conduje, condujiste, condujo, condujimos, condujisteis,
   condujeron
FUT. IND. conduciré   **CONDITIONAL** conduciría
IMPERATIVE conduce, conducid
PRES. SUBJ. conduzca, conduzcas, conduzca, conduzcamos, conduzcáis,
   conduzcan
IMPF. SUBJ., -ra FORM, condujera   **-se FORM,** condujese

143.   cubrir to cover

PAST PART. cubierto
      (Other forms regular)

144.   dar to give

PRES. PART. dando   **PAST PART.** dado
PRES. IND. doy, das, da, damos, dais, dan
IMPF. IND. daba
PRET. IND. di, diste, dió, dimos, disteis, dieron
FUT. IND. daré   **CONDITIONAL** daría
IMPERATIVE da, dad
PRES. SUBJ. dé, des, dé, demos, deis, den
IMPF. SUBJ., -ra FORM, diera   **-se FORM,** diese

145.   decir to say

PRES. PART. diciendo   **PAST PART.** dicho
PRES. IND. digo, dices, dice, decimos, decís, dicen
IMPF. IND. decía
PRET. IND. dije, dijiste, dijo, dijimos, dijisteis, dijeron
FUT. IND. diré   **CONDITIONAL** diría
IMPERATIVE di, decid
PRES. SUBJ. diga, digas, diga, digamos, digáis, digan
IMPF. SUBJ., -ra FORM, dijera   **-se FORM,** dijese

146.   escribir to write

PAST PART. escrito
      (Other forms regular)

147.   estar to be

PRES. PART. estando   PAST PART. estado
PRES. IND. estoy, estás, está, estamos, estáis, están
IMPF. IND. estaba
PRET. IND. estuve, estuviste, estuvo, estuvimos, estuvisteis, estuvieron
FUT. IND. estaré   CONDITIONAL estaría
IMPERATIVE está, estad
PRES. SUBJ. esté, estés, esté, estemos, estéis, estén
IMPF. SUBJ. -ra FORM, estuviera   -se FORM, estuviese

148.   haber to have

PRES. PART. habiendo   PAST PART. habido
PRES. IND. he, has, ha (impers. hay), hemos, habéis, han
IMPF. IND. había
PRET. IND. hube, hubiste, hubo, hubimos, hubisteis, hubieron
FUT. IND. habré   CONDITIONAL habría
IMPERATIVE (he), habed
PRES. SUBJ. haya, hayas, haya, hayamos, hayáis, hayan
IMPF. SUBJ., -ra FORM, hubiera   -se FORM, hubiese

149.   hacer to make

PRES. PART. haciendo   PAST PART. hecho
PRES. IND. hago, haces, hace, hacemos, hacéis, hacen
IMPF. IND. hacía
PRET. IND. hice, hiciste, hizo, hicimos, hicisteis, hicieron
FUT. IND. haré   CONDITIONAL haría
IMPERATIVE haz, haced
PRES. SUBJ. haga, hagas, haga, hagamos, hagáis, hagan
IMPF. SUBJ., -ra FORM, hiciera   -se FORM, hiciese

150.   imprimir to print

PAST PART. impreso
(Other forms regular)

151.   ir to go

PRES. PART. yendo   PAST PART. ido
PRES. IND. voy, vas, va, vamos, vais, van
IMPF. IND. iba, ibas, iba, íbamos, ibais, iban
PRET. IND. fuí, fuiste, fué, fuimos, fuisteis, fueron

FUT. IND. iré   **CONDITIONAL** iría
IMPERATIVE ve, id
PRES. SUBJ. vaya, vayas, vaya, vayamos (vamos), vayáis, vayan
IMPF. SUBJ., -ra FORM, fuera   **-se FORM,** fuese

152.   **oír** to hear

PRES. PART. oyendo   **PAST PART.** oído
PRES. IND. oigo, oyes, oye, oímos, oís, oyen
IMPF. IND. oía
PRET. IND. oí, oíste, oyó, oímos, oísteis, oyeron
FUT. IND. oiré   **CONDITIONAL** oiría
IMPERATIVE oye, oíd
PRES. SUBJ. oiga, oigas, oiga, oigamos, oigáis, oigan
IMPF. SUBJ., -ra FORM, oyera   **-se FORM,** oyese

153.   **placer** to please (impersonal)

PRES. PART. placiendo   **PAST PART.** placido
PRES. IND. place
IMPF. IND. placía
PRET. IND. plugo
FUT. IND. placerá   **CONDITIONAL** placería
PRES. SUBJ. plega or plegue
IMPF. SUBJ., -ra FORM, pluguiera   **-se FORM,** pluguiese

154.   **poder** to be able

PRES. PART. pudiendo   **PAST PART.** podido
PRES. IND. puedo, puedes, puede, podemos, podéis, pueden
IMPF. IND. podía
PRET. IND. pude, pudiste, pudo, pudimos, pudisteis, pudieron
FUT. IND. podré   **CONDITIONAL** podría
IMPERATIVE (lacking)
PRES. SUBJ. pueda, puedas, pueda, podamos, podáis, puedan
IMPF. SUBJ., -ra FORM, pudiera   **-se FORM,** pudiese

155.   **poner** to place

PRES. PART. poniendo   **PAST PART.** puesto
PRES. IND. pongo, pones, pone, ponemos, ponéis, ponen
IMPF. IND. ponía
PRET. IND. puse, pusiste, puso, pusimos, pusisteis, pusieron

FUT. IND. pondré   CONDITIONAL pondría
IMPERATIVE pon, poned
PRES. SUBJ. ponga, pongas, ponga, pongamos, pongáis, pongan
IMPF. SUBJ., -ra FORM, pusiera   -se FORM, pusiese

156.   prender to catch

PAST PART. prendido *or* preso

(Other forms regular)

157.   proveer to provide

PAST PART. proveído *or* provisto

(Other forms regular)

158.   querer to wish, be fond of

PRES. PART. queriendo   PAST PART. querido
PRES. IND. quiero, quieres, quiere, queremos, queréis, quieren
IMPF. IND. quería
PRET. IND. quise, quisiste, quiso, quisimos, quisisteis, quisieron
FUT. IND. querré   CONDITIONAL querría
IMPERATIVE quiere, quered
PRES. SUBJ. quiera, quieras, quiera, queramos, queráis, quieran
IMPF. SUBJ., -ra FORM, quisiera   -se FORM, quisiese

159.   romper to break

PAST PART. rompido *or* roto

(Other forms regular)

160.   saber to know

PRES. PART. sabiendo   PAST PART. sabido
PRES. IND. sé, sabes, sabe, sabemos, sabéis, saben
IMPF. IND. sabía
PRET. IND. supe, supiste, supo, supimos, supisteis, supieron
FUT. IND. sabré   CONDITIONAL sabría
IMPERATIVE sabe, sabed
PRES. SUBJ. sepa, sepas, sepa, sepamos, sepáis, sepan
IMPF. SUBJ., -ra FORM, supiera   -se FORM, supiese

161. **salir** to go out

PRES. PART. saliendo   PAST PART. salido
PRES. IND. **salgo, sales, sale, salimos, salís, salen**
IMPF. IND. salía
PRET. IND. salí
FUT. IND. **saldré**   CONDITIONAL **saldría**
IMPERATIVE **sal**, salid
PRES. SUBJ. **salga, salgas, salga, salgamos, salgáis, salgan**
IMPF. SUBJ., -ra FORM, saliera   -se FORM, saliese

162. **ser** to be

PRES. PART. siendo   PAST PART. sido
PRES. IND. **soy, eres, es, somos, sois, son**
IMPF. IND. **era, eras, era, éramos, erais, eran**
PRET. IND. **fuí, fuiste, fué, fuimos, fuisteis, fueron**
FUT. IND. seré   CONDITIONAL sería
IMPERATIVE **sé**, sed
PRES. SUBJ. **sea, seas, sea, seamos, seáis, sean**
IMPF. SUBJ., -ra FORM, fuera   -se FORM, fuese

163. **tener** to have

PRES. PART. teniendo   PAST PART. tenido
PRES. IND. **tengo, tienes, tiene,** tenemos, tenéis, **tienen**
IMPF. IND. tenía
PRET. IND. **tuve, tuviste, tuvo, tuvimos, tuvisteis, tuvieron**
FUT. IND. **tendré**   CONDITIONAL **tendría**
IMPERATIVE **ten**, tened
PRES. SUBJ. **tenga, tengas, tenga, tengamos, tengáis, tengan**
IMPF. SUBJ., -ra FORM, tuviera   -se FORM, tuviese

164. **traer** to bring

PRES. PART. **trayendo**   PAST PART. traído
PRES. IND. **traigo,** traes, trae, traemos, traéis, traen
IMPF. IND. traía
PRET. IND. **traje, trajiste, trajo, trajimos, trajisteis, trajeron**
FUT. IND. traeré   CONDITIONAL traería
IMPERATIVE trae, traed
PRES. SUBJ. **traiga, traigas, traiga, traigamos, traigáis, traigan**
IMPF. SUBJ., -ra FORM. trajera   -se FORM, trajese

165. **valer** to be worth

PRES. PART. valiendo   PAST PART. valido
PRES. IND. **valgo,** vales, vale, valemos, valéis, valen
IMPF. IND. valía
PRET. IND. valí
FUT. IND. **valdré**   CONDITIONAL **valdría**
IMPERATIVE **val** or vale, valed
PRES. SUBJ. **valga, valgas, valga, valgamos, valgáis, valgan**
IMPF. SUBJ., -ra FORM, valiera   -se FORM, valiese

166. **venir** to come

PRES. PART. **viniendo**   PAST PART. venido
PRES. IND. **vengo, vienes, viene,** venimos, venís, **vienen**
IMPF. IND. venía
PRET. IND. **vine, viniste, vino, vinimos, vinisteis, vinieron**
FUT. IND. **vendré**   CONDITIONAL **vendría**
IMPERATIVE **ven,** venid
PRES. SUBJ. **venga, vengas, venga, vengamos, vengáis, vengan**
IMPF. SUBJ., -ra FORM, **viniera**   -se FORM, **viniese**

167. **ver** to see

PRES. PART. viendo   PAST PART. **visto**
PRES. IND. **veo,** ves, ve, vemos, veis, ven
IMPF. IND. **veía, veías, veía, veíamos, veíais, veían**
PRET. IND. vi, viste, vió, vimos, visteis, vieron
FUT. IND. veré   CONDITIONAL vería
IMPERATIVE ve, ved
PRES. SUBJ. **vea, veas, vea, veamos, veáis, vean**
IMPF. SUBJ., -ra FORM, viera   -se FORM, viese

168. **yacer** to lie

PRES. IND. **yazco, yazgo,** or **yago,** yaces, yace, yacemos, yacéis, yacen
IMPERATIVE yace or **yaz,** yaced
PRES. SUBJ. **yazca, yazga,** or **yaga,** etc.

(Other forms regular)

INDEX OF IRREGULAR VERBS

169. In this list are included all irregular verbs in the first five thousand words of Buchanan, *A Graded Spanish Word Book*, except those in -car, -gar, and -zar that have no irregularities other than the changes in spelling treated in Article 123. The numbers refer to articles.

aborrecer hate, 124
abreviar (abrevio) abridge, 126 2
abrir open, 137
abstenerse abstain, 163
acaecer happen, 124
acariciar (acaricio) caress, 126 2
acertar (ie) hit the mark, 128
acoger receive, 123 6
acontecer happen, 124
acordar (ue) agree, 128
acostar (ue) put to bed, 128
acrecentar (ie) increase, 128
actuar (actúo) act, 127
adherir (ie-i) adhere, 131
adormecer lull to sleep, 124
adquirir (ie-i) acquire, 132 2
advertir (ie-i) take notice of, 131
aferrar (ie) grasp, 128
afligir afflict, 123 6
agradecer thank, 124
agraviar (agravio) wrong, 126 2
alentar (ie) encourage, 128
aliviar (alivio) lighten, 126 2
almorzar (ue) breakfast, 128 ; 129
amanecer dawn, 124
andar walk, 138
anegar (ie) inundate, 128 ; 129
angustiar (angustio) afflict, 126 2
anochecer grow dark, 124
ansiar (ansío) desire anxiously, 126 1
anteponer place before, 155
anunciar (anuncio) announce, 126 2

aparecer appear, 124
apetecer long for, 124
apostar (ue) wager, 128
apreciar (aprecio) appreciate, 126 2
apremiar (apremio) urge, 126 2
apretar (ie) compress, 128
aprobar (ue) approve, 128
apropiar (apropio) appropriate, 126 2
arrepentirse (ie-i) repent, 131
ascender (ie) ascend, 128
asentar (ie) seat, 128
asentir (ie-i) acquiesce, 131
asir seize, 139
asociar (asocio) associate, 126 2
atender (ie) heed, 128
atenerse abide by, 163
aterrar (ie) demolish, 128
atraer attract, 164
atravesar (ie) cross over, 128
atribuir attribute, 125
auxiliar (auxilio) aid, 126 2
avenir reconcile, 166
avergonzar (ue) shame, 128 ; 129
averiguar verify, 123 3

bendecir bless, *like* decir, 145, *except fut., cond., and past part., which are regular, and imperative singular* (bendice)
caber be contained, 140
caer fall, 141

calentar (ie) warm, 128
calumniar (calumnio) slander, 126 2
carecer lack, 124
cegar (ie) make blind, 128; 129
ceñir (i-i) gird, 133; 134
cerner (ie) sift, 128
cerrar (ie) close, 128
cocer (ue) boil, 124 1; 128; 129
codiciar (codicio) covet, 126 2
coger catch, 123 6
colar (ue) strain, 128
colgar (ue) hang up, 128; 129
comenzar (ie) begin, 128; 129
compadecer pity, 124
comparecer appear (before a judge), 124
competir (i-i) compete, 133
complacer please, 124
componer compose, 155
comprobar (ue) verify, 128
concebir (i-i) conceive, 133
concertar (ie) adjust, 128
concluir conclude, 125
conducir conduct, 142
confesar (ie) confess, 128
confiar (confío) confide, 126 1
conmover (ue) disturb, 128
conocer know, 124
conseguir (i-i) attain, 133; 134
consentir (ie-i) consent, 131
consolar (ue) console, 128
constituir constitute, 125
construir construct, 125
contar (ue) count, 128
contener contain, 163
continuar (continúo) continue, 127
contraer contract, 164
contrariar (contrarío) oppose, 126 1
contribuir contribute, 125
convencer convince, 123 5
convenir agree, 166

convertir (ie-i) convert, 131
copiar (copio) copy, 126 2
corregir (i-i) correct, 133; 134
costar (ue) cost, 128
crecer grow, 124
creer believe, 123 8
criar (crío) rear, 126 1
cubrir cover, 143

dar give, 144
decir say, 145
deducir deduce, 142
defender (ie) defend, 128
degollar (ue) decapitate, 128; 130 4
demostrar (ue) demonstrate, 128
deponer put aside, 155
derretir (i-i) melt, 133
desafiar (desafío) challenge, 126 1
desaparecer disappear, 124
descender (ie) descend, 128
descollar (ue) overtop, 128
descomponer disarrange, 155
desconcertar (ie) disconcert, 128
desconfiar (desconfío) distrust, 126 1
desconocer fail to recognize, 124
describir describe, 146
descubrir discover, 143
desenvolver (ue) unwrap, 128; 130 5
desfallecer grow weak, 124
deshacer undo, 149
desmentir (ie-i) give the lie to, 131
desolar (ue) lay waste, 128
desollar (ue) skin, 128
despedir (i-i) discharge, 133
despertar (ie) awaken, 128
despreciar (desprecio) despise, 126 2
desterrar (ie) exile, 128
destruir destroy, 125
desvanecer disintegrate, 124

desviar (desvío) deflect, 126 1
detener detain, 163
devolver (ue) return (*trans.*), 128;
  130 5
diferenciar (diferencio) differen-
  tiate, 126 2
diferir (ie-i) defer, 131
dirigir direct, 123 6
disminuir diminish, 125
disolver (ue) dissolve, 128; 130 5
disponer dispose, 155
distinguir distinguish, 123 7
distraer distract, 164
distribuir distribute, 125
divertir (ie-i) amuse, 131
doler (ue) feel pain, 128
dormir (ue-u) sleep, 131

efectuar (efectúo) effect, 127
ejercer exercise, 123 5
elegir (i-i) elect, 133; 134
embestir (i-i) attack, 133
empezar (ie) begin, 128; 129
encarecer enhance, 124
encender (ie) kindle, 128
encerrar (ie) lock up, 128
encoger shrink, 123 6
encomendar (ie) recommend, 128
encontrar (ue) meet, 128
encubrir conceal, 143
enfriar (enfrío) cool, 126 1
enfurecer irritate, 124
enloquecer madden, 124
enmendar (ie) improve, 128
enmudecer hush, 124
enriquecer enrich, 124
entender (ie) understand, 128
enternecer move to compassion,
  124
enterrar (ie) bury, 128
entreabrir leave ajar, 137
entretener entertain, 163
entristecer sadden, 124
envejecer grow old, 124

enviar (envío) send, 126 1
envidiar (envidio) envy, 126 2
envolver (ue) wrap up, 128; 130 5
equivaler be of equal value, 165
erguir raise up straight, 135 1
errar wander, 130 2
escarmentar (ie) take warning,
  128
escarnecer mock, 124
esclarecer enlighten, 124
escoger choose, 123 6
escribir write, 146
esforzarse (ue) exert oneself, 128;
  129
esparcir scatter, 123 5
establecer establish, 124
estar be, 147
estremecer shake, 124
estudiar (estudio) study, 126 2
exceptuar (exceptúo) except, 127
excluir exclude, 125
exigir demand, 123 6
expedir (i-i) forward, 133
exponer expose, 155
extender (ie) extend, 128
extinguir extinguish, 123 7
extraer extract, 164
extraviar (extravío) mislead, 126 1

fallecer die, 124
fastidiar (fastidio) annoy, 126 2
favorecer favor, 124
fiar (fío) trust, 126 1
fingir feign, 123 6
florecer flower, 124
forzar (ue) overpower, 128; 129
freír fry, 135 3
fruncir pucker, 123 5

gemir (i-i) groan, 133
gobernar (ie) govern, 128
graduar (gradúo) gauge, 127
gruñir growl, 123 9
guiar (guío) guide, 126 1

premiar (premio) reward, 126 2
prender grasp, 156
presenciar (presencio) witness, 126 2
presentir (ie-i) forebode, 131
prevalecer prevail, 124
prevenir prearrange, 166
prever foresee, 167
principiar (principio) begin, 126 2
probar (ue) prove, 128
producir produce, 142
pronunciar (pronuncio) pronounce, 126 2
proponer propose, 155
proscribir proscribe, *like* escribir, 146, *except past part.* proscrito *or* proscripto
proseguir (i-i) prosecute, 133; 134
proteger protect, 123 6
proveer provide, 157
provenir originate, 166
pudrir rot; *inf.* podrir *or* pudrir, *past part.* podrido, *otherwise regular*

quebrar (ie) break, 128
querer wish, 158

rabiar (rabio) suffer from hydrophobia, 126 2
realizar realize, 123 4
recaer fall back, 141
recoger gather, 123 6
recomendar (ie) recommend, 128
reconocer recognize, 124
recordar (ue) remind, 128
reducir reduce, 142
referir (ie-i) refer, 131
reforzar (ue) strengthen, 128; 129
refugiar (refugio) shelter, 126 2
regar (ie) irrigate, 128; 129
regir (i-i) rule, 133; 134
reír laugh, 135 2
relucir glow, 124
remediar (remedio) remedy, 126 2

remendar (ie) repair, 128
remover (ue) stir, 128
renacer be born again, 124
rendir (i-i) subdue, 133
renegar (ie) disown, 128; 129
renovar (ue) renew, 128
renunciar (renuncio) renounce, 126 2
reñir (i-i) quarrel, 133; 134
repetir (i-i) repeat, 133
reponer replace, 155
reproducir reproduce, 142
requerir (ie-i) court, 131
resentirse (ie-i) resent, 131
resolver (ue) resolve, 128; 130 5
resonar (ue) resound, 128
resplandecer glisten, 124
restablecer re-establish, 124
restituir restore, 125
retener retain, 163
retorcer (ue) twist, 128; 129
reventar (ie) burst, 128
revestir (i-i) clothe, 133
revolver (ue) turn over, 128; 130, 5
rociar (rocío) sprinkle, 126 1
rodar (ue) roll, 128
roer gnaw, 123 8
rogar (ue) entreat, 128; 129
romper break, 159
rugir roar, 123 6

saber know, 160
saciar (sacio) satiate, 126 2
salir go out, 161
satisfacer satisfy, 149
seducir seduce, 142
segar (ie) reap, 128; 129
seguir (i-i) follow, 133; 134
sembrar (ie) sow, 128
sentar (ie) seat, 128
sentir (ie-i) feel, 131
ser be, 162
servir (i-i) serve, 133

THE CONNECTING PREPOSITION

170. As a connective between a finite verb and a dependent infinitive or between a verb and a substantive, Spanish uses very frequently **a, de, en,** and less commonly **con** and **por.** Often no connective is required before the infinitive. With each verb the proper connective must be learned, for no rule is of much service. With regard to the connecting preposition between verb and substantive, the chief difficulty arises from the fact that many English verbs which take an object directly have as their Spanish equivalents verbs which do not, and vice versa; for example, compare, in the list below, **acercarse *a*** (to approach) and **aprovechar** (to take advantage *of*).

On this and the following pages is an alphabetical list of the verbs that the student is likely to use in his first years of study, together with connecting prepositions and illustrative sentences.

171. *Alphabetical List of Verbs with Connecting Prepositions*

abandonarse a: **Se abandonó a sus vicios.** He gave himself up to his vices.

acabar con: **Pronto acabó con todo su dinero.** He soon spent all his money.

acabar de:

El viajero acaba de llegar. The traveler has just arrived.

En cuanto acabe de hablar. As soon as I finish speaking.

Acababa de darle la noticia. I had just given him the news.

Esta tan delicada reserva acabó de cautivarla. Such delicate reserve finally captivated her.

acabar por: **Acabaron por no buscarse.** In the end they ceased to seek each other.

acercarse a: **Tuve tentaciones de acercarme a ellas.** I was tempted to approach them.

acertar a: **Claudia acertó a entrar.** Claudia chanced to enter.

acordar: **Acordaron no venderle más huevos.** They agreed to sell him no more eggs.

237

acordarse de: **Me acuerdo bien de aquel día.** I remember that day well.

acostumbrar: **Acostumbro levantarme tarde.** I am in the habit of getting up late.

acostumbrarse a: **Se acostumbraban a la miseria.** They were getting used to poverty.

agradecer a: **Se lo agradezco a Juan.** I am grateful to John for it.

alcanzar a: **Muy poco alcanzó a ejecutar.** He succeeded in accomplishing very little.

alegrarse de: **Se alegraba de haber tropezado conmigo.** She was glad to have happened upon me.

alejarse de: **Se alejó de la ciudad.** He withdrew from the city.

antojarse: **No se me antoja ponerlo en letras de molde.** It does not suit me to put it into print.

apartarse de: **Se apartó de nosotros.** He kept away from us.

apoderarse de: **Los carlistas se apoderaban del pueblo.** The Carlists were taking possession of the village.

apoyarse en: **Se apoyó en la pila bautismal.** She leaned against the baptismal font.

aprender a: **Aprendo a leer el francés.** I am learning to read French.

apresurarse a: **Se apresuraron a manifestar su desprecio.** They hastened to show their scorn.

aprovechar: **Aprovecharon todas las ocasiones.** They took advantage of all opportunities.

arrepentirse de: **Se arrepintió luego de su crimen.** He soon repented of his crime.

asistir a: **Sentía deseos de asistir a teatros.** He wanted to go to theaters.

asomarse a: **El príncipe se asomó al balcón.** The prince appeared on the balcony.

atreverse a: **No se atrevió a salir a la calle.** He did not dare to go out into the street.

ayudar a: **Le ayudaban a descender.** They were helping him descend.

burlarse de: **Se burlaba de todos.** He made fun of everybody.

cambiar de: **Hay que cambiar de tren en Irún.** It is necessary to change trains at Irún.

cansarse de: **Se cansa de tanto trabajar.** He is getting tired of working so much.

carecer de: **Carece de reverencia.** He is lacking in reverence.

casarse con: **Debía casarse con la sobrina.** He was to marry the niece.

cesar de: **Cesó de hacerme deletrear.** He stopped making me spell.

comenzar a: **Comenzaba a nevar.** It was beginning to snow.

complacerse en: **Se complacía en referir cuanto pasaba.** He took pleasure in telling all that happened.

condenar a: **Le condenaron a morir.** They condemned him to die.

confesar: **Confesó haber robado al viejo.** He confessed to having robbed the old man.

confiar en: **Confiaban en Dios.** They trusted in God.

consistir en: **La vida no consiste en la abundancia de los bienes.** Life does not consist in abundance of wealth.

contar con: **Cuento con su amistad.** I am counting on your friendship.

convenir en: **Habíamos convenido en ir a su despacho.** We had agreed on going to your office.

convertirse en: **La duda se convirtió en certidumbre.** The doubt was changed into certainty.

convidar a: **Le convidé a cenar conmigo.** I invited him to sup with me.

correr a: **Corrió a verlos.** He ran to see them.

creer: **Creo verle todavía.** I think I see him yet.

creer en: **No creo en nada de eso.** I do not believe in anything of that sort.

cuidar de: **Cuidó mucho de la buena policía.** He gave much attention to good policing.

dar a: **La puerta da a la calle.** The door opens on the street.
   Lo dió a entender. He let it be understood.

dar con: **Dió con la ronda.** He ran into the guard.

dar por: **Lo dió por perdido.** He considered it lost.

deber: **Debo confesarlo.** I must confess it.

deber de: **Debió de hacerle un gran bien.** It must have done her much good.

decidir: **Decidió ponerse lo más guapa posible.** She decided to look her prettiest.

decidirse a: **Se decidió a hacer un viaje.** He decided to make a journey.

dedicarse a: **Se dedicó a vigilar a su hija.** She gave herself up to watching over her daughter.

dejar: **No les dejaba hablar a solas.** She did not let them speak alone.

dejar de: **Sin dejar de correr me llamó.** Without stopping running, she called to me.

desear: **Deseo conocerla.** I wish to meet her.

despedirse de: Se despidió de todos. He took leave of all.

detenerse a: Se detuvo a hablarme. He stopped to talk to me.

dirigirse a: Se dirigió a la puerta. He went toward the door.

disponerse a: El padre se disponía a insistir. The father was getting ready to insist.

divertirse en: Se divertía en leer. He amused himself by reading.

dudar de: Dudo de la verdad de lo que dijo. I doubt the truth of what he said.

echar a: Echó a correr calle abajo. He began to run down the street.

echar de: Eché de verle. I happened to see him.

echarse a: Yo me eché a reír. I began to laugh.

empeñarse en: Se empeñaba en perseguir a los judíos. He persisted in persecuting the Jews.

empezar a: Empezaron a sonar las campanadas de las diez. It began to strike ten.

enamorarse de: Se enamoró de la viuda. He fell in love with the widow.

encargarse de: Se encargó de alimentar a los huérfanos. He took it upon himself to feed the orphans.

encontrarse con: Se encontró con Aquilino. She came upon Aquilino.

enseñar a: Me enseñó a hablar español. He taught me to speak Spanish.

enterarse de: Al enterarse de lo ocurrido. On being informed of the happening.

entrar en: Un soldado entró en la casa. A soldier entered the house.

enviar a: Le envió a comprar carne. He sent him to buy meat.

esperar: No esperaba yo escapar tan bien. I did not hope to escape so well.

estar para: Estaba para casarse. He was about to be married.

faltar a: No falta a sus clases. He does not miss his classes.

fiarse de: No me fío de él. I have no confidence in him.

figurarse: Se figuraba que todos eran criados. She imagined that all were servants.

fijarse en: No se fija en nada. He does not pay attention to anything.

fingir: Benedicta fingió creerlo. Benedicta pretended to believe it.

gozar de: Gozarás de bienes. You will enjoy good things.

gustar a: A mí me gustaba la hermana. I liked the sister.

haber de: He de cobrar venganza. I am going to take vengeance.

hacer: Hizo llamar al médico. He had the doctor called.

impedir: La pobreza no le impide ser honrado. Poverty does not keep him from being honest.

inclinarse a: Me inclino a creerlo. I am inclined to believe it.

insistir en: Insistió en acompañarme. He insisted on accompanying me.

intentar: El preso intentó evadirse. The prisoner tried to escape.

invitar a: Me invitó a visitarle. He invited me to visit him.

ir a: Iba a amanecer. Day was about to break.

jugar a: Jugaban a los naipes. They were playing cards.

jurar: Juró vengarse. He swore to avenge himself.

lograr: Logró trasladarse a España. He succeeded in getting over to Spain.

llegar a: Llegué a dominar su idioma. I succeeded in mastering its language.

mandar: Mandó colgar de las antenas a los dos cabecillas. He ordered the two leaders hanged from the yards.

merecer: Usted merece ser feliz. You deserve to be happy.

meterse en: Se mete en lo que no le toca. He interferes in things that do not concern him.

necesitar: Tú necesitas quedarte en casa. You need to remain at home.

negarse a: Los soldados se negaban a batirse. The soldiers refused to fight.

obligar a: Me obligaron a dejar la universidad. They compelled me to leave the university.

ocuparse de: Nadie se ocupó de don Ángel. No one paid attention to Don Ángel.

ocurrirse: No se me ocurrió preguntarlo. It did not occur to me to ask about it.

oír: Le oigo respirar. I hear him breathing.

olvidarse de: Se olvidó de hacer la cruz. She forgot to make the sign of the cross.

oponerse a: Siempre se opone a mis deseos. He always opposes my wishes.

pararse a: Se paró a mirar. He stopped to look.

parecer: Me parece estarlo oyendo. I seem to be hearing it.

parecerse a: Se parece mucho a su madre. She looks much like her mother.

pensar: Pienso marcharme mañana. I intend to go away tomorrow.

pensar de: ¡Qué piensa usted de mí! What do you think of me!

pensar en: **No pensaba más que en comer bien.** He thought only of eating well.

permitir: **No me permitieron trabajar.** They did not let me work.

poder: **No puedo olvidarlo.** I cannot forget it.

ponerse a: **Se puso a rezar.** He began to pray.

preferir: **Prefirió tomar el velo.** She preferred to take the veil.

pretender: **Pretende ganar mi amistad.** He is trying to win my friendship.

privarse de: **Se priva de lo más necesario.** He deprives himself of the most necessary things.

procurar: **Procuro dominarme.** I try to control myself.

prometer: **Prometió ayudarme.** He promised to aid me.

proponerse: **Me propongo hacer un largo viaje.** I intend to take a long trip.

quedarse a: **Te quedarás a almorzar con nosotros.** You will stay to lunch with us.

quedarse con: **Se quedó con el libro.** He kept the book.

quejarse de: **Se quejaba de todo.** He complained about everything.

querer: **Quiso saber dónde estaba.** He wished to know where he was.

recordar: **No recuerdo haberle visto.** I do not recall having seen him.

referirse a: **No se refiere a su honradez.** His honesty is not in question.

reírse de: **Se rió de la carta.** He made fun of the letter.

resolverse a: **Se resolvió a abandonar la patria.** He resolved to leave his native land.

retirarse a: **Se retiró a Cataluña.** He retired to Catalonia.

saber: **Sabe hablar español.** He can speak Spanish.

salir a: **Salió a pasearse.** He went out to take a walk.

sentarse a: **Se sentaron a la mesa.** They sat down at the table.

sentir: **Yo sentiré molestar a ustedes.** I shall be sorry to trouble you.

separarse de: **Se separó de sus amigos.** He left his friends.

servir de: **El molinero me sirvió de guía.** The miller acted as my guide.

servir para: **No sirve para nada.** It is not good for anything.

servirse: **Sírvase usted acompañarme.** Please come with me.

servirse de: **Se sirve de un lápiz para escribir.** He uses a pencil to write.

soler: **Solía visitarme.** He used to visit me.

soñar con: **Soñaba con la riqueza.** He was dreaming of riches.

subir a: **Subió al tren.** He boarded the train.

tardar en: **No tardó en calmarse.** She was not long in quieting down.

temer: **Teme salir de noche.** He is afraid to go out at night.

tocar: **Ahora me toca a mí reír.** Now it is my turn to laugh.

tratar de: **Trataron de hacerle hablar.** They tried to make him talk.

tratarse de: **Se trataba de asistir a algún enfermo.** It was a question of treating some sick person.

tropezar con: **Tropezamos con ellas.** We came upon them.

valerse de: **Se vale de todo.** He makes use of everything.

venir a: **Vendrá a vivir con nosotros.** He will come to live with us.

ver: **Le vió llegar.** He saw him arrive.

volver a: **Volví a verla.** I saw her again.

SPANISH–ENGLISH VOCABULARY

The sign ∽ indicates the word printed in black type at the head of the paragraph; thus ∽s under **abuelo** means **abuelos**.

a to, at, on
abandonar to abandon
abril *m.* April
abrir to open
la abuela grandmother
el abuelo grandfather; los ∽s grandparents
abundar to abound
el acento accent
aceptar to accept
acerca de concerning, about
acercarse (a) to approach
acompañar to accompany
acostarse (ue) to go to bed
acostumbrarse (a) to become accustomed (to)
actual present
admirar to admire, wonder (at)
agosto *m.* August
agradable agreeable
agradablemente agreeably
el agua *f.* water
ahora now
el aire air
la alcoba bedroom
la aldea village
alegrarse (de) to rejoice, be glad
algo something; *adv.* somewhat
alguien someone, anyone
alguno, algún, alguna some, any
el alma *f.* soul, spirit
almorzar (ue) to lunch
el almuerzo lunch
alrededor de around
alto -a high, tall
la altura height

el alumno, la alumna, pupil, student
allí there
amable likable, obliging
la América del Sur South America
el amigo friend
ancho -a broad, wide
el animal animal
anoche last night
antes de before
anunciar to announce
el año year
aprender to learn
aquel, aquella, aquellos, aquellas that, the former, those
aquél, aquélla, aquello, aquéllos, aquéllas that one, that, the one, the former, those
aquí here; ∽ tiene(n) usted(es) here is (are)
el árbol tree
arreglar to settle
así thus
el asiento seat
asistir (a) to be present (at), attend
aunque although
el automóvil automobile
el autor author
la avena oats
ayer yesterday
ayudar to aid, help
el azúcar sugar
azul blue

bajar to go down; ∽ de to get off
bañarse to take a bath

245

el **baño** bath
barato -a cheap
bastante, ∽**s,** enough, somewhat, fairly, numerous
la **batalla** battle
el **baúl** trunk
beber to drink
bello -a beautiful
la **biblioteca** library
bien well
el **billete** ticket
blanco -a white
la **bondad** kindness
bonito -a pretty
el **brazo** arm
buen(o) -a good
buscar to look for

el **caballo** horse; **a** ∽ on horseback
la **cabeza** head
cada each; ∽ **uno -a** each one
el **café** coffee; café
el **calor** heat
la **calle** street
la **cama** bed
la **camisa** shirt
la **campanilla** little bell
el **campesino** countryman
el **campo** country, field
cansado -a tired; **estar** ∽ to be tired
cansarse to tire oneself, get tired
la **caña** cane; ∽ **de azúcar** sugar cane
el **capítulo** chapter
la **cara** face
característico -a characteristic
cargado -a loaded
cariñoso -a affectionate
Carlos Charles
la **carne** meat
la **carnicería** butcher shop
el **carnicero** butcher

el **carro** cart, wagon
la **carta** letter
la **casa** house; **en** ∽ at home; **a** ∽ (toward) home; ∽ **de campo** country house
casi almost, nearly
el **caso** case
el **castillo** castle
católico -a Catholic
la **causa** cause; **a** ∽ **de** on account of
Cayo Hueso Key West
la **central** sugar mill
el **centro** center; **al** ∽ downtown
cerca *adv.* near, near by; ∽ **de** *prep.* near (to)
cerrado -a closed
el **cielo** sky
cien(to) (one) hundred
cierto -a certain
cinco five
cincuenta fifty
el **cinematógrafo** *or* **cine** movingpicture show
la **ciudad** city
claro -a clear, evident
la **clase** class; kind; ∽**s** school
la **cocina** kitchen
el **coche** carriage, cab
el **cochero** coachman
coger to catch, gather
Colón Columbus
el **color** color
el **comedor** dining room
comer to eat, dine; **dar de** ∽ **a** to feed (animals)
el **comerciante** merchant
la **comida** dinner, meal
como like, as, since
cómo *interrog. and excl.* how
completo -a complete
la **compra** purchase
comprar to buy
comprender to understand

común common; **por lo** ∼ ordinarily

con with; ∼ **tal que** provided

conmigo with me, with myself

conocer to meet, be acquainted with, know (a person)

consigo with himself, with herself, with themselves, *etc.*

consiguiente: por ∼ in consequence, consequently

consolar (ue) to console

contar (ue) to count, relate

contestar to answer

contigo with thee, with thyself, with you, with yourself

continuar to continue

la conversación conversation

la corbata necktie

cordialmente cordially

correctamente correctly

correr to run

cortar to cut

corto -a short

la cosa thing

la cosecha harvest, harvesting

costar (ue) to cost

la costumbre custom

crecer to grow

creer to believe

la criada servant

el cuaderno notebook

cual: el ∼ *etc.* who, whom, which

cuál -es *interrog.* which, what

cuando when

cuándo *interrog.* when

cuanto -a as much, as many; all that

cuánto -a *interrog. and excl.* how much, how many; **a** ∼**s estamos del mes** what day of the month is it

cuarto -a fourth

el cuarto room; quarter (of an hour); ∼ **de baño** bathroom

cuatro four

Cuba *f.* Cuba

cubano -a Cuban

cubierto -a *past part. of* **cubrir** covered

la cuenta account, bill

el cuento story

el cuerpo body

el cuidado care, worry; **tener** ∼ **(de)** to be careful (to); **una cosa de** ∼ a serious thing

cultivar to cultivate

chico -a small

dar to give; ∼ **de comer a** to feed (animals); ∼ **de propina** to tip; ∼ **un paseo** to take a walk

de of, from

deber to owe, be under obligation, ought

debiera *impf. subj. of* **deber** ought

décimo -a tenth

decir to say, tell; **se dice** it is said

dejar to leave, let, permit

delante de in front of

demás: lo, los, las ∼ the rest, the others

demasiado too, too much; ∼**s** too many

dentro de within

desagradable unpleasant

desayunarse to breakfast

el desayuno breakfast

descansar to rest

describir to describe

descubrir to discover

desde since, from

desear to wish, desire

despedirse de (i-i) to take leave of, say good-by to

despertar (ie) to awaken (another); ∼**se** to wake up

después *adv.* afterwards; ∽ **de**
prep. after

detrás de behind

el día day; **buenos** ∽s good day;
todos los ∽s every day

el diccionario dictionary

dice (he) says

diciembre *m.* December

diciendo *pres. part. of* **decir** saying

diez ten; **las** ∽ ten o'clock

la diferencia difference

difícil difficult

la dificultad difficulty

el difunto the deceased

dije (I) said

dijeron (they) said

dijo (he) said

diligente diligent, industrious

el dinero money

dirigirse (a) to turn (to), speak
(to), go (toward)

distinguir to distinguish

distintamente distinctly

distinto -a different

divertir (ie-i) to divert, amuse

dividir to divide; ∽se to be divided

la docena dozen

el dolor pain, grief

el domingo Sunday

donde where

dónde *interrog.* where; **a** ∽ (to)
where; **de** ∽ (from) where

dormir (ue-u) to sleep

Dorotea Dorothy

dos two

dudar to doubt

durante during

la edad age

el edificio building

el efecto: en ∽ in fact

el ejercicio exercise

el the

el (la, lo, los, las) *followed by* **de** *or*
que that, the one, those

él he, it, him

ella she, it, her

ello it

ellos -as they, them

embargo: sin ∽ nevertheless

empezar (ie) to begin

el empleado employee, official,
agent

en in, on, into, at

el encargo errand, commission

encontrar (ue) to meet, find; ∽se
to be found

enero *m.* January

la enfermedad sickness

enfermo -a sick

enfrente opposite, in front

Enrique Henry

enseñar to teach, show

entender (ie) to hear, understand

entonces then

entrar to enter; ∽ **en (la casa)** to
enter (the house)

entre between, among

enviar to send

era (he) was

es (he) is

la escalera stairway

escribe (he) writes

escriben (they) write

escribir to write

escrito -a *past part. of* **escribir**
written

escuchar to listen

la escuela school, schoolhouse

ese, esa, esos, esas that, those
(near you)

ése, ésa, eso, ésos, ésas that one
(near you), that, those; **por eso**
therefore

España *f.* Spain

español Spanish; **el ∾** the Spaniard, the Spanish language

esperar to wait, wait for, expect, hope

la estación season; station

los Estados Unidos the United States

estar to be

este, esta, estos, estas, this, these, the latter

éste, ésta, esto, éstos, éstas, this, this one, these, the latter

el estudiante student

estudiar to study

el estudio study

Europa *f.* Europe

excesivo -a excessive

la excursión excursion

el éxito success; **tener ∾** to succeed

explicar to explain

extranjero -a foreign

la fábrica factory, refinery

fácil easy

la falta mistake

faltar to be lacking

la familia family

famoso -a famous

la farmacia drugstore

febrero *m.* February

Fernando Ferdinand

el ferrocarril railway

el fin end; **al ∾** finally

la finca farm

la flor flower

la forma form, shape

formar to make, form

la frase sentence

fresco -a cool, fresh

el fresco coolness, cool weather; **hace ∾** it is cool weather

el frío cold; **hace ∾** it is cold

la fruta fruit

la gallina hen

la gana desire; **tener ∾s** to want to

las gracias thanks

la gramática grammar

grande big, large, tall, great

la guerra war

gustar to be pleasing; **me gusta I** like (it)

el gusto pleasure

la Habana Havana

haber to have; **∾ de** to be (expected) to, have to; **∾ que** (*impers. only*) to be necessary to

había there was (were)

la habitación room

hablar to speak, talk

hacer to make, do; **∾se** to be made; **hace calor, frío,** *etc.* it is warm, cold, *etc.*; **hace muchos años** many years ago

hallar to find; **∾se** to find oneself, be

el hambre *f.* hunger; **tener ∾** to be hungry

hasta even

hasta que until

hay there is (are); *see* **haber**

hecho *past part. of* **hacer** made

el heno hay

la hermana sister

el hermano brother; **los ∾s** brothers, brother(s) and sister(s)

hermoso -a beautiful, handsome

el hielo ice

la hierba grass

la hija daughter

el hijo son; **los ∾s** sons, son(s) and daughter(s)

la historia history

la hoja leaf

el hombre man

la hora hour; **a qué ∾** at what time

hoy today
el huevo egg
húmedo -a humid

el idioma language
la iglesia church
importante important
inglés English; el ∽ the Englishman, the English language
inmenso -a immense
inteligente intelligent
interesante interesting
interesar to interest
el invierno winter
la invitación invitation
invitar to invite
ir to go; ∽ a to be going to; ∽ a
pie to walk, go on foot
Isabel Isabella
la isla island

jamás never
el jardín yard, garden
Jorge George
José Joseph
Josefa Josephine
joven young; un ∽ a young man
Juan John
el jueves Thursday
julio m. July
junio m. June

el kilo(gramo) kilogram (about
two pounds)

la the
la her, you, it
el lápiz pencil
las the
las them, you
lavar to wash; ∽se to wash (oneself)
le to him, to her, to it, to you; him,
it, you

la lección lesson
la lectura reading
la leche milk
lee (he) reads
leen (they) read
leer to read
la legumbre vegetable
lejos far
la lengua language
lentamente slowly
les to them, to you; you
levantarse to get up
leyendo pres. part. of leer reading
la librería bookstore
el librero bookseller
el libro book; ∽ de lectura reader;
∽ de ejercicios exercise book,
workbook
limpio -a clean
listo -a ready
lo it, him, you; so
los the
los them, you
el lugar place
el lunes Monday

llamar to call; ∽se to be called, be
named
la llegada arrival
llegar to arrive
lleno -a full
llevar to carry, take with one
llover (ue) to be raining
la lluvia rain

la madre mother
maduro -a ripe
la maestra teacher, schoolmistress
el maestro teacher, schoolmaster
el maíz corn
mal badly
la maleta valise
malo -a bad, poor; estar ∽ to be sick
mandar to order

la **mano** hand

mañana tomorrow; la ∾ morning, forenoon

María Mary

el **martes** Tuesday

marzo *m.* March

más more, most; ∾ que more than

mayo *m.* May

mayor larger; older

me to me, to myself; me, myself

el **médico** doctor

la **medida** measure

medio -a half; en ∾ de in the midst of

mejicano -a Mexican; el ∾ the Mexican

Méjico *m.* Mexico

mejor better

menor smaller; younger

menos less

menos que less than

el **mercado** market, market place

el **mes** month

la **mesa** table

meter to place, put within

mi, mis my

mí me, myself

el **miedo** fear; tener ∾ to be afraid

mientras while

el **miércoles** Wednesday

mil (one) thousand

el **minuto** minute

mío -a my, mine

mirar to look, look at, watch

mismo -a same

el **modo** way, manner; de ∾ que so that

el **momento** moment

montar to mount; ∾ a caballo to ride on horseback

morir(se) (ue-u) to die

Morro: el Castillo del ∾ Morro Castle

mostrar (ue) to show; ∾se to show oneself

el **mozo** waiter

la **muchacha** girl

el **muchacho** boy

mucho -a much, a great deal of; ∾s many

la **muerte** death

muerto -a *past part. of* morir died, dead

la **mujer** woman; wife

mundial of the world

el **mundo** world; el **Nuevo Mundo** the New World, America

muy very

nacer to be born

nada nothing

nadie no one, (not) anyone

la **naranja** orange

la **naturaleza** nature

necesario -a necessary

necesitar to need

negar (ie) to deny

los **negocios** (*pl.*) business

negro -a black

ni nor; ni . . . ni neither . . . nor

la **nieve** snow

ninguno, ningún, ninguna, no, none, no one, not any

el **niño** child

no not, no

la **noche** night, evening; esta ∾ tonight

el **nombre** name

el **norteamericano** North American; American (of the United States)

nos to us, to ourselves, to each other; us, ourselves, each other

nosotros -as we, us

la **nota** grade, note, trait

notar to take note of, notice

la **novela** novel

noveno - a ninth
noviembre *m.* November
nuestro -a our, ours
Ñueva York *f.* New York
nueve nine; a las ∽ at nine
o'clock
nuevo -a new
nunca never

o or
observar to observe
octavo -a eighth
octubre *m.* October
ocupado -a busy; estar ∽ to be
busy
la oficina office
el ojo eye
olvidar to forget
la oportunidad opportunity
os to you, to yourselves, to each
other; you, yourselves, each
other
el otoño autumn
otro other, another

el padre father; los ∽s parents
pagar to pay
la página page
el país country
el paisaje landscape
el pájaro bird
la palabra word
el palacio palace
la palma palm
el pan bread
la panadería bakery, baker's shop
el panadero baker
ei panecillo roll
el papel paper
el par pair
para for, in order to; ∽ que in
order that
pararse to stop
parecer to appear

la parte part; por todas ∽s everywhere
partir to depart, leave
pasado -a past
pasar to pass; spend (time); go;
happen
el paseo walk; dar un ∽ to take
a walk
la patata potato
el patio court, patio
pedir (i-i) to ask for (a favor), to
request
pensar (ie) to think, intend
peor worse, worst
pequeño -a little, small
la pera pear
perder (ie) to lose
el periódico newspaper
permitir to permit
pero but
la peseta peseta (monetary unit
of Spain, normally worth about
twenty cents)
el pie foot; ir a ∽ to walk, go on
foot
pintoresco -a picturesque
la pizarra blackboard
el plan plan
la planta plant
la plaza public square
la pluma pen
pobre poor
poco -a little, few; *adv.* little
poder to be able
poner to put, place
pongo *from* poner (I) place, put
poquísimo *from* poco very little
por by, for, through, about, during,
on account of, for the sake of; ∽
todas partes everywhere; ∽ eso
therefore; ∽ qué *interrog.* why
por qué why
porque because
posible possible

preciso -a necessary
preferir (ie-i) to prefer
la pregunta question; hacer una ∾ to ask a question
preguntar to ask
preparar to prepare
presentar to introduce
el presidente president
la primavera spring
primer(o) -a first
primero *adv.* (at) first
el primo cousin
principal principal
la prisa haste; tener ∾ to be in haste
probable probable
el producto product
el profesor teacher
prometer to promise
pronto soon
pronunciar to pronounce
la propina tip, gratuity; dar de ∾ to tip
propio -a own
próximo -a next, near by
publicar to publish; ∾se to be published
pudiera *impf. subj. of* poder could
el pueblo people, race; town
puedo, puede, *from* poder, (I) (he) can
la puerta door
el puerto port
el punto point; a ∾ de on the point of

que *rel. pron.* who, whom, which, that
que: el (la, lo, los, las) que *rel. pron.* he who, that which, *etc.*
que *conj.* that, than, for; tener ∾ to have to
qué *interrog. and excl.* what (a), how

quedar(se) to remain
querer to wish, be fond of
querido -a dear
quien -es who, whom
quién -es *interrog.* who, whom
quiero *from* querer (I) wish
quinto -a fifth
quisiera *impf. subj. of* querer (I) should like, (he) would like

rápidamente rapidly
rápido -a rapid, fast
un rato a short time
la raza race
recibir to receive
reciente recent
recoger to gather, harvest
recorrer to go through, roam about
el recuerdo remembrance, souvenir; ∾s regards
la regla rule
la reina queen
el reinado reign
reinar to reign
repetir (i-i) to repeat
el restaurante restaurant
retirarse to retire, withdraw
reunirse to meet, gather, assemble
el rey king
rico -a rich
rojo -a red
la ropa clothing

el sábado Saturday
saber to know (a fact)
sacar to take out, extract
la sala living room, parlor; ∾ de clase classroom; ∾ de lectura reading room
salgo *from* salir (I) go out
la salida departure
salir to go out, depart
saludar to salute, greet
Santa Clara *f.* a city in Cuba

el sastre tailor
la sastrería tailor's shop
se himself, herself, itself, yourself;
themselves, yourselves; to himself, *etc.*; to him, to her, to them,
etc.
seco -a dry
seguida: en ∾ at once
seguir (i-i) to follow, continue
segundo -a second
seis six
la semana week
sentarse (ie) to sit down
sentir (ie-i) to feel, feel sorry;
siento mucho I feel very sorry;
∾se **bien** to feel well
el señor sir, Mr., gentleman
la señora madam, Mrs., lady
septiembre (*pronounced* setiembre)
m. September
séptimo -a (*pronounced* sétimo)
seventh
ser to be
servir (i-i) to serve; ∾se to be
kind enough to, please
sexto -a sixth
si if
sí yes
sí himself, herself, itself, yourself,
themselves, yourselves
siempre always
siempre que whenever
el siglo century
siguiente following
la silla chair
simpático -a likable
sin without; ∾ **embargo** nevertheless; ∾ **que** without
el sol sun; **al** ∾ in the sun
el soldado soldier
sólo only
el sombrero hat
son (they) are
sonar (ue) to sound, ring

su, sus, his, her, its, their, your
subir to go up, get into
el sudamericano South American
el suelo ground, floor
el sueño sleep; **tener** ∾ to be
sleepy
suplicar to entreat, request
suyo -a his, her(s), its, their(s),
your(s)

el tabaco tobacco
tal such, such a; **con** ∾ **que** provided that
también also
tan so, such, as
tanto -a as much, so much, as
many, so many
tarde *adv.* late
la tarde afternoon
la taza cup
te to thee, to you, to thyself, to
yourself; thee, you, thyself, yourself
el teatro theater
temprano early
el tendero shopkeeper
tener to have; ∾ **que** to have to
tercer(o) -a third
tercio third (*in fractions*)
terminar to finish
ti thee, thyself, yourself
la tía aunt
el tiempo time; weather
la tienda shop, store
tiene (he) has
tienen (they) have
la tierra earth, land
la tinta ink
el tío uncle; **los** ∾s uncle and aunt
la tiza chalk
todavía yet, still
todo -a all; everything; ∾s **los días**
every day
toma (he) takes

tomar to take, get; buy (*a ticket*);
eat; drink
el tomate tomato
trabajar to work
traducir to translate
traer to bring
el traje suit of clothes
tranquilo -a tranquil, quiet
el tranvía street car
tratar (de) to try (to)
el tren train
tres three; **las ~** three o'clock
el trigo wheat
triste sad
la tristeza sadness
tropical tropical
tu, tus, thy, your
tú thou, you
tuyo -a thy, your, thine, yours

último -a last
un, una, a; **unos, unas,** some
un(o), una, one
la universidad university
usted -es you
útil useful

la vaca cow
vale (it) is worth
valen (they) are worth
valer to be worth
el valor value
el vapor steam, steamship
varios -as various, several
el vaso glass
Vd. = usted; **Vds.** = ustedes
ve (he) sees
veíamos *impf. ind. of* **ver** (we)
were seeing
vencer to conquer, overcome
el vendedor, la ~a, vender, seller
vender to sell
venir to come

la ventana window
la ventanilla (car) window
ver to see
el verano summer
el verbo verb
vestirse (i-i) to dress oneself
la vez time; **de ~ en cuando** from
time to time; **en ~ de** instead
of; **a veces** at times; **otra ~**
again; **muchas veces** often
viajar to travel
el viaje journey, voyage, trip
el viajero traveler
la vida life
viejo -a old; **un ~** an old man; **los**
~s old people
viene *from* **venir** (he) comes
el viento wind; **hace ~** it is
windy
el viernes Friday
el vino wine
la visita visit; **tener ~** to have a
visitor *or* visitors
visitar to visit
visto -a *past part. of* **ver** seen
vivía (he) lived, was living
vivían (they) lived, were living
vivir to live
volver to turn, return
vosotros -as you, ye
la vuelta turn, return
vuelto *past part. of* **volver** returned
vuestro -a your, yours

y and
ya now, already
yo I

la zapatería shoe shop
el zapatero shoemaker, shoe
dealer
el zapato shoe

ENGLISH–SPANISH VOCABULARY

The numbers in black type after certain verbs refer to articles

abandon abandonar
able: be ∾ poder **154**
abound abundar
about de, acerca de
absence la ausencia
absent ausente
accent el acento
accompany acompañar
according to según
account la cuenta; **on** ∾ **of** a causa de, por
accustom acostumbrar
acquainted: get *or* be ∾ **with** conocer **124**
actress la actriz
admire admirar
affect afectar
affectionate cariñoso
afraid: be ∾ **of** tener miedo de
after después de, después que
afternoon la tarde; **in the** ∾ de *or* por la tarde
afterwards después
again otra vez; **do a thing** ∾ volver a hacer una cosa
age la edad
agent el empleado
ago: three days ∾ hace tres días
agreeable agradable
agreeably agradablemente
aid ayudar
air el aire
Alice Alicia
all todo, todos; ∾ **the**, ∾ **that**, cuanto(s)
almost casi
alms la limosna
along por
already ya

also también
altar el altar
although aunque
always siempre
Amazon (River) el Amazonas
America América
American americano
among entre
amuse divertir (ie-i); ∾ **oneself** divertirse
ancient antiguo
and y; e *before* i- *or* hi-
animal el animal
announce anunciar
another otro
answer contestar
any algun(o); *(after a negation)* ningun(o); *often unexpressed*
anyone alguien
anything algo; **not** ∾ nada
apparatus el aparato
appear parecer **124**
apple la manzana
approach acercarse a **123 1**
April abril *m.*
Argentina la Argentina
arm el brazo
around alrededor de
arrival la llegada
arrive llegar **123 2**
artist el artista
as como, tan, tanto, de; ∾ **good** ∾ tan bueno como
ashes la ceniza
ask: ∾ *(a favor)*, ∾ **for**, pedir (i-i); ∾ *(a question)* preguntar; ∾ **a question** hacer una pregunta
assassin el asesino
at a, en, contra, por

257

atom el átomo
attend asistir (a)
August agosto *m.*
aunt la tía
author el autor
automobile el automóvil
autumn el otoño
avaricious avaro
avoid evitar
awaken despertar (ie)

bad malo
badly mal
baker el panadero
bakery la panadería
ball la pelota
bark ladrar
basket la cesta
bath el baño
bathe bañarse
bathroom el cuarto de baño
battle la batalla
be ser **162**; estar **147**; hallarse;
  ∽ hot, cold, hacer calor, frío;
  tener calor, frío; ∽ ten years old
  tener diez años; ∽ sorry sentir;
  we are to attend hemos de asistir
beautiful bello, hermoso
because porque; ∽ of a causa de
bed la cama; go to ∽ acostarse (ue)
bedroom la alcoba, el dormitorio
before *prep.* antes de, delante de;
  adj. pasado; *adv.* antes
begin empezar (ie), principiar **126 2**
behind detrás de
believe creer **123 8**
bell la campana; little ∽ la campanilla
besides *adv.* además; *prep.* además de
best mejor, más
better mejor, más
between entre
bid good-by (to) despedirse (de) **133**

big grande
bill la cuenta
bird el pájaro
black negro
blackboard la pizarra
blow soplar
blue azul
board (*blackboard*) la pizarra
boatman el barquero
body el cuerpo
book el libro
bookseller el librero
bookstore la librería
born: be ∽ nacer
both ambos
box la caja
boy el muchacho; ∽ student el
  alumno
brave valiente
bread el pan
breakfast el desayuno; eat *or*
  have ∽ desayunarse
bridge el puente
bring traer **164**
broad ancho
brother el hermano; ∽(s) and
  sister(s) los hermanos
building el edificio
busy: be ∽ estar ocupado
but pero, mas, sino
butcher el carnicero
butcher shop la carnicería
buy comprar; ∽ a ticket tomar
  un billete
by por, de, en

cab el coche
cabin la barraca
Cadiz Cádiz *f.*
café el café
cage la jaula
call llamar; be ∽ed llamarse
calm la calma; *v.* calmar
can poder **154**; saber **160**

Canada el Canadá
cane la caña; sugar ∾ la caña de
azúcar
capital la capital
captain el capitán
car (automobile) el automóvil
care el cuidado
careful: be ∾ tener cuidado
carefully cuidadosamente
caress acariciar 126 2
carriage el coche
carry llevar; ∾ away llevarse
cart el carro
case el caso
castle el castillo
catch coger 123 6
Catholic católico
cause la causa
cave la cueva
cease cesar (de)
center el centro
central central
Central America la América Central
certain cierto
certainly ciertamente
chair la silla
chalk la tiza
chapter el capítulo
characteristic característico
Charles Carlos
chatterbox el charlador
cheap barato
child el niño, el hijo
Christopher Cristóbal
church la iglesia
city la ciudad
class la clase; Spanish ∾ la clase
de español
classroom la sala de clase
clean limpio
clear claro
clearly claramente
climate el clima

close cerrar (ie); ∾ to cerca de;
∾ (by) cerca
clothes, clothing, la ropa
coach el coche
coachman el cochero
coat la chaqueta
coffee el café
coin la moneda
cold frío; I am ∾ tengo frío; it is
∾ hace frío
collar el cuello
color el color
Columbus Colón
come venir 166; ∾ in entrar; ∾
into entrar en; ∾ out salir 161
command mandar
commission el encargo
companion el compañero
complain quejarse
complete completo
concerning acerca de
conquer vencer 123 5
consequently por consiguiente
console consolar (ue)
construct construir 125
continue continuar 127; seguir 134
conversation la conversación
convert convertir (ie-i)
cool fresco
coolness el fresco
cordially cordialmente
corn el maíz
correct correcto
correctly correctamente
cost costar (ue)
count contar (ue)
country el país, el campo; adj. de
campo
countryman el campesino
court el patio
cousin el primo
cover cubrir 143
cow la vaca
coward el gallina, el cobarde

cross la cruz
Cuban el cubano
cultivate cultivar
culture la cultura
cup la taza
cure curar
current la corriente
custom la costumbre
cut cortar

danger el peligro
dangerous peligroso
dare (to) atreverse (a)
date la fecha
daughter la hija; ∽-in-law la nuera
day el día; good ∽ buenos días
deal: a great ∽ mucho
dear querido; **Dear Sir** Muy señor mío
death la muerte
debt la deuda
deceased el difunto
December diciembre *m.*
decide decidir
demand pedir (i-i)
deny negar (ie)
depart partir
departure la salida, la partida
describe describir 146
deserve merecer 124
desire el deseo, la(s) gana(s); *v.* desear
desk el pupitre
destroy destruir 125
devotion la devoción
dictionary el diccionario
die morir (ue-u)
difference la diferencia
different diferente, distinto
difficult difícil
difficulty la dificultad
diligent diligente
dining room el comedor

dinner la comida
discover descubrir 143
disease la enfermedad
distinctly distintamente, claramente
distinguish distinguir 123 7
divert divertir (ie-i)
divide dividir
do hacer 149
doctor el médico
dog el perro
Dominic Domingo
door la puerta
Dorothy Dorotea
doubt dudar
down: go ∽town ir al centro
dozen la docena
drama el drama
dress vestir (i-i), vestirse
drink beber
drugstore la farmacia
dry seco
during durante, por

each cada; ∽ one cada uno
early temprano
earn ganar
earth la tierra
easily fácilmente
easy fácil
eat comer; ∽ breakfast, luncheon, dinner, desayunarse, almorzar (ue), comer
editor el redactor
education la educación
egg el huevo
eight ocho
either . . . or o . . . o; (*after a negative*) ni . . . ni
eldest el mayor
emperor el emperador
employee el empleado
empress la emperatriz
end el fin; *v.* terminar

energy la energía
English inglés; the ∼ los ingleses
enough bastante(s)
enter (into) entrar (en)
entreat suplicar 123 1
errand el encargo
Esperanto esperanto (*a universal language*)
Europe Europa
even aun, hasta; ∼ if, ∼ though, aunque
evening la noche; in the ∼ por *or* de la noche
ever jamás
every cada; ∼ day todos los días
everything todo
everywhere por todas partes
evident claro
example el ejemplo
exceedingly sumamente; ∼ beautiful hermosísimo
excessive excesivo
excursion la excursión
exercise el ejercicio
exercise book el libro de ejercicios
exist existir
expect esperar
expensive caro
explain explicar 123 1
expression la expresión
extract sacar 123 1
extremely muchísimo; ∼ rich riquísimo
eye el ojo

face la cara
fact: in ∼ en efecto
factory la fábrica
fairly bastante
fall el otoño; *v.* caer 141
family la familia
famous famoso
far lejos
farm la finca

farmer el campesino
fast rápido; *adv.* rápidamente, de prisa
father el padre
favorite favorito
fear el miedo; *v.* temer, tener miedo
February febrero *m.*
feed dar de comer
feel sentir (ie-i), sentirse; ∼ sorry sentir; ∼ like (*desire to*) tener ganas de
Ferdinand Fernando
fertile fértil
few pocos, algunos
fewer menos
field el campo
fierce feroz
fifteen quince
fifty cincuenta
finally al fin
find encontrar (ue), hallar, buscar 123 1
finish terminar
fire el incendio; *v.* (∼ *a gun*) disparar
first primero; *adv.* primero
fish el pez
five cinco
floor el suelo
flower la flor
fluently corrientemente
follow seguir (i-i) 134
following siguiente
food la comida
foot el pie
for para, por; *conj.* porque, puesto que; he has been there ∼ ten minutes hace diez minutos que está allí
foreign extranjero
forest el bosque
forget olvidar
form la forma; *v.* formar

former: the ~ aquél
four cuatro
fox la zorra
France Francia *f.*
French francés; **the** ~ los franceses
fresh fresco
Friday el viernes
friend el amigo, la amiga
friendship la amistad
from de, desde
front: in ~ enfrente; **in** ~ **of** delante de
fruit la fruta
full lleno
fundamental esencial

gain ganar
garden la huerta, el jardín
gate la puerta
gather coger, recoger 123 6
general el general
generally por lo común
gentleman el señor, el caballero
George Jorge
German alemán
get: ~ **a ticket** tomar un billete; ~ **the cows** buscar las vacas; ~ **off from,** ~ **out of** (*a train, an automobile*) bajar de; ~ **into** (*a train etc.*) subir a; ~ **up** levantarse
girl la muchacha; ~ **pupil** *or* **student** la alumna; **little** ~ la niña
give dar 144
glad: be ~ alegrarse, estar contento
glass el vaso
glove el guante
go ir 151; ~ **away** irse; ~ **to bed** acostarse (ue); ~ **down** bajar; ~ **up** subir; ~ **out** salir 161, arrancar 123 1
God Dios
gold el oro

good bueno; ~ **day,** ~ **morning,** buenos días
good-by: bid *or* **say** ~ **to** despedirse (i-i) de
government el gobierno
grade la nota
grain el grano
grammar la gramática
grandfather el abuelo
grandmother la abuela
grass la hierba
great grande; **a** ~ **deal** mucho
Greece Grecia
greet saludar
grief el dolor
ground el terreno, el suelo
group el grupo
grow crecer 124
guard el guardia
guide el guía; ~**book** la guía

hair los cabellos
half *adj.* medio; *noun* la mitad
hand la mano
handsome hermoso
happen pasar, suceder
happily felizmente
happy feliz, alegre
hard difícil; *adv.* mucho
harvest recoger
harvest, harvesting, la cosecha
haste la prisa
hat el sombrero
Havana la Habana
have haber 148; tener 163; ~ **to** tener que
Havre el Havre
hay el heno
head la cabeza
health la salud
hear oír 152
heat el calor
height la altura
help ayudar

hen la gallina
Henry Enrique
here aquí; ~ **are** aquí están, aquí tiene(n) usted(es)
high alto
Himalayas los (montes) Himalaya
himself se, él mismo
history la historia
home la casa, el hogar; **at** ~ en casa; **take** ~ llevar a casa; **go** ~ ir a casa
honest honrado
honestly honradamente
nonesty la honradez
hope esperar
horrible horrible
horse el caballo
hot: it is ~ hace calor
hour la hora
house la casa
how como, lo; (*interrog. and excl.*) cómo; ~ **much,** ~ **many** (*interrog. and excl.*) cuánto(s); ~ **pretty** (*excl.*) qué hermoso
humid húmedo
hundred cien, ciento
hunger el hambre *f.*
hurry: be in a ~ tener prisa
husband el esposo, el marido

ice el hielo
idea la idea
if si
ignorant ignorante
immediately en seguida
immense inmenso
important importante
impossible imposible
in a, en, por, de
indicate indicar **123** 1
information los informes
ink la tinta
inkstand el tintero

inquisitive preguntón
insist (on) insistir (en)
instantly inmediatamente, al momento
instead of en vez de
intelligence la inteligencia
intelligent inteligente
intend pensar (ie)
interest interesar
interesting interesante
into a, en
introduce presentar
invitation la invitación
invite invitar
Isabella Isabel
island la isla
Italian italiano
Italy Italia *f.*

January enero *m.*
Jericho Jericó
Jerusalem Jerusalén
jesting *adj.* burlón
John Juan
Joseph José
Josephine Josefa
journey el viaje
judge el juez; *v.* juzgar **123 2**
July julio *m.*
June junio *m.*
just justo; I have ~ **seen him** acabo de verle

Key West Cayo Hueso
kill matar
kilogram el kilogramo, el kilo
kind la clase; *adj.* bondadoso; **be** ~ **enough to** sírvase Vd.
kindness la bondad
king el rey
kitchen la cocina
knee la rodilla
know (*a person*) conocer **124**; (*a fact*) saber **160**

labor el trabajo
lack faltar
lady la señora
land la tierra
landscape el paisaje
language la lengua, el idioma
large grande
last último; ~ month el mes pasado; v. durar, continuar 127
late tarde
latter: the ~ éste
law la ley
lazy holgazán
leaf la hoja
learn aprender
least menor
leather el cuero
leave dejar; intrans. marcharse, partir, salir de (una casa etc.); take ~ of despedirse de
less adv. menos; adj. menor or menos
lesson la lección
let dejar, permitir; ~ us speak hablemos
letter la carta
liberty la libertad
library la biblioteca
life la vida
light rubio
likable amable, simpático
like adv. como; I ~ it me gusta; ~ to querer 158
lion el león
listen escuchar
little adj. pequeño; adj. and adv. poco; a ~ un poco; very ~ poquísimo
live vivir
living la vida
living room la sala
loaded cargado
log el tronco
long largo

look mirar; ~ at mirar; ~ for, ~ up, buscar 123 1
lose perder (ie)
Louise Luisa
love amar
loyalty la lealtad
Lucky Fortuna
lunch(eon) el almuerzo; v. almorzar (ue)

madam señora; Dear Madam Muy señora mía
major el comandante
make hacer 149
man el hombre; business~ el hombre de negocios
many muchos; too ~ demasiados; as ~ tantos
map el mapa
March marzo m.
market place el mercado
marry casarse con
Mary María
master don
matter el asunto; v. importar
May mayo m.
meal la comida
measure la medida
meat la carne
meet encontrar (ue), tropezar (ie) con, conocer 124; intrans. reunirse
merchant el comerciante
messenger el mensajero
Mexican el mejicano
Mexico Méjico m.
middle el medio
midst: in the ~ of en medio de
milk la leche
mill la fábrica; sugar ~ la fábrica, la central
minute el minuto
miss señorita
mistake la falta
model el modelo

moderation la moderación
moment el momento
Monday el lunes
money el dinero
month el mes
more más; the ∾ . . . the ∾
cuanto más . . . (tanto) más
morning la mañana; in the ∾ por
or de la mañana
Morro Castle el Castillo del Morro
most más; los más
mother la madre
mount montar
mountain la montaña
mouse el ratón
mouth la boca
movie el cine
moving-picture show el cinematógrafo, el cine
Mr. señor
Mrs. señora
much mucho; too ∾ demasiado;
as ∾ tanto; how ∾ (interrog. and
excl.) cuánto
must deber, tener que, haber que

named llamado; be ∾ llamarse
Napoleon Napoleón
nation la nación
nature la naturaleza
near cerca de; ∾ (by) cerca,
próximo; ∾er más cerca (de),
más acá
nearly casi
necessary necesario; be ∾ ser
necesario or preciso
necklace el collar
necktie la corbata
need necesitar
neighbor el vecino
neither: ∾ he nor she ni él ni ella
net la red
never nunca, jamás
nevertheless sin embargo

new nuevo
newspaper el periódico
New York Nueva York f.
next siguiente, próximo
night la noche; last ∾ anoche
nine nueve; at ∾ o'clock a las
nueve
no no, ningun(o); ∾ one nadie
nobody nadie
noise el ruido
none ningun(o)
nor ni
north el norte
North America la América del
Norte
North American el norteamericano
nose la nariz
not no
note la nota; take ∾ of notar
notebook el cuaderno
nothing nada; ∾ but no más que
notice notar
novel la novela
November noviembre m.
now ahora, ya
numerous bastantes
nun la monja

oats la avena
obliging adj. amable
observe observar
occupation el oficio
occur ocurrir
o'clock: at nine ∾ a las nueve
October octubre m.
of de
offer ofrecer 124
office la oficina
often muchas veces, a menudo
old viejo; ∾er mayor; ∾ fellow
)tío; ∾ people los viejos; be ten
years ∾ tener diez años
on en, sobre, encima de, de; ∾ entering al entrar (en)

once una vez; **at** ~ en seguida
one un(o); **the** ~ el; **no** ~ nadie
only sólo, solamente; *adj.* único
open abrir **137**
opportunity la oportunidad
opposite enfrente de
or o; u *before* o- *or* ho-
orange la naranja
order mandar; **in** ~ **to** para; **in** ~
that para que
ordinarily por lo común
other otro; **the** ~s los demás
ought deber
outside fuera (de)
over sobre, encima de
overcome vencer **123 5**
overtake alcanzar **123 4**
owe deber
own propio

Pacific el Pacífico
page la página
pain dolor
pair el par
palace el palacio
palm la palma
paper el papel, el periódico
pardon perdonar
parents los padres
Paris París
parlor la sala
part la parte; el papel
pass pasar
passenger el viajero
past pasado
patriot el patriota
Paul Pablo
pay pagar **123 2**
pear la pera
pen la pluma
pencil el lápiz
penknife el cortaplumas
people la gente, el pueblo
perish perecer **124**

permit permitir
person la persona
Peru el Perú
peseta la peseta (*a Spanish coin,
normally worth about twenty cents*)
Peter Pedro
Philip Felipe
physician el médico
picturesque pintoresco
pity la lástima
place el lugar
plan el plan
plant la planta
Plata (River) el Plata
play jugar (ue)
please tenga Vd. la bondad de,
sírvase Vd.
pleasing: **be** ~ gustar
pleasure el gusto
poem el poema
poetess la poetisa
poetry la poesía
point el punto; **on the** ~ **of** en
punto de
poor pobre, malo
poorly pobremente
Pope el Papa
port el puerto
possible posible
potato la patata
praise alabar
preach predicar **123 1**
prefer preferir (ie-i)
prepare preparar
present *adj.* (*referring to time*)
actual; **be** ~ **at** asistir a
president el presidente
pretty hermoso, bonito
priest el cura
prince el príncipe
princess la princesa
principal principal
probable probable
problem el problema

produce producir **142**
product el producto
professor el profesor, el maestro
prohibit prohibir
promise prometer
pronounce pronunciar **126 2**
pronunciation la pronunciación
property: his ∾ lo suyo
Protestant protestante
provided (that) con tal que
publish publicar **123 1**
pupil el alumno, la alumna
purchase la compra; *v.* comprar
put poner **155**; ∾ **on** ponerse; ∾ **into** meter; ∾ **to bed** acostar (ue)

quarter el cuarto
queen la reina
question la pregunta; **ask a** ∾ hacer una pregunta; *v.* preguntar
quiet tranquilo
quite bastante

race la raza, el pueblo
railroad, railway, el ferrocarril; ∾ **ticket** el billete de ferrocarril
rain la lluvia; *v.* llover (ue)
rapidly rápidamente
reach llegar (a) **123 2**
read leer **123 8**
reader el libro de lectura
reading la lectura
ready listo
reason: for that ∾ por eso
receive recibir
recent reciente
red rojo
refinery la fábrica
regards los recuerdos
regret sentir (ie-i)
reign el reinado; *v.* reinar
relate contar (ue)
relative el pariente
remain quedar

remember recordar (ue)
remembrance el recuerdo
repeat repetir (i-i)
reply la respuesta; *v.* contestar
request pedir (i-i); rogar (ue) **129**; suplicar **123 1**
require costar (ue), necesitar
resemble parecerse a **124**
resources los recursos
respect el respeto; *v.* respetar
rest: the ∾ lo(s) demás; *v.* descansar
restaurant el restaurante
retire retirarse, acostarse (ue)
return la vuelta; *v.* volver; *trans.* devolver **130 5**
rich rico
ride (on horseback) montar (a caballo)
ridiculous ridículo
ring sonar (ue)
ripe maduro
rise (*of the sun*) salir **161**
river el río
road el camino
roam (about) recorrer
roll el panecillo
Rome Roma *f.*
roof el techo
room el cuarto, la habitación; **class**∾ la clase, la sala de clase; **be** ∾ **for** caber **140**
root la raíz
round redondo
royal real
rule la regla
run correr; **at a** ∾ corriendo

sad triste
sadness la tristeza
saint el santo
sake: for the ∾ **of** por
salute saludar
same mismo

Saturday el sábado
say decir 145; ∿ **good-by (to)**
 despedirse (i-i) (de)
school la escuela, las clases
schoolhouse la escuela
schoolmaster el maestro
seaport el puerto de mar
search (for) buscar 123 1
season la estación
seat el asiento; **be** ∿**ed** sentarse
 (ie), estar sentado
see ver 167
seek buscar 123 1
seem parecer 124
Seine el Sena
seldom raramente
sell vender
seller el vendedor
send enviar 126 1
sentence la frase
sentinel el centinela
September septiembre (*pronounced*
 setiembre) *m.*
series la serie
serious grave, serio, sensato; **a** ∿
 thing una cosa de cuidado
servant el criado, la criada; ∿ **girl**
 la criada
serve servir (i-i)
settle arreglar
seven siete
several varios
shade la sombra
sheep la oveja
shirt la camisa
shoe el zapato; ∿ **dealer** el zapatero; ∿ **shop** la zapatería
shoemaker el zapatero
shop la tienda
short corto
should deber
show mostrar (ue), enseñar
shut cerrar (ie)
sick: be ∿ estar malo *or* enfermo

sickness la enfermedad
silent: keep ∿ callar
since desde, desde que, como; **it is**
 a year ∿ hace un año que
sing cantar
sir señor, caballero; **Dear Sir** Muy
 señor mío
sister la hermana
sit: ∿ **down** sentarse (ie)
six seis
sky el cielo
sleep el sueño; *v.* dormir (ue-u)
slowly lentamente
small pequeño, chico
smoke fumar
snow la nieve; *v.* nevar (ie)
so así, tan; ∿ **large as** tan grande
 como; ∿ **many** tantos; ∿ **that**
 para que
soldier el soldado
some algun(o), algunos, unos; *often*
 unexpressed in Spanish
somebody, someone, alguien
something algo
sometimes algunas veces, a veces,
 de vez en cuando
somewhat algo
son el hijo
soon pronto, dentro de poco
sorry: I am ∿ (lo) siento
soul el alma *f.*
sound sonar (ue)
South America la América del Sur
South American el sudamericano
souvenir el recuerdo
Spain España *f.*
Spaniard el español
Spanish español; ∿ **class** la clase
 de español
speak hablar
spend (*time*) pasar; (*money*) gastar
spirit el alma *f.*
sport el deporte
spring la primavera

square cuadrado ; public ∾ la plaza
stairs, stairway, la escalera
start partir
state el estado
station la estación
stay quedar(se)
steamer, steamship, el vapor
steps las gradas, la escalera
still todavía, aún ; ∾ others otros
todavía
stone la piedra
stop parar, pararse
store la tienda
storekeeper el tendero
storm la tormenta
story el cuento
strange extraño
street la calle ; ∾car el tranvía
stroll pasearse
strong fuerte, vigoroso
student el alumno, la alumna, el
estudiante
study el estudio ; v. estudiar
stupid tonto
succeed tener éxito
success el éxito
such tal, tan
suddenly de repente
sufficient bastante
sugar el azúcar ; ∾ cane la caña de
azúcar ; ∾ mill la central
suit el traje
suitcase la maleta
summer el verano
sun el sol ; in the ∾ al sol
Sunday el domingo
supper la cena
surprise sorprender ; be ∾d (at)
admirarse (de)
swamp el pantano
swim nadar

table la mesa
tail el rabo, la cola

tailor el sastre ; ∾'s shop la sastrería
take tomar ; ∾ a walk dar un
paseo ; ∾ a trip hacer un viaje ;
∾ a bath bañarse ; ∾ (with one)
llevar ; ∾ out sacar 123 1
talk hablar
talkative hablador
tall alto
tame manso
tea el té
teach enseñar
teacher el maestro, la maestra, el
profesor
telegram el telegrama
tell decir 145
ten diez
Texas Tejas m.
than que, de
thank agradecer 124
thanks las gracias
that dem. adj. ese, aquel ; dem.
pron. ése, aquél, el ; rel. pron. que ;
conj. que ; so ∾ para que
theater el teatro
then entonces
there allí, ahí ; ∾ is, ∾ are, hay
therefore por eso
thing la cosa
think pensar (ie), creer 123 8
third tercero
this este
Thomas Tomás
though aunque
thousand mil
three tres ; at ∾ o'clock a las tres
through por
Thursday el jueves
thus así
ticket el billete ; ∾-seller el empleado
tie la corbata
tiger el tigre
time el tiempo ; (in a series) la vez

a long ~ mucho tiempo; a short
~ un rato; what ~ is it? ¿qué
hora es? at ~s a veces; from ~
to ~ de vez en cuando
timid tímido
tip la propina; v. dar de propina
tire trans. cansar; intrans. cansarse; be ~d estar cansado
to a, hasta, para
tobacco el tabaco
today hoy
together juntos
tomato el tomate
tomorrow mañana
tonight esta noche
too demasiado, también; ~ much
demasiado
top: on ~ of encima de
tower la torre
town el pueblo; down~ al centro
train el tren
trait la nota
tranquil tranquilo
translate traducir 142
travel viajar
traveler el viajero
tree el árbol
tremble temblar (ie)
trip el viaje
tropical tropical
true verdadero; it is ~ es verdad
trumpeter el trompeta
trunk el baúl
truth la verdad
try tratar
Tuesday el martes
turn la vuelta; v. volver (ue) 130 5;
volverse; ~ to dirigirse a 123 6
twenty veinte
two dos

umbrella el paraguas
uncle el tío; ~(s) and aunt(s) tíos
under debajo de

understand entender (ie), comprender
union la unión
United States los Estados Unidos
university la universidad
unless a menos que
unpleasant desagradable
until hasta; hasta que
upon en
use usar
useful útil

valise la maleta
valor el valor
value el valor
various varios
vegetables las legumbres
vender el vendedor
verb el verbo
very muy
Vesuvius el Vesubio
village la aldea
virtue la virtud
visit la visita; v. visitar
visitor: have ~s tener visita
voice la voz
volume el tomo

wagon el carro
wait esperar; ~ for esperar
waiter el mozo
wake up trans. despertar (ie); intrans. despertarse
waken despertar (ie)
walk el paseo; v. ir a pie, andar 138
want querer 158, desear, tener
gana(s) de
war la guerra
warm caliente; I am ~ tengo
calor; it is ~ hace calor
wash lavar; ~ oneself lavarse
waste perder (ie)
watch el reloj (pronounced reló); v.
mirar

water el agua *f.*
wear llevar
weather el tiempo
weather vane la veleta
Wednesday el miércoles
week la semana
well bien ; **be** ∾ estar bueno
western occidental
what *interrog. and excl.* qué ; *interrog.* cuál ; (= *that which*) lo que ; ∾ **is good** lo bueno ; ∾**ever** cualquiera (que)
wheat el trigo
when cuando, mientras que ; *interrog.* cuándo
whence de donde ; *interrog.* de dónde
whenever siempre que
where donde ; *interrog.* dónde ; (= *whither*) *interrog.* adónde ; (= *whence*) *interrog.* de dónde
whether si
which *rel. pron.* que, el cual, el que ; *interrog.* cuál, qué
while mientras, mientras que
white blanco
who *rel. pron.* que, quien, el cual, el que ; *interrog.* quién ; ∾**ever** quien, quienquiera (que)
whole todo
whose cuyo ; *interrog.* de quién
why por qué ; pues
wide ancho

wife la esposa, la mujer
wild salvaje
will la voluntad
wind el viento
window la ventana ; **car** ∾ **la** ventanilla
windy : it is ∾ hace viento
wine el vino
winter el invierno
wish desear, querer **158**
with con
within dentro de
without sin ; *conj.* sin que
wolf el lobo
woman la mujer
word la palabra
work el trabajo ; *v.* trabajar
workman el obrero
world el mundo ; *adj.* mundial
worry el cuidado
worse peor
worst el peor
worth : be ∾ valer **165**
wrap envolver **130** 5
write escribir **146**

year el año
yes sí
yesterday ayer
yet todavía
young joven ; ∾**er** menor ; ∾ **man** el joven

INDEX

Reference is to paragraphs

273

PRINTED IN THE UNITED STATES OF AMERICA